1977

The people side of systems
The human aspects of computer systems

The people side of systems

The human aspects of computer systems

Keith R. London

London · New York · St Louis · San Francisco · Auckland ·
Düsseldorf · Johannesburg · Kuala Lumpur · Mexico ·
Montreal · New Delhi · Panama · Paris · São Paulo ·
Singapore · Sydney · Tokyo · Toronto

Published by

McGRAW-HILL Book Company (UK) Limited

MAIDENHEAD · BERKSHIRE · ENGLAND

LC# 76-372578

07 084463 1

Printed and bound in Great Britain

To: PPG at WCC, 1973

Table of contents

Introduction

Computers and computer systems are playing an ever-increasing role in commerce, industry, and government. Census data on the world-wide use of computers is difficult to obtain, but probably expenditure on computers and related services this year is in the order of $60 000 million with over 100 000 computers installed in the United States and Western Europe. This makes the computer industry the third largest in the world, after motor cars and chemicals. There are many statistics on expenditure and installations, on hardware and software usage, and on applications and usage by industry, but in this book we are interested in the impact of computers on *people* in their working environment. Here the statistics become even more difficult to obtain, but are worth considering. In the United States, for example, it is estimated that 10 per cent of the working population deal with computers. This represents about 20 million people.

Statistics will never show the personal impact of a computer-based system on the managers and workers. Organizations using computers have had to deal not only with the technical problems of exploiting a new technology, but also adjusting and adapting to the impact of that technology.

In some companies, the introduction of a computer (especially in marketing, accounting, administrating, and personnel) may represent a first venture into 'high technology' with all the problems of monitoring project development, authorizing high capital expenditure and managing the introduction of radical changes in jobs, procedures, and reporting. In other companies, the introduction of a computer has required management to analyse its own function, undertake forward planning and control, and specify information requirements to a level of formality and detail never before necessary. In decision making, the manager may become more and more reliant on computer-produced reports, in which he must have confidence. In addition to dealing with accountants, organization and methods analysts, industrial engineers, and so on, the manager is now faced with new groups of technocrats: systems analysts and designers, programmers, operations personnel, and software specialists.

The impact of computers on workers has been of no less significance. The fears of large-scale redundancy through computerization, prevalent in some industries in the 1950s, have been somewhat quelled. But to the worker the computer can be seen as both a menace and helper. The attitudes of workers have been conditioned not only by the day-to-day operational impact of systems but also by the way systems were introduced As a menace, the computer has been seen vaguely as a very complex and sophisticated machine run by educated technocrats well steeped in machine theory but lacking 'working experience'. In practical terms, the workers have reacted as follows:

'Can I cope?'

'My job is running a machine/supervising a store/selling, not filling in all these forms.'

'Before, I could see the job as a whole, now I just feed the blackbox with input and get paper back—I have no knowledge or control of what goes on in between.'

'It's all meant more work with nothing in it for me.'

'Computers relieving me of boring, repetitive clerical work? The amount of repetitive clerical work has gone down. What I'm left with is even more boring than before, and I've just created more work to fill the gaps in my time left by the computer.'

'Computers? Marvellous excuse. Best excuse since "Don't you know there's a war on?". If anything goes wrong, blame the computer. The public sympathize all the time.'

For over 20 years of computing, technical problems with hardware and software have come and gone. Many of the problems of designing systems for people remain. The personnel who analyse and design computer systems are generally well versed in the technical aspects of computing; knowledge of and training in the people side of systems has been inadequate. It is that gap which this book attempts to fill.

This book puts the technical aspects of computing to one side and focuses on problems of developing and implementing systems which meet the requirements of the organization and satisfy the people who work in it. It has two practical aims. The first is to get project leaders and system analysts *thinking* about the people side of systems—a reorientation away from the hardware/software aspects of computer systems. The second is to present practical advice on tackling the day-to-day tasks of developing and running systems.

Any study of people at work must take into account many disciplines: industrial psychology, theory and practice of motivation, management decision-making techniques, and the behaviour of groups, for example. This book presents a series of practical suggestions and specific techniques on how and why the project leader, systems analyst or system designer can undertake many of the people-oriented tasks in systems development. No one book can present in detail a review of *all* the conflicting theories of man at work, views of management in practice, and studies on industrial relations of the last 50 years. I have attempted to extract from the massive volume of research and published work on the behavioural sciences a selected slice of the theory that is relevant to the work of a typical project leader or systems analyst. To the hard-pressed working systems analyst it is a practical, self-contained handbook. For the student it can be used as first reader, a compendium from which he can progress as required on to more specialized works.

The book is organized into three parts. The first part, 'People and systems', looks at people at work and the general problems and solutions of organizing systems development work. The second part, 'Project techniques', describes methods for carrying out five crucial people-oriented tasks in developing and implementing a system. The third part, 'Communication techniques', discusses methods for improving communications within a project team and between the project leader and the users.

In writing this book I have been able to draw on many sources of knowledge and experience: from my own experience of developing systems and that of my colleagues, from the many students I have lectured to on courses, and from research undertaken for my clients. Individual acknowledgments would fill a book in itself. If only one acknowledgement is to be given, it is to the many users who have educated me in the people side of systems.

KEITH R. LONDON

Part I

People and systems

1
The project, systems analysis, and people

The project

Every organization that uses computers evolves from experience its own methods for developing systems. Eventually these methods are formalized into standard practices. An organization structure is created and lines of communication are established to enable a multitude of people to work together on the development of a system.

A general structure is shown in Figure 1.1. On the one hand, there is the consultation and decision-making process within one user area (within administration, within personnel, within production, within marketing, etc.), from senior management to the most junior clerical or manual worker. On the other is the mechanism for a number of users to work together on the same or related systems, informal senior or line management consultations between a number of departments, or a more formal steering committee or working party. A parallel structure is created within the group that has the responsibility for the actual development work. This is called variously, the computer department, the management services department or the data processing department. This structure enables the different functions within the department to work together: systems analysis, systems design, programming, support (software, standards and training), forward planning, and operations. Finally, there is the mechanism whereby the user and data processing department work together. The standard practices for developing systems and the organization of the personnel undertaking this work vary from company to company, and from government department to government department. Before examining various systems techniques, it is necessary to review how companies organize their development work. This can be reviewed under a number of headings, as summarized in Figure 1.2.

The policies and procedures for developing systems as shown in Figure 1.2 will be determined by the characteristics of the organization as a whole. Figure 1.3 summarizes the factors which affect the development of new systems. All the factors themselves are, of course, interrelated. The following

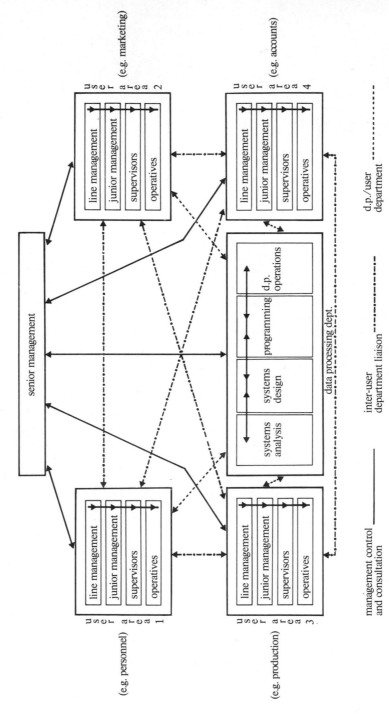

Figure 1.1: Communications in system development

Figure 1.2:   Approaches to systems development

---

1.   *Systems development cycle*
   (a) *What* are the tasks in developing a system from first inception to live running and thereafter?
   (b) *What* are the checkpoints (decision-making points) at which the following are agreed?
   - economic viability
   - operational suitability
   - technical feasibility.

2.   *Responsibilities*
   (a) *Who* has the responsibility to *authorize* the start of a project or task within a project?
   (b) *Who* has the responsibility to *approve* the quality and quantity of work during a project?
   (c) *Who* must be *consulted* during a project?

3.   *Organization*
   (a) *How* are the tasks and checkpoints in 1(a) and 1(b) carried out?
   - within a user area
   - between user areas
   - within data processing department
   - between data processing department and user areas.
   (b) *How* are the job functions within the data processing department divided among individuals and how is the data processing department organized?

Example 1: A large US manufacturing and distribution company operating also in Europe and Africa

examples, based on actual organizations, illustrate how radically the systems development policies and procedures can vary based on the factors shown in Figure 1.3.

The national operating companies had a high standard of management, good industrial relations, and progressive personnel policies. Considerable control was exercised over the operating companies, despite a policy of autonomous self-control. The company overall had four or five major applications. The characteristics of its system development were as follows:

1. Systems standards were originated in the head office, with strong pressure applied for their use in operating companies.

2. In three major application areas, the requirement was for common systems which could be implemented in most operating companies. International system project teams were created for these projects.

3. Local projects, of which there were many, were undertaken in different ways within each operating company. Systems analysts were allowed access to all user personnel from senior management to junior clerks, and there was no fear of the unorthodox. User management were capable of specifying in detail their business and information requirements, a reflection of the planning and objective-setting cycle that was an integral part of a manager's job.

5

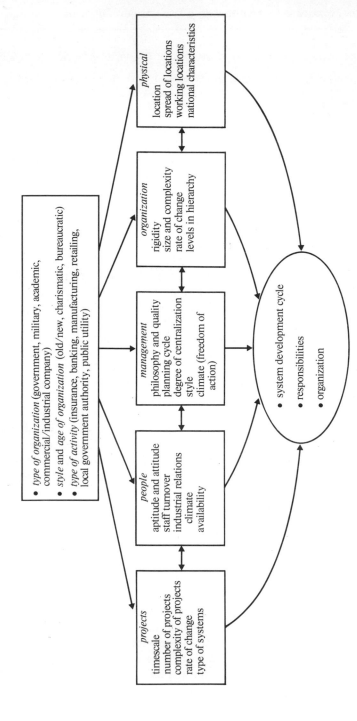

Figure 1.3: Factors determining system development approach

4. In each operating company, the structure of the data processing department and the job functions within it became standardized to enable staff to move between companies, an incentive to the d.p. staff.

5. Computers had been used in the company from the very day of its formation and were recognized as being an integral part of the business. The data processing department was recognized as being of vital importance to the success of the business.

Example 2: A large government authority in London

The organization had the typical working environment and structure of a local authority in a city: formalized organization structure and job grading, the reconciliation of democratic government via its elected members and the efficient running of its affairs via professional civil servants. The authority operated within the rules and conventions of local government. Salaries were below the local norm and working conditions were difficult.

1. There were a large number of diverse complex applications from engineering to education, from social services to cleansing, from town planning to rating. Applications were developed for a specific user, reflecting parochial user management attitudes.

2. Analysts had access to low and middle level management, rarely to higher levels of management. This reflected the status consciousness of the organization.

3. Checkpoints were time-consuming activities, proposals being referred to a plethora of committees and management levels.

4. Conservative attitudes preserved the *status quo*. Problem analysis was superficial; user managers had rather vague objectives and rarely admitted that problems existed or that their activities had scope for improvement. Data processing was thought by some to be a 'parasite', a necessary evil remote from the *real* work of the authority.

Example 3: A US military installation

The organization had a rigid structure of command and detailed, formalized procedures. Operationally, there were very precisely defined objectives. Forward planning was a remote function, and senior personnel rarely saw themselves performing 'senior management' functions.

1. The rigidity of structure and formalized procedures were carried into systems development. For example, methods standards occupied five volumes, each two inches thick. Checkpoints were very formal.

2. It was accepted that personnel would 'follow the rules'. Systems were designed on the basis that they would be followed to the letter. User attitudes at lower levels were discounted; users did as they were told.

3. There was a limited number of applications, mainly concerned with record keeping and low-level control. Management reporting was a small part of a system structure with the exception of standard budgetary control reports.

4. The data processing department was organized with the same rigorous rules and thoroughness as the operational areas. The job of the systems analyst was very limited, with user contact regulated according to precise rules.

These three examples illustrate how data processing policies and methods are a reflection of the total environment. Nevertheless, there are a number of policies and procedures for developing computer-based systems that are common to most organizations. The difference lies in the quality of work, and how the policies and procedures are implemented. Perhaps the most important factor is the definition of the series of tasks to develop and implement a system, from first thoughts to operational running. This is the *system development cycle.*

Figure 1.4 shows an 11 step system development cycle. The steps may be called by other names, but the structure is typical of many organizations. Figure 1.5 shows the standard steps with additional tasks for the project initiation and project development of a large job. The diagram also shows the major documents produced and the management checkpoints. (Each of the steps will be further sub-divided into more detailed tasks for the purposes of project planning and control.) The work performed at each step and the contents and format of the documentation produced will depend on the project and the organization. There are, however, standard functions that must be performed if the resultant system is to be effective and realistic. *Effective* in that it makes a positive contribution to the organization (profits in a company, service level in a government department), and *realistic* in that it is capable of being run by both users and data processing operations.

The techniques discussed later in this book must be related to an overall framework of systems development. The framework chosen is the 11 step cycle shown in Figure 1.4. The functions of each of the steps are summarized below.

STEP 1—USER REQUEST

This is also called *exploratory study* and *problem definition.* It is the first formal step in the systems development cycle, but will probably have been preceded by informal reviews and negotiations between user staff and between users and the data processing department. Regardless of the casual discussions at the inception of a project, it is vital to document formally the business requirements for a new system, to specify detailed terms of reference for any future work. In this respect the terms 'user request' and 'problem definition' taken together provide an excellent description of the work involved, which is to produce a statement of problems from the user's point of view, and a request for assistance in solving them.

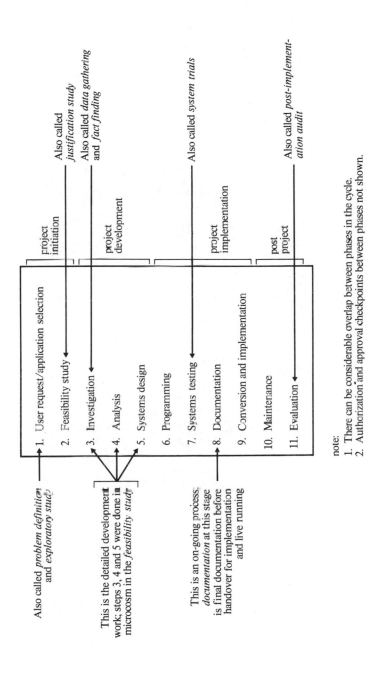

Also called *problem definition*
and *exploratory study*

1. User request/application selection — project initiation

2. Feasibility study — Also called *justification study*

3. Investigation — Also called *data gathering and fact finding*

4. Analysis — project development

5. Systems design

This is the detailed development work; steps 3, 4 and 5 were done in microcosm in the *feasibility study*

6. Programming

7. Systems testing — Also called *system trials*

8. Documentation — project implementation

This is an on-going process; *documentation* at this stage is final documentation before handover for implementation and live running

9. Conversion and implementation

10. Maintenance — post project

11. Evaluation — Also called *post-implementation audit*

note:
1. There can be considerable overlap between phases in the cycle.
2. Authorization and approval checkpoints between phases not shown.

Figure 1.4: 11 step system development cycle

A. *Project initiation*

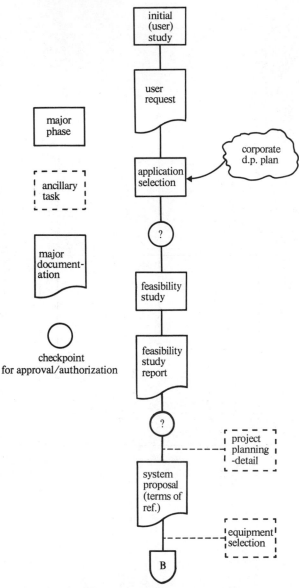

Figure 1.5:   System development cycle, with documentation and checkpoints

10

B. *Project development*

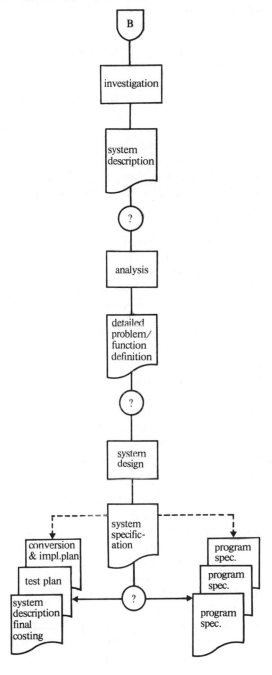

The exact contents of the user request depend on local standards, but typically, the following are required:

- *objectives*: what the new system must achieve: for example, cost reductions, better service levels, ability to deal with workload increases. The objectives are thus business performance targets which any new system must meet. They are only meaningful if they are quantified, i.e. presented as specific, attainable targets.
- *boundaries and constraints*: what the new system must not do. These are restrictions imposed on any solution from the business point-of-view. A boundary could be an organizational limit: an area where a solution is required with other areas left (preferably) unchanged. A constraint could be any restriction (budgetary, personnel, other resource) on the development work or in the operation of the new system.
- *timescale*: when a solution is required. This is the target date for the new system, again derived from the business requirements. It could be based on the release of a new product or on a reorganization, or it could be determined by the date of annual stocktaking or the start of a financial year, or by the impending collapse of existing methods.
- *mandatory documents/reports*: outputs which must be produced by the new system, operational documents, and management reports. For example, the format and content of some documents may be restricted by convention or legislation. Mandatory management reports, derived from examination of business needs, are those which any new system must produce.
- *identified problems*: problems in the existing environment (current and future) that any new system must solve.
- *suggested solutions*: general solutions considered by the user management.

The user request is thus a formalized specification of what any new system must and must not do. This is rarely prepared by the users unaided; usually it is the product of the user with the assistance of a senior systems analyst. Some companies, realizing that the user request is principally concerned with business and management (as opposed to computers and other technical solutions), employ *business analysts*—internal management consultants who assist in the preparation of such documents.

Most companies have some form of application selection procedure, where user requests are submitted to a steering committee for evaluation. The steering committee approves projects for further work, assigns priorities, and ensures that all departmental interests are considered.

The user request states the problems, the feasibility study proposes solutions. The objectives of the feasibility study (also called a *justification study*) are two-fold: to validate the user request, and to present alternative solutions for further development.

Figure 1.6:   Sample contents of feasibility study

---

1. Terms of reference

    1. Introduction and scope
    2. Method
    3. Objectives, boundaries and constraints

2. Existing system

    1. Summary description
    2. Growth and future trends
    3. Problem analysis

3. Alternative solutions (for each solution)

    1. Outline description
    2. Outline development plan
    3. Cost/benefit analysis
    4. Advantages and disadvantages

4. Conclusions and recommendations

Appendices

A. Key statistics and volumes
B. Sample documents and reports
C. Detailed costing figures

This phase will include investigation, analysis, and design—*all in outline*. Subsequent development work (steps 3, 4, and 5 in Figure 1.4) will repeat these steps in detail. Both user management and the data processing department must agree an outline solution prior to undertaking detailed development work, for three reasons:

1. All parties must be assured that a chosen solution is apparently economically viable, operationally suitable, and technically feasible prior to incurring further expenditure.
2. It is difficult, sometimes impossible, to assure user cooperation and involvement without an agreed sense of direction.
3. The greater the expenditure before a basic 'go/no go' decision is taken, the more the decision is pre-empted to 'go' to justify a return from the expenditure already incurred.

An example table of contents is shown in Figure 1.6. Although the report will contain recommendations from the team who prepared it, typically systems analysts from the data processing department, it should present, as objectively as possible, alternative courses of action. It is then a user management decision as to which solution is acceptable to them and is to be pursued with their backing.

The chosen solution is extracted from the report, a more detailed project plan prepared, and this document, the 'system proposal', becomes the detailed terms of reference for subsequent work.

The concept of a feasibility study as a study in outline, not detail, requires the establishment of *checkpoints* at which the findings can be validated and agreed after more detailed work has been done. These checkpoints take place after steps 3, 4, and 5 in Figure 1.4.

In many commercial and government systems it is the steps of 'programming', 'systems testing', and 'conversion and implementation' which consume most of the project budget, i.e. steps 6, 7, and 9 in Figure 1.4. The major checkpoint is thus based on the study of the system specification after step 5, 'systems design'. This is the final point at which a 'go/no go' decision can be taken before incurring the expenditure of the implementation steps.

STEP 3—INVESTIGATION

The investigation carried out during the feasibility study was intentionally superficial. It concentrated on the upper levels of management, with only selected data being checked in detail, such as key data volumes and times. The investigation at step 3, on the other hand, is a thorough and exhaustive review. This step is also called 'data gathering' and 'fact finding'. The objective is a complete understanding of the existing environment and how it will change in the future. The output will be a complete specification of:

- *the data*—its uses, volumes, and characteristics
- *the procedures*—what is done, where, when, and how, including all error and exception cases
- *the people*—who does what, when, and how, their aptitudes and attitudes
- *the future*—growth rates of the business and their impact on data and workload volumes
- *management reports*—requirements for new reports and their contents, accuracy, and timeliness.

The time and resources for this step depend on the age and type of the existing system. For example, if the existing system is a manual one which has been in operation for 20 or 30 years, has never been formally reviewed or even documented, and has continually been changed in a haphazard way, then the investigation may take several man-years. If, on the other hand, the existing system is a batch computer system implemented in the past five years, has not been subject to much maintenance, and has remained well documented, then the investigation will require far less effort.

A major investigation which includes a review of many activities in an old, manual system may require an additional step, that of *data organization*. This is the formal documentation of all the findings, including:

- organization charts and job descriptions
- document and functional flowcharts
- data analysis charts
- procedure specifications.

This will form the basis of a major user checkpoint. This user checkpoint can be expressed as follows: before going further and incurring more expenditure on analysis and design, do we (user and data processing) agree that this is a complete and accurate description of the existing system, the future of the business and new reporting requirements?

STEP 4—ANALYSIS

At its simplest, the analysis step determines *what* the new system must do, prior to the design step which determines *how* the new system will do it. The output from analysis will include a detailed list of *functions*—what any new system must do—a list of *problems*—what the new system must solve—and a description of the *data*—what any new system will use. This may form the basis of a formal user checkpoint prior to embarking on step 5, 'design'. Again, this checkpoint can be described as: before spending any time and effort on design, do we (user and data processing) agree that this is what the new system must do, the problems it must solve and the data available to do it?

STEP 5— SYSTEM DESIGN

The major output from the design step is the 'system specification'. Some companies require the design phase to be split into two parts. The first, sometimes called 'business system design', is concerned with the detailed user input and output procedures, and a general description of the files maintained on the computer. The second part, 'technical system design', is concerned with the computer sub-system, i.e. detailed file contents and formats and the sub-division of the system to the program specification level. Note that the system specification must not only describe the new system but also provide the basis for a final cost/benefit assessment and a plan for the subsequent project implementation steps. An example table of contents for a full system specification is shown in Figure 1.7.

STEPS 6, 7 AND 9—PROGRAMMING, SYSTEMS TESTING, CONVERSION, AND IMPLEMENTATION

The work in these steps can overlap considerably. Based on the program specifications, the programming step will produce programs coded and tested to the specification, using programmer-generated test data. Systems testing (using selected live data) will progress from suite or linkage testing to user acceptance trials in which *all* activities are tested.

Conversion will include all tasks prior to the actual implementation of the new system. Conversion tasks include:

- file conversion
- user training
- preparing operating instructions/user manuals
- printing new stationery
- delivery and installation of new hardware.

Again, many of these tasks will overlap with implementation of the new system by parallel, pilot, or gradual changeover.

Figure 1.7: Sample summary contents of systemal specification

1. System summary
   1. Management summary
   2. System flowchart
   3. Narrative description
   4. Cost–benefit analysis

2. Data specifications
   1. Files
   2. Inputs
   3. Outputs

3. Processing specifications
   1. Manual
   2. Computer

4. System test plan
   1. Test organization
   2. Test schedule

5. Conversion plan
   1. Conversion tasks and responsibilities
   2. File data sources and preparation method
   3. Conversion schedule

STEP 8—DOCUMENTATION

This is shown as a separate step in Figure 1.4 but is an on-going process throughout steps 3 through 10. Documentation at step 8 is *final documentation* before handover for implementation and live running. This will therefore include all data processing operating instructions and user operating procedures. It also includes the tidying up of all systems and program documentation for later systems maintenance.

Poorly documented systems have been the scourge of some data processing departments, leading principally to inefficient and ineffective maintenance. The continuous documentation of work done at steps 3 through

9 and the subsequent up-dating of the documentation at step 10 is vital for the success of the data processing department as a whole.

STEP 10—MAINTENANCE

Invariably the new system will be subject to change, probably from the first week of live running. Some changes will have to be made to eliminate residual bugs left from the testing phase; other changes (hopefully minimal) will have to be made because the specification as accepted was incorrect, ambiguous, or incomplete. Most maintenance, however, will be concerned (or *should* be concerned) with keeping the system in step with changes in the business structure and management; for example, new business methods, reorganization, statutory changes, new products or services, corporate acquisitions.

STEP 11—SYSTEMS EVALUATION

This, the final step in the system development cycle is also called the 'post-implementation audit'. It is the formal review of the system after it has been in operation for some time and sets out to answer three main questions:

1. Has the system achieved what the users wanted it to achieve, as in the user request (step 1)?
2. Have the requirements for the system changed, and if so, how has the system performed within these changed objectives and how should it be modified or extended? (This can lead into a repeat of the systems development cycle for a new system from step 1.)
3. Was the development work done effectively? This is an evaluation of how well the system was developed, such as, were schedule or cost targets missed or met? It can also include a technical evaluation of system performance (program sizes and execution times, validity and performance of file structures, etc.), as well as a review of user satisfaction with day-to-day procedures.

This 11 step development cycle will thus provide the basis for describing the systems techniques later in the book. The next task here is to review the job of the systems analyst.

Systems analysis

So far in this chapter it has been shown that the systems development methods in an organization are but a reflection of the type of organization, its structure, its operating methods, and its management. The structure of the data processing department, the organization of project teams, and the job content of systems analysis and programming, will in turn be a reflection of these methods. Although most companies have adopted or are moving toward an 11 step cycle as described previously, no two organizations seem to agree exactly on what the job of a systems analyst is, how a project team should be organized, or what the reporting structure should be.

The job title 'systems analyst' and the function 'systems analysis' are industry standards but examination of the work content shows that these are misnomers. The typical systems analyst will be concerned with investigation, design, testing, implementation, and maintenance—analysis *per se* forms only a small part of his work.

phase	method				
	1	2	3	4	5
user request	"progalysts"	systems analyst	systems analyst	business analysts	business analysts
feasibility study					systems analysts
investigation				systems analyst	
analysis			systems designers		
system design		programmers		systems designer	systems designer
programming			programmers		systems assurance / programmers
systems testing		systems analyst	systems analysts	systems designer	
documentation		programmers	systems analysts	systems analysts	systems analysts
conversion and implementation			maint./prog. analysts	maint. progalysts	systems analysts
maintenance				systems analysts	operational enhancements and improvements
evaluation					

* Major responsibilities shown; consultation not shown.

Figure 1.8: System development cycle—example job responsibilities

Figure 1.8 shows five job structures related to the 11 step systems development cycle. These five ways of dividing the project work represent the most commonly used approaches in commerce and government. The jobs shown are concerned with the main systems development functions. Support functions are not shown, but can include:

- standards and training
- software support
- data base administration
- documentation library and clerical support
- forward resource planning (hardware/software evaluation and
- selection)
- forward system planning (long-range corporate systems planning)
- network control (for on-line systems).

Method 1—the programmer/analyst or 'progalyst' approach is now out of favour, except in small organizations where neither the budget nor the workload will permit any specialization. The advantages and disadvantages of the 'jack of all trades' can be summarized as follows:

Minimal staff and lowest cost—but with capacity for only a limited number of simple projects. The progalyst approach appears to be suitable for the two- to four-man development organization (with working managers). There will generally be only three or four applications, and these will be simple in structure, such as the straight computerization of existing systems. This approach will thus tend to be used in small manufacturing and distribution companies, small merchant banks, small local government authorities, and so on. These will have a visual record computer, or a 370/125 computer or similar machine.

Simplified communication between phases, because there is no handover of specifications between functions at the end of the various phases, as between systems design and programming. This can have the disadvantage of careless or inadequate documentation, creating problems when an individual leaves.

Technically realistic systems, because the man who designs the system will have to program, test, and implement it.

Workload imbalance, because one systems analyst can generate work for a number of programmers. The progalyst may thus be supported by two or three full-time programmers. When the workload increases, however, the progalyst functioning as a programmer will form a bottleneck. Similarly, as more and more work goes on the computer, maintenance will increase substantially. Much of this maintenance work will be revisions to programs, again creating an imbalance of development effort and resources.

Consistency of quality of work in all phases: The aptitude, skills, and experience required at each of the phases in the development cycle are different. Contrast, for example, the work involved in dealing with users, the investigation and systems analysis tasks, and the coordination and control of conversion activities with the technical functions of file design and programming. Consistently high performance in *all* these tasks must be a contradiction in terms.

At the other end of the spectrum, there is the very large organization using method 5 in Figure 1.8. Such an installation will have a wide range of complex applications, a high rate of change, and very tight development schedules. The organization has a high degree of job specialization:

- business analysts
- systems analysts
- systems designers
- programmers
- systems assurance officers

- operational improvements and enhancement staff (a euphemism for specialist maintenance staff).

There are, in addition, support functions such as standards and training, as well as the various levels of management and supervision within each activity. This will solve many of the problems of the progalyst approach but will introduce others:

- arranging workable handover points between groups
- developing and enforcing rigorous documentation standards for interphase communication
- coordinating all activities between and within the different groups
- creating meaningful jobs of sufficient depth and interest to provide satisfaction to all employees
- preventing an imbalance of power and authority between groups.

Perhaps the most common approaches are methods 2 and 3 in Figure 1.8. These recognize the differences in workload, work content, and skill required at each of the steps, at the same time minimizing the number of different groups.

In summary, a typical job specification for a senior systems analyst (working within methods 2 and 3 in Figure 1.8) is shown in Figure 1.9 and that for a systems analyst in Figure 1.10. This book is based generally on the job of a systems analyst as defined in these job specifications.

What type of person is employed as a systems analyst? This is an important question, for it will determine the quality of the organization's systems.

In the 20 years or so since the job of computer-oriented systems analyst was created, no standard has emerged for the selection and training of analysts. Indeed, it is still a controversial subject. For example, a preliminary study on systems analyst selection published in 1970 contained the following conclusions and recommendations:

'1. Many potentially successful systems analysts are lost if only graduates are considered for selection.
2. It was rare to find systems analysts assessed as having high ability in all aspects of the work: it is therefore important to consider the particular contributions they can make in relation to the jobs for which they are selected.
3. No useful relationships were found between the biographical information obtained and assessments of job performance.
4. Standard tests of intelligence, verbal aptitude, and logical thinking are likely to be useful in selecting systems analysts.
5. Scores on certain tests of personality were related to assessments of performance but proof of their value for selection depends on the results of further study.

General responsibility
Responsible to the data processing manager for assisting other managers in determining the information requirements to improve planning, direction, and control of the organization, for directing the design and justification of computer-based systems that will meet such needs, and for reviewing the progress of such jobs until they are in production. He regularly reviews operational jobs, controls the system designers and determines the interface between jobs split amongst them.

Detailed responsibilities
(a) Estimates the cost of carrying out an appraisal.
(b) Appraises the organization's information needs in an area defined by management.
(c) Appraises the available information, both internal and external, in relation to the needs of the organization and particularly of its management.
(d) In the light of these appraisals defines, in conjunction with management, the information required to meet the current and expected needs of the organization.
(e) To meet the information needs, designs an 'information system'; provides an outline plan showing the flow of information, the processing required, and the equipment which may be needed; where appropriate, prepares a model or advocates a pilot scheme. This design will include block diagrams, broad flow charts, and narrative suitable for presentation to managers concerned.
(f) Estimates the time required to develop and implement the proposed system.
(g) Estimates the resources required for and the total costs of developing the system design and related manual and other procedures, and of introducing, implementing, and operating the proposed system, based on detailed estimates prepared by the systems staff.
(h) Estimates, in conjunction with the user departments, the direct savings resulting from the proposed system of processing information; assesses the value of other quantifiable benefits, and describes any non-quantifiable benefits or disadvantages.
(i) Submits the justification report through the data processing manager to obtain top management's approval to proceed with the project; conducts any formal presentation.
(j) Controls the progress of projects by regular review meetings.
(k) Monitors the operation of the installed system and compares results, including costs, with the justification report.
(l) Keeps under continuous re-appraisal the effectiveness of the information system in relation to the changing needs of the organization, and to equipment becoming available.
(m) Assists in recruiting systems personnel and in their training; reviews their performance.
(n) Keeps abreast of all relevant developments.
(o) Lays down standards and techniques to be observed in systems work and ensures conformity with them.

This job description was prepared by the Department of Trade and Industry in consultation with computer users, computer manufacturers, and the National Computing Centre.

6. A further study is needed in which new recruits to systems analysis are tested and interviewed to see if their subsequent performance may be correctly predicted'. (Margret Crawley and Jennifer Morris, *Systems Analyst Selection—A Preliminary Study*, p. 8, National Institute of Industrial Psychology and the National Computing Centre, Manchester, England, 1970.)

Certainly, there is no accepted industry aptitude tests for analysts (as opposed to those for programmers or operators). Neither are there truly national or international academic qualifications for analysts, but there has been increasing activity in this field, for example, the British Computer Society examinations and National Computing Centre certificates in systems analysis in the UK. In selecting systems analysts, therefore, many

Figure 1.10: Example job description:
systems designer or analyst

General responsibility
Responsible to the chief/senior systems designer for the detailed design of part or the whole of a computer-based information processing system. May control the implementation of a project.

Detailed responsibilities
- (a) Participates in the feasibility study and in particular does any necessary fact finding.
- (b) Examines the proposed information system and defines in detail the input and output requirements, the file contents, and the relationship between them.
- (c) Prepares, in a form suitable for programmers, a specification of the processes to be carried out (elaborating as required the broad flow charts), and agrees the contents with the user parties concerned.
- (d) Assesses the input, output and file volumes, and the frequency of each of the various processes, in conjunction with programming and operating staff, so that the time and cost for implementing and operating the system can be estimated.
- (e) Collaborates with auditors to ensure the necessary controls are incorporated in the system.
- (f) In conjunction with users and other computer staff, designs the forms for input data and output results.
- (g) Specifies any required manual or non-computer processing, the information required for it, and the controls necessary to minimize and correct inaccuracies in transferring data to and from the computer.
- (h) Provides instructions or a manual of the revised procedure for user-departments. Specifies requirements and provides test data for trying out the system, and arranges the trials. May control or assist in the implementation of the system.
- (i) Checks that the system in operation meets the specification.
- (j) May control junior staff assisting in all or some of the above duties.
- (k) Devises and supervises the education and training of all user personnel concerned with the project.

This job description was prepared by the Department of Trade and Industry in consultation with computer users, computer manufacturers, and the National Computing Centre.

organizations rely on various interpretations of previous academic attainments and job performance to indicate potential for success in systems work. Training courses, linked to on-the-job training, are now provided by many academic institutions, professional bodies, and commercial training companies.

In the absence of conclusive, formal research programmes into the selection and development of systems analysts, we have to rely on the general reactions of employers.

First, the source of systems analysts. An analysis was done by the author of 520 students, currently employed as systems analysts, attending practical training courses; their backgrounds are categorized in Figure 1.11.

1. Recruited as trainees straight from school, college or university as first jobs, i.e. direct entry.
2. Recruited from other, user, areas of the same organization.
3. Recruited from other, user, areas (totally different disciplines) outside the company.
4. Recruited from other problem-solving advisory functions, i.e. work study, industrial engineering or organization and methods.
5. Recruited from other *technical* branches within data processing, i.e. operations or programming.

Figure 1.11:   Analysis of source of systems analysts*

Source	Number	Percentage
Direct entry	115	22
User areas: (within organization)	62	12
User areas: (outside organization)	36	7
Other advisory areas: (e.g. work study, O&M)	109	21
Technical d.p. (e.g. programmers, operations)	198	38
	520	100

* Based on survey of 520 systems analysts (trainees, juniors, seniors, and progalysts) attending courses. The analysts came from a wide range of organizations: banking, local and central government, retail and distribution, engineering, etc. A further 28 analysts did not fit easily into any of the above categories.

The numbers in each category are shown in Figure 1.11. Unfortunately, it was not possible to measure job performance against these categories by any objective yardstick. It appeared, however, that the contribution made by an analyst differed according to his background. The ex-programmers concentrated and performed well on the technical design aspects of a system, but often required considerable assistance in user negotiations, business problem solving, form design techniques, and so on. Experienced users trained in systems techniques did well in business problem analysis and outline design, but relatively poorly on the technical aspects of design. Where it was not possible to compensate by giving additional assistance, the system suffered accordingly.

Because the job of a systems analyst has been defined in so many ways by different organizations, the employers' assessment of 'what makes a good analyst' is difficult to correlate. In 1971, one survey carried out by the author asked employees to list the six *abilities* of analysts they considered most

Figure 1.12: Analysis of employer-rating of relative importance of abilities

- *Communication:* ability to get information and cooperation from, and to present information to, all levels of user staff and management, as well as own team, programmers, operations staff, etc.
- *Analysis:* ability to sub-divide complex systems, procedures, and data as a whole into their constituent parts, and to define problems and requirements therefrom
- *Discipline:* ability to follow an orderly, neat approach, and to organize and monitor own performance
- *Social sensitivity:* ability to perceive and analyse the interaction between individuals, and between people and automated processes
- *Detail:* ability, within taking a broad approach, to follow one line of thought in detail, taking a step-by-step logical approach, considering all combinations of data and processing conditions
- *Coordination:* ability to plan, apply, and control resources, as in systems testing, conversion, and implementation

Note: Various personality characteristics were very common, such as tenacity, assertiveness, stamina, strength of character, sense of purpose.

Figure 1.13: Analysis of employer-rating of relative importance of knowledge and experience

- *Hardware/software capabilities and techniques:* including program logic design, back-up and recovery, application program construction, validation techniques, software availability, timing and response
- *Input techniques:* including forms design, data preparation methods, checking and validation techniques, data control functions, document reading methods
- *Management problems and techniques:* including styles of management, decision making, functions of management (by application area), MBO, budgeting, management sciences, use of MIS
- *Communication and analytical techniques:* including interviewing, report preparation, presentations, group meetings and activities, user liaison, team meetings
- *Business problems and techniques:* including business economics, business climate, organization structures, forecasting, business technology and methods (by application area)
- *Individual and group processes:* including leadership, job enrichment, introducing change, interaction between individuals, group psychology

essential for the successful system analyst in the relative order of importance. A summary is given in Figure 1.12. (Note that in this survey the six most common stated abilities were taken for the final table, and the relative rating in the scale adjusted. For example, if an employee rated the abilities as A, B,

X, Y, C, D, with A, B, C, and D being the most commonly quoted abilities but with X and Y not, the relative importance of A, B, C, D was given as 1, 2, 3, 4, not 1, 2, 5, 6.)

The employers were then asked to give their assessment of the relative importance of knowledge and experience of hardware characteristics, software characteristics, programming, user management, and business methods. This produced results summarized in Figure 1.13. An interesting contradiction emerged. Although the ability to communicate (such as in user liaison) was rated high in the table in Figure 1.12, knowledge of hardware and software was rated high in the table in Figure 1.13. Unfortunately, it was not possible to take this particular research project further. We can, however, draw on the work of Richard D. Arvey and Joseph C. Hoyle (*Evaluating Computing Personnel*, pp. 69 to 71, 73, Datamation, July 1973).

Working with a midwestern computer manufacturer employing some 3000 computer personnel in the US and Canada, they catalogued the major dimensions of job behaviour and their definitions for programmer/analysts and systems analysts. This is reproduced in Figure 1.14(a). The average importance ratings for these twelve dimensions of job behaviour for systems analysts and programmer/analysts are shown in Figure 1.14(b). Note that the dimensions considered more important for systems analysts than for programmer/analysts were:

maintaining customer relations (user liaison)
maintaining communications
assessing customer needs
conducting presentations
training others
providing supervision and leadership.

All indications thus suggest that the ideal analyst (as seen from the employer's point of view) is an 'all-rounder', a person who has the balance of abilities and knowledge between machine and people, between the technical and the human, with the emphasis, if any, towards the human.

People

Programmers often see an organization in black and white: the nuts and bolts of document flow, clearly defined file data element characteristics, precise logical program branches, rigid computer operations schedules. The very nature of the computer itself requires that a program be specified in precise, formal terms. He is, in his everyday work, seeing only the formalized tip of an iceberg. If such a programmer becomes a systems analyst, he would now investigate and analyse. If he were to maintain his mechanistic perception of a system, his work would be doomed to failure. For he would still see only the tip of the iceberg of the formal procedures and data. The bulk of the iceberg in systems terms is the people, their jobs, and their attitudes.

Figure 1.14:   Dimensions of job behaviour and their relative importance for systems analysts and programmer/analysts (Arvey and Hoyle)

(a) Major dimensions of job behaviour for systems analysts and programmer/analysts

1. *Technical knowledge:* keeping abreast of and retaining familiarity with software and hardware, learning new languages, application, utility routines, and/or executives, learning about central processors, peripherals, and other input/output media.

2. *Planning, organizing, and scheduling:* effective utilization of time, planning, and scheduling of current and future work, reacting to potential problems, making schedules, etc.

3. *Maintaining customer relations:* trying to please the customer, answering customer questions in an understandable manner, 'holding up' under customer demands and abuse, presenting new techniques on 'selling' the customer whenever appropriate, providing continuing customer service, providing advice, assistance, and updating to the customer.

4. 4. *Providing supervision and leadership:* giving technical work direction, directing and delegating assignments, motivating and utilizing personnel, calling meetings, coordinating activities, preparing cost estimates, and project schedules, etc.

5. *Training others:* providing instruction and guidance to customer personnel, co-workers, and/or subordinates, etc.

6. *Documentation:* providing formal narratives describing a program and/or system in sufficient detail so that others can understand and use the program and/or system.

7. *Maintaining communications:* providing information through the use of written or verbal channels, such as letters to colleagues, established procedures, using the telephone, etc.

8. *Assessing customer needs and providing recommendations:* studying and determining customer and/or internal management problems and requirements including the isolation, definition, and analysis of problem and need areas. Recommending software and hardware to solve these problems and/or meet their requirements.

9. *Job commitment and effort:* putting in long hours and extra time, working on own time to acquire knowledge, putting in a full week's work, performing tasks that might be considered beyond the 'call of duty', being committed to doing a good job.

10. *Debugging:* using various techniques (CRAM analysis, tracing of logic, etc.) in connecting the logic and associated problems in order to make a program or system operation.

11. *Program and/or systems modification and/or development:* modifying and/or developing programs and/or systems that reflect unique solutions and/or a certain degree of 'creativity'.

12. *Conducting presentations:* formally providing information and/or materials to interested personnel, illustrating how a system works, developing seminars, etc.

(b) Average importance ratings for 12 dimensions of job behaviour for
systems analysts and programmer/analysts

importance ratings

dimensions   1 2 3 4 5 6 7 8 9 10 11 12 13 14 15

technical knowledge

planning, organizing
and scheduling

*maintaining customer
relations

providing supervision
and leadership

training others

*documentation

*maintaining communications

*assessing customer needs
and providing recommendations

job commitment and effort

*debugging

*program and/or systems modi-
fication and/or development

*conducting presentations

*The difference between the systems analysts and programmer/analyst on this
dimension is statistically significant such that a difference this large would only occur
less than 1 time out of 20.

☐ systems analysts   ■ programmers

A company, a government department, and an academic institution are all social groups. If we examine the workings of a commercial company, what we would find would be the product of ideas and efforts of many individuals. More importantly, it would be the product of individuals interacting with each other. The reporting structure, the job responsibilities, the procedures, and the documentation are all the results of human attitudes and aptitudes, not just of current employees, but of all employees in the past, possibly generations of them. The job of the systems analyst is to define, design formalize, and specify a computer-based system, and this cannot be done in isolation from the people in the organization and the interactions between them. Rarely, if ever, can the analyst totally demolish the iceberg and rebuild it completely anew. Rather, he must work within the existing environment, building or remodelling a system within the constraints of the organization.

The analyst must have an awareness and understanding of the total environment within which he works. He must consult, negotiate, and advise. His product—a proposed new system—must be suitable for the environment in which it is to operate. He may recommend changes to the environment, but the impact of these changes must be carefully considered and they must, like the new system itself, be realistic.

Successful computer users recognize that the systems analyst is an *adviser*, an instrument of change. But the management of the change itself—the introduction of a new system—is the responsibility of users. An analyst can never totally re-create an environment. He cannot, for example, totally change both management structure and management, or the attitudes of workers. Nor can he restructure the entire reporting structure, or business methods and procedures. He must work within the organization. If there are bad industrial relations, possibly the accumulation of decades of social and business problems, can the analyst (or indeed management for that matter!) make them better in the two-year duration of a development project? Is it his job to do so? If there is little or no forward planning, can the analyst in a short space of time re-educate management, change their attitudes, and their aptitudes? Again, is it his job to do so?

A systems analyst, even a junior one, will have an influence on how an organization develops. How great that influence is will depend on the responsibilitity given to him, his exposure in the company and his personal credibility to management. It is not the analyst's job to perpetuate bad practices, to promote incompetent staff, nor to preserve anomalous organization structures. But he must recognize that changes are made through *user* management's decisions and actions, not his own. No matter how bright, enthusiastic, and energetic an analyst is, he cannot change the organization overnight.

The speed and scope of change are constrained by many factors in an organization, and it is important to review these.

Quality of management: The writings of the management theorists and practitioners would probably fill a good-sized office block or factory. Many write about 'good' versus 'bad' management. One of the best definitions of a manager was given by Peter Drucker in *The Practice of Management*:

'The manager is the dynamic lifegiving element in every business. Without his leadership the resources of production remain resources and never become production. In a competitive economy all the managers determine the success of a business, indeed they may determine its survival. For the quality and performance of its managers is the only effective advantage an enterprise in a competitive economy can have.'

Good management could be defined as management which creates a stable (but not stagnant) commercially successful company. This implies it will stay in business, continue to produce a satisfactory return on investment and live up to expectation of both employees and shareholders.

A more specific definition of management is:

'The term "management" is used . . . in the sense of a controlling activity: the managers of a firm are concerned with the use of the firm's resources to satisfy the aims of the firm. To do this successfully they must:
—identify objectives and set them in order of importance;
—design and construct a means by which those objectives may be attained; and
—measure from time to time the progress being made.' (*Training and Development of Managers . . . Further Proposals*, p. 3, Report by the Management Training and Development Committee, Department of Employment and Productivity, HMSO, London, 1969.)

So specifically, we must say that 'good' management is management which tries and succeeds in doing this, and 'bad' management is management which doesn't. It has long been realized that computerization will have little or no effect on the success of an organization if there is, by this definition, bad management.

Listed below are some real-life examples of 'bad' management. These are examples from the author's experience quoted virtually verbatim:

'Yes, I'm the Sales Manager. I don't have time for planning and all that. My job's that of a super-salesman. I go out and call on our most prestigious customers.'

This could be a fault of the organization structure (e.g. insufficient staff and time) or an excuse for not undertaking the management function.

'Information for planning? I've got two legs, two eyes and two ears. When something goes wrong and I want to know anything I get up and out, look and listen.'

There is nothing wrong with the collection of information informally from many sources, or by personal contact. But why wait until something has gone wrong?

> 'Ah yes, a new production system. Well, don't come and waste my time. I've got my hands full just trying to keep the plant running and meeting my quotas. I've got enough problems trying to solve yesterday's problems today, let alone tomorrow's.'

This was from a *senior* production manager. Let us hope someone, somewhere, *was* thinking about the future.

> 'Objectives? Well, certainly. Let me tell you what we *do*.'

This was a department in local government. In fact, there were no objectives, no agreed statement of what the department had to achieve. There were, on the other hand, volumes of procedure manuals and standing orders which stated *what* had to be done and how. Why were things done that way? Well, they always had been. Looking at the objectives of this manager, they could best be expressed as:

> 'To arrive at the office at 09.00,
> To leave the office at 17.00,
> *and not to rock the boat in the intervening period.*'

Indeed, as it turned out, the entire department of more than 50 people was organized and run with this objective—to preserve the *status quo*—in mind.

> 'Ah yes, management information from the new computer system. What I would like is . . .'

This statement was followed by a catalogue of new reports, a few of which made sense, most of which were irrelevant, duplications or just meaningless. The manager had never really thought about his job and was intellectually incapable of doing so.

This is the negative—but not uncommon—side of the picture.

Good management, as defined earlier, does exist. And where it does, the job of the systems analyst is simplified and the resultant system will probably make a major contribution to the organization. There is also another factor which comes into play. This is the exposure that management has had to projects similar to the development of computer systems. That is, long-term 'research and development' projects, involving expensive capital equipment. In a manufacturing company most management have had considerable exposure to such projects. They realize the importance of good forward planning, and that in the 'high technology' area costs invariably escalate and deadlines are difficult to meet. Consider an insurance company that has no machines more sophisticated than typewriters and adding machines. Management and staff have had little exposure to high technology projects similar to developing computer-based systems. They may not be completely aware of the function of a feasibility study, or the importance of checkpoints or, indeed, the importance of long-term planning and project control.

Management climate: In the above examples, the quality of management was partly determined by the capabilities of the individuals and partly by the constraints imposed upon them. The management climate is the sum of these constraints. In many cases, this is simply how much a manager is allowed to manage.

Quoting again from the report referred to on page 29:

'Where the climate within the firm is favourable certain characteristics are evident, e.g.,

—managers are allowed to manage and to learn from the consequences of their decisions;
—they know that achievement will be recognized and rewarded;
—enterprise and new ideas are encouraged and there is no fear of the unorthodox;
—the senior managers not only talk to their staff but they also listen to them.'

The management climate in a company evolves gradually, sometimes from the personality and style of one or two individuals, sometimes as a function of the type of organization, sometimes as a result of political or trading conditions.

Staff relations climate: When referring to personnel relations, most people think in terms of management–worker industrial relations, with the manager in his office confronting, or not, the workers on the shop floor. Here we are concerned not only with the hierarchy (vertical relations) but also with horizontal relations. Further, we must think of interaction not only between management and worker in the sense of manual workers, but also in terms of clerical, technical and administrative staff. We must also consider the vertical interaction at senior and intermediate management levels, not just within the lower levels of the hierarchy.

The relationships between staff, horizontally and vertically, can be categorized in many ways; for example:

good = trust, respect, confidence; based on consultation, 'fair dealing', and delegation of responsibility with authority.
bad = mistrust, mockery, anger, resentment, lack of confidence; based on 'arbitrary' decisions, deceit, and interference.

This climate may be conditioned by how people interact over many years, or may be changed by critical events in a short time. In a large multinational chemical company, for example, there were excellent staff relations for over 70 years, but within a year of a merger, and at a time of a statutory pay freeze, relations turned very sour indeed.

The analyst will have to work within the existing climate, good or bad. He may improve the situation a little, but he can aggravate it considerably. Again, some practical examples relations are useful to illustrate this:

From an intermediate manager, talking about his superior:

'This computer project is typical. My boss gets a bee in his bonnet about a new system. Probably he was sold the idea by somebody else. Out of the blue, without consultation, he announces that a new system must go in by the end of next year.'

From a supervisor, talking about his intermediate superior:

'So my boss signs-off on the specification for a new system. We down here never saw the specification, we weren't even asked about it. He doesn't really have a clue what we do down here. And we're the ones who have got to live with the new system. For years.'

From a clerk, talking about his management in general:

'The new system? Well, you can bet your bottom dollar that if its the "management" that thought it up, it will be a mess. All *their* ideas are half baked.'

From a storeman about his management generally:

'The new system *must* mean more work for the same money. Or, they want to save money and the only way they can do that is to get rid of some of us. I'd like to see them try. I'm not going to wait around to be fired. I'm looking for another job now.'

The relationships between staff at the same level horizontally may also be good or bad. If good, there is sympathy and trust, and a good team spirit. If bad, there are parochial attitudes, petty squabbles over trivia, empire building for self aggrandisement, and a drive to 'get the other man before he gets me'.

Quality of staff: This means the ability of the staff to deal with a new system. From the analyst's point of view, most employees can be divided into two categories: those whose primary function is to run the computer system, supply input, and interpret output, and those to whom these functions are secondary to their real jobs. The obvious examples of the former lie within the operations area—data control, data preparation, computer operators, the library, and so on. The less obvious are some clerical sections in the user area whose primary function may be to prepare input, such as coding, editing, manual verification, capture of data in hardcopy from telephone calls, and the operating of on-line terminals as a full-time job.

Examples of the second category are any staff to whom the computer-based system is incidental. The primary function of a salesman is to sell, to explain the goods and services in their best light and to persuade potential customers to buy; a *secondary* activity could be to complete an order, to fill in a call-sheet, and so on. A machine operator on the factory floor is paid to keep his machine loaded and to produce work of an acceptable quality. He may receive computer-produced job dockets to initiate an operation and he may have to complete a 'work done' docket (hours, scrap, quantity produced), but these are secondary. If the system is too complex to handle or interferes with his primary activity, it will not be successful. Quality of staff is therefore their ability to deal with the secondary activities. This is, of course, relative; it is possible to design a system of such complexity, that even somebody in the top one per cent of MENSA could not operate it. It is also possible to design a system which a person with an IQ of 80 could operate—but at a cost.

Aptitude (the ability to do a task) and attitude (the willingness to do it) are closely related, and it is often not possible to separate them. We shall consider this in more detail later.

Some quotations, this time from users and systems analysts, will illustrate the constraints of staff quality.

An analyst working on a distribution system for a medium-sized oil company:

> 'Those drivers can turn a 50 foot tanker on a penny. But get them to fill up a form correctly and it's asking for the moon.'

An accountant in a local talking about installing visual display units in a clerical office (not under his control):

> 'Those idiots can't even fill in a simple form, let alone operate that kind of equipment. This authority doesn't have the type of staff we want to run the current procedures. With the shortage of clerical staff in this area, the money we pay, and our reputation, it's not surprising that we end up with low calibre people.'

A data processing manager talking about the problems of designing systems in his 200-year-old insurance company:

> 'We have to design systems for the lowest common denominator, and in this place, that is pretty low. Most of our people do boring, repetitive, mind-destroying jobs requiring no imagination and little intelligence. You have to be thick to do the job; you'd go mad otherwise. Mind you, they're mainly a happy bunch; good workers.'

A systems analyst talking about designing on-line systems in the foreign exchange department of a merchant bank:

'It's marvellous. We can really do things here. All the staff, from filing clerks to secretaries to senior dealers are bright. They can handle complex, conditional logic and follow very rigorous rules on data formats.'

Simply, the quality of staff as defined above does vary from company to company, as well as between different departments. An understanding of the quality of staff is thus an important element in understanding the working environment as a whole.

Summary

This chapter has been concerned with definitions: how organizations develop systems, the job of a systems analyst, and the company or institution as a social group. The ideas and techniques presented in this book will be based on these definitions. Specifically, the following will be assumed:

1. The way an organization arranges its systems development depends on many factors (as summarized in Figure 1.3). This book will assume an 11 step system development cycle of:

1 ● user request
2 ● feasibility study
3 ● investigation
4 ● analysis
5 ● design (business and technical)
6 ● programming
7 ● testing
8 ● documentation
9 ● conversion and implementation
10 ● maintenance
11 ● evaluation.

2. There can be considerable overlap between these steps, and they do not necessarily represent a strict chronological sequence. In the pre-programming steps, however, each step should be completed before work on the next step begins. Formal checkpoints (i.e. review steps) take place after each step, to approve the work in that step, before it progresses.

3. The development of a system is a joint effort between user and data processing. The overall co-ordination of work, such as the setting of priorities, is the responsibility of a top-level steering committee.

4. The jobs within the data processing department vary (as in Figure 1.8), based on the size of organization, and the number, scope, and complexity of applications. The job of a systems analyst will be assumed as defined in the job specification in Figure 1.9.

5. There is, at present, no single source for recruiting systems analysts, nor nationally or internationally accepted qualifications or training programmes. The previous working background of the analyst will influence how he tackles a job and the quality of the system produced. Abilities related to people, however, are strongly rated by employers.

6. The systems analyst must strike a balance in attitude, knowledge, and experience between 'business and social' versus 'technical'.
That is:

business/social	*technical*
● business methods	● hardware characteristics
● management	● software characteristics
● user negotiations	● programming techniques
● information requirements	● data preparation techniques
● analysis of procedural and organizational problems, etc.	● file structures, etc.

This book deals exclusively with the business/social side of the systems analyst's job.

7. The analyst, in developing systems, must work within the existing environment of the organization. He is aided or constrained by factors which have evolved within the organization as a whole. By and large, he cannot alter this situation by himself.

8. The environment within which the analyst must work is determined by:

● quality of management
● management climate
● staff relations climate
● quality of staff.

9. In developing a system, the analyst must recognize that to many of the people who will use the system, the computer is incidental. It is not an end in itself, and it has a secondary role that must not interfere with primary job activities.

10. Staff aptitude and attitude are both major contributors to job performance, and are often inseparable to the casual observer. The calibre of staff is a major asset or hindrance to the work of the systems analyst.

2
Systems good
and systems bad

Criteria for success

The systems analyst is constantly striving to produce *good* systems. This chapter is concerned with answering four questions:

- what is a good system?
- what is a bad system?
- how does a good or bad system come about?
- how is this related to the people side of systems?

If the characteristics of good and bad systems can be specified and their causes defined, techniques can be developed to ensure success (or at least to prevent disaster).

A good system is one that achieves the objectives set for it. By meeting the objectives, the system is of benefit to the organization. This, of course, presupposes that the objectives set for the system were beneficial to the organization in the first place. To be classed as successful, a system must not only meet its objectives in terms of overall performance, such as a better customer service, less cost, better planning, etc., but also must be technically and operationally sound.

Three specific criteria may therefore be set:

1. *Economic viability*: the system meets its objectives, financial benefits are realized (directly or indirectly) at an acceptable cost.
2. *Operational viability*: the system is satisfactory in its day-to-day operation by staff.
3. *Technical viability*: the system works efficiently within the constraints of hardware and software.

Items 2 and 3 are usually prerequisites to 1. But a system may be partially economically viable without, in the short term, being operationally viable.

Systems bad—the faults

To examine the specific characteristics of a good system, especially one that qualifies as operationally viable, it is useful to examine the faults in a bad system. This we may do by looking at working systems which are rated by both users and data processing as having operational faults.

Figure 2.1 lists the eight most common faults identified in 25 systems running in eight commercial companies. The cumulative result of these faults will be that the systems fail to meet their objectives. For example:

Higher costs because of

- excessive maintenance to get the system working as it should
- more hardware to deal with extra processing
- more staff to deal with the volume of work.

Lower benefits because

- problems were not effectively solved or new problems were created
- management information not used
- full potential of system not used.

The result could be anything from general disenchantment with the system to outright antagonism, with people trying to beat it. It is important, therefore, to explore these systems faults in more detail, to examine their impact and probable causes.

Figure 2.1:   Operational system faults

- reports for management are inadequate/redundant
- low data accuracy
- missed schedules
- exceeded capacity
- existing system retained
- not all processing/data conditions catered for in new system
- system is over restrictive and too inflexible
- staff under more pressure

Reports for management are inadequate

A system starts live running; reports are produced and sent to management. They are expensive to produce, not just in machine time for printing them, but in file storage, coding techniques, and so on. Some reports may be found to be redundant. They come off the line printer, go via a messenger to a manager, and then straight into the waste-paper basket because the format, content, accuracy, and timescale are wrong. They either contain too much information or too little. Or, the user may struggle to make the system work. In one company, two additional clerks were employed to recast management reports—using adding machines. In extreme cases, it has been found that complete reports were entirely omitted from the new system. The impact here will obviously be expensive maintenance to get the reports right (as the manager wants them) as well as possible dissatisfaction with the system.

So far, we have considered known reporting requirements. There will also be cases where new reports are needed because of changes in the business, its organization, methods, or trading climate, but the system doesn't include them. Here are six common causes for this:

- The manager didn't know what to expect from a computer system, so he didn't know what to ask for.
- The manager didn't have time to analyse his requirements; he didn't think it important anyway because it was so far in the future and a bit theoretical.
- The manager thought he should specify something (so as not to appear antagonistic or apathetic) but his ideas were ill-conceived and hazy.
- The manager didn't have the analytical ability to define his requirements properly.
- The analyst thought he knew best, and the manager relied on him.
- The analyst saw the information was in the system, and so produced a report anyway.

These six points thus arise from the limitations in the manager's capabilities, his personality, the way in which he was consulted, and the interaction between analyst and manager. This is obviously one area where the people side of systems is important, and techniques for dealing with this situation are presented in Part II.

Low data accuracy

Errors in input data will occur in any system. When the input error rate is high, there will be additional costs of correction and re-entry. This may also create delays that have an impact elsewhere in the system. Alternatively, the incorrect data may pass further into the system and affect the files and output, causing wrong actions and decisions to be taken, a poorer service to customers (e.g. more complaints about errors in invoices), and a general lack of confidence in the system and its data.

There are various causes for these problems:

- The input procedure is too complex for the staff.
- The input procedures interfere with the user's primary activity, making their day-to-day work harder.
- The users have the attitude: 'If it's wrong someone else, or the computer, will pick it up, so why should I worry?'

- The users have no interest in the system; placid resistance: 'It doesn't do anything for me, I don't know why it's being done—it's *their* system', etc.
- The users are antagonistic to the system and won't make it work; possibly, they will try to actively make it fail.

The problems here are in two categories. The first is the realism of the systems design; that it is not geared to the environment. The second is in *how* the system was developed and implemented.

Missed schedules

This is similar to the faults of low data accuracy; data is consistently late arriving for processing. The causes and, as we shall see, the solutions are the same.

Exceeded capacity

The projected workload exceeds the proposed hardware capacity. This will result in an upgrading of hardware and software, more people to run the system or a degraded service (such as longer run times in a batch system or slower response rates in an on-line system). The causes of exceeded capacity may lie outside the scope of the system itself, such as changes in business methods or trading conditions. There are also the 'problems of success', as in a credit card company that had 50 per cent more applications for cards than was expected. Some cases of exceeded capacity, however, are caused by the way users interact with the system. For example, in an on-line order processing system in a chemical company, the message volume was double that expected, caused mainly by operators' fumbling. This was not a short-term problem: it persisted for over two years until the system was revised. In a local government authority, the volume on two on-line applications was ten times as high as initial estimates; this was partly because of operator errors, but mostly because users found new uses for the systems, 'browsing' via enquiry transactions, and so on.

Some causes of exceeded capacity are thus 'technical': increases in business and over-optimistic estimates of hardware performance. Others, however, are caused by the way people apply themselves to the system.

Existing system retained

This can be a serious problem. The system which was due to be replaced by the new, computer-based system is, in whole or part, retained. The two systems run side-by-side, sometimes without the knowledge of management. The reasons given for not relinquishing the existing system may be that the new one doesn't give the users the information or service they had before, or that the users have no confidence in the new system, or that the new system creates anomalies which can only be resolved by the old system.

The cost of duplicating systems effort can erode many of the benefits claimed for the new system. Indeed, the effort directed in supporting the old system may leave insufficient time and effort to support the new. For example, in a medium-sized engineering company, a manual stock recording system was replaced with a batch computer system. In the manual system, stock cards were updated almost immediately when a stock movement occurred and the cards were available for immediate inspection to answer queries. This was what staff claimed they needed to do their jobs effectively—as proved by the fact that the manual system, implemented more than 20 years ago, had played a major role in the success of the company. The new computer system produced a stock listing five days in arrears. (For example, stock movements submitted to the computer on Monday were incorporated in the stock listing returned from the computer on Friday. Stock movements on Tuesday through Friday were not included.) The existing system was therefore necessary (it was claimed) to record *all* movements so that the computer report could be updated. In fact, the whole of the manual system was retained, with the computer-produced report being assigned immediately to a filing cabinet! The input error rate was very high, because of the attitude of 'why bother to send in accurate input when the results are useless?'. This situation existed for about two years. The computer-based system had some benefits for management, such as the production of stock movement statistics, the maintaining of stock re-order levels and the setting of re-order quantities. The decision was finally taken to go on-line, and to provide the record-keeping service which would satisfy the operational needs of staff. A major design consideration was this: if the new, on-line system did not satisfy the lower level staff requirements, then the manual system would still be retained. If this happened, then the quality of input submitted continuously via visual display units would be as low as in the batch system.

How did this situation come about? There were three main reasons:

- The new system was supposed to satisfy batch record-keeping and control (management) requirements. The timescale and accuracy requirement of the two systems were radically different. Only the control (management) aspect of the system was considered in detail.
- The service and performance level expected of the record-keeping system by the user was based on experience and previous expectation. The service level of the existing system was, in fact, too sophisticated; a lower performance level would have met business needs. But the expectations of the people were never reconciled with the business objectives.

- There was a three-way conflict: *us* (the clerical users), *them upstairs* (the management) and *them over the road* (the computer people).

The faults stemmed from a lack of consultation between user managers and staff and a lack of understanding on the part of the analyst of quantified business aims (the theoretical performance level required) and the staff's perception of the service required.

Omissions in new system

Computer-based systems include both automated and manual procedures. The computerized procedures must be rigorously specified. If any processing or data conditions are omitted from, or ambiguously stated in, the program specifications, then the operational programs will be invalid. Expensive maintenance will be required to correct the programs or additional manual procedures will have to be introduced to compensate for the omissions. The resulting unplanned increase in manual work as well as delays in making yet further changes, can cause user dissatisfaction and loss of confidence.

Omitted conditions or incorrect processing are usually caused by inadequate investigation by the analyst and careless checking or authorization of specifications by user staff.

System is over restrictive and too inflexible

'Before the computer system, all we salesmen had to do to get our expenses was to complete a form, get it authorized and present it to the cashier at virtually any time. Now we have to complete the form with all sorts of codes, once a month. We have to put the form in by the last Friday of the month. Then, eventually, we get a cheque—up to three weeks later. Some service these computers give.'

'If I wanted stock, I'd call Fred in the Stores and he'd send it over—do the paper work later. It did get done, you know. Now it's fill in a form in triplicate, all these codes. It wastes a lot of time.'

'I used to update this ledger from just a scribbled note. I could recognize all the handwriting—even the scribbled abbreviations. Now the ledger is on the computer, it's all filling in little boxes, counting this and counting that. And the ledger is no more up-to-date than ever it was.'

'It's all rules and regulations nowadays with the computer. You can't do this because the paper's got to go through the computer first. You can't do that because the code isn't quoted.'

'If I wanted to know a customer's balance, his payment record, and a bit of general background, I could call any of the sales ledger clerks.

Now I have to wait up to 48 hours for a balance; the sales ledger clerks have lost touch with what customers are doing.'

'If I wanted to make a change in the old manual system, I would issue a memo to the staff and the staff would be working to the new procedures within 24 hours. With the computer I've had to wait up to six weeks for even a simple change. It's something to do with a shortage of programmers, problems with computer time or something.'

'Yes, I certainly do get better information from the computer. But there's a very long lead time to change a management report. It's even tougher to change the system.'

These are all user comments on the rigidity and inflexibility of computer-based systems, as seen by them. By their very nature, computer-based systems tend to formalize previously loose procedures. It is possible, however, to design a system which is too rigid and over restrictive. Many systems need 'manual over-ride' procedures for exceptional cases. An over restrictive system is commonly the result of putting the system first and the job second, putting the computer first and people second.

It is important to differentiate between systems which are really over restrictive in operation and those systems which are merely claimed to be. There may be reasons for closer controls and more rigid timescales that are not understood. Take the first example quoted above—the payment of salesman's expenses. The objective of the payment system *as seen by the salesman*, is to pay money owed (i.e. to reimburse money spent on behalf of the company) on demand, in cash. The objective of the payment system from the *accounting point of view* is radically different. For example:

1. There are problems in handling cash because of security, and a cheque is preferable.
2. A cheque is preferable to cash because of the additional administrative effort and responsibilities of collecting it from a bank, and reconciling cash with accounts records.
3. One expense form a month per salesman simplifies recordkeeping (and cuts down the cost of raising too many cheques).
4. The fixed time enables 'cost of sale' statistics to be compiled against a standard accounting period. The codes are also necessary for the production of these reports.
5. It is cheaper and easier to do one computer run per month, than a run two or three times per week.

What is 'over restrictive' to one user (the salesman) is an 'economic rationalization' to another (the accountant). In this case, the formality and rigidity of the computer system is almost incidental to the introduction of the policy of a monthly payment by cheque.

Irrespective of whether the rigidity or inflexibility of the system is actual or perceived, the results can be the same: a lack of interest and enthusiasm in running the new system, or a short-circuiting or bypassing the standard procedures (even beating the system). This dissatisfaction may result in a barrier to further systems development in the future, as well as immediate operational problems of poor data accuracy, misused output, and missed timescales.

Staff under more pressure

This is a claim made by user staff who are dissatisfied with the new system. Again, it may be actual or only perceived. The system may create more work, or create peaks of work, the reasons for which are not immediately apparent. Perhaps the benefits of new procedures lie in other departments or in higher levels of management. Consider the following examples:

System A: A payroll system for weekly paid staff. Run late on Thursday afternoon. Unexpected high error rate. Errors to be cleared by payroll section by 21.00 hours. This meant that payroll clerks had to work to at least 20.00 hours. Staff in this section rarely, if ever, worked overtime in the old system. No warning had been given during systems development that this would be necessary. Tension and conflict developed between data processing staff and the payroll staff and their management.

> *payroll staff*:
> 'We never had all this in the old system.'
> 'We work these hours to fit in with the computer.'
> 'In this system, the computer and its schedule comes first, we and our time come a very bad second.'

> *data processing staff*:
> 'The evening/night is the only time we have to run this job on a very tight computer schedule.'
> 'If *they* didn't make so many errors then *they* wouldn't have to spend all this time cleaning-up the data.'
> 'It's *their* system. So why shouldn't *they* put in this work. They're not doing us a favour, you know.'

System B: An on-line order entry system run by 11 clerks, drawn from 18 clerks who ran the original batch system. (The other seven clerks were 'redeployed to other sections' after the advent of the new system). If the system had worked according to initial estimates and specification, the workload for staff would have been marginally lighter than in the original system. For a number of reasons, however, the workload increased drastically. This meant that all staff had to be present for the system to operate effectively.

43

With the exception of carefully planned annual holidays, time off for special leave, sickness, training courses, time off in lieu of overtime, etc., made the system very difficult to operate. Staff, therefore, felt resentment not only towards working hours, but also to the restriction of 100 per cent attendance. Because part of the justification for the new system was the 50 per cent cut in staff, management would not agree to any staff increase.

The causes of the additional workload included: the complexity of display and input, slower response times than expected, and the time required for the manual reconciliation of batched source documents to computer-held balances. The system was based on the assumption that 40 per cent of staff time was spent on terminal operation, 60 per cent on other duties. The terminal operation, however, accounted for over 70 per cent of staff time. Other duties also increased because the number of staff had been reduced. Because these duties did not directly affect the operation of the computer-based procedures, the systems analyst had not studied them. No allowance had been made for the time spent on on these duties.

System C: A sales system (batch) in which orders were completed on customer's site by salesmen. A new system was introduced to reduce order turnaround time. The new order form (form B) was radically different from the old (form A). Form A included more complex coding for customer, delivery requirements, products, and product quantities. There were a number of checking procedures to be performed by salesmen (line counts, hash total of product code, total of quantities).

Salesmen claimed that the form and its processing took too much of their time, to the detriment of their selling activities. Over a period of about a year, a clerical section was formed at Sales Head Office. The salesmen went back to using form A and the clerks, up to ten at one point, transcribed orders from form A to form B. This eroded the claimed benefits for the system: no significant decrease in order turnaround time or decrease in operating costs.

When senior management learned of the new Head Office clerical section, they insisted it should be disbanded. This put the pressure back on to the salesmen. Some salesmen resigned from the company, others expressed considerable dissatisfaction.

System D: A job allocation and reporting system for inspectors in a local government authority. Inspectors were in very short supply. A rough apportionment of their time showed: general administration = 15 per cent, travel = 30 per cent, inspection and action = 45 per cent, dead time (unaccounted for) = 10 per cent. The objective of the new system was to reduce time spent on administration and travel and to raise active time from 45 per cent to 70 per cent. This target was accepted by line management, who made promises of better service to senior management. Technically, the system worked well. Detailed investigation showed, however, that there was no significant increase in active time.

The reason was as follows: the inspectors had a very difficult job in which they were abused and obstructed; they felt constrained by various political decisions and limited support resources. They claimed that they could not be expected to devote greater than 50 per cent of their time to inspections. For the remainder of the time they wanted to 'come in from the cold'. The new system thus fell quickly into disrepute, and line management were embarrassed that their promises were not fulfilled. Inspectorate staff were unhappy that the new system had failed and that, by implication, they had failed.

There are common themes in these problem systems. First, the systems had been developed without considering the working environment as a whole. Second, optimistic estimates had been made of workload and generous assumptions had been made about user ability to operate the new systems. Finally, management, having accepted the claims for the new systems, insisted that they operate according to specification despite the problems caused at the working level.

Causes of failure and their prevention

Figure 2.2 summarizes the system faults discussed above, with a review of possible causes. These faults exist in the systems as a whole and, of course, do not include the various technical problems that can arise with hardware and software. The latter are more immediately apparent and must obviously be corrected if the system is to operate at all. The faults as shown in Figure 2.2 are difficult to correct; prevention is better than cure.

It is impossible to categorize the root causes of all failures into neat, separate compartments. It is possible, however, to generalize the most common causes of failure and their prevention. Figure 2.3 lists the five major causes of system faults as described above. All are interrelated in some way, but for the sake of simplicity and clarity are discussed separately below.

Machine orientation

There are many pressures and constraints acting on the systems analyst in the development and implementation of a system. The relative importance of these constraints and the pressure exerted depends very much on the project and the company. A typical cross-section of constraints is shown in Figure 2.4. To illustrate the interaction of these constraints on the analyst and his job, a modification of the Blake Managerial Grid® can be used.

Dr Robert R. Blake and Dr Jane S. Mouton, formerly professors at the University of Texas (and President and Vice-President respectively in the consulting firm of Scientific Methods, Inc., Austin, Texas) developed the Managerial Grid (Gulf Publishing Co., 1964) as a means of analysing

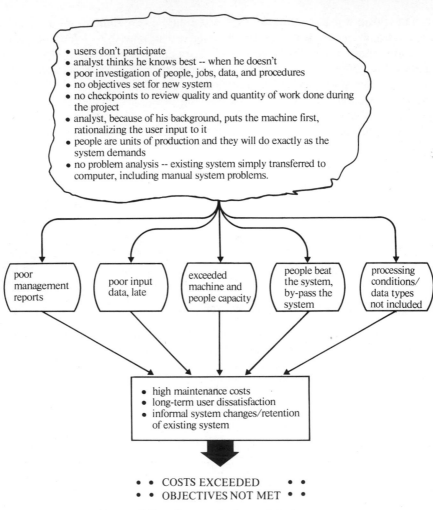

Figure 2.2: *System faults and their causes*

Figure 2.3: *Five major causes of system faults*

- machine orientation in development approach and design
- lack of user cooperation and involvement
- insufficient investigation
- lack of specific, quantified system objectives
- inadequate forward planning on the impact of the system on the individual

managerial style. Mechanically, the grid is a nine-by-nine matrix as shown in Figure 2.5. It is used to measure two variables: concern for people, 1 to 9 vertically, and concern for production, 1 to 9 horizontally. The grid approach is based on two premises:

1. Management can be measured according to these two variables, and
2. The best management is team management (9,9 on grid).

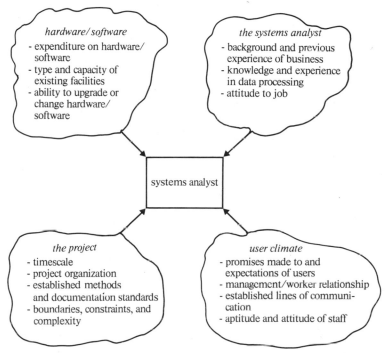

Figure 2.4:   Constraints acting on the systems analyst and his job

The authors discuss five styles of management:

9,1   task management
1,9   country club management
1,1   impoverished management
5,5   dampened pendulum management
9,9   team management.

The characteristics of these management styles are described briefly below.

9,1: TASK MANAGEMENT

A strong emphasis on the task to be performed. The authoritarian style of leadership with the manager seeing the members of the team purely as units of production—almost as automatons. Subordinates must execute orders unquestioningly and can be replaced should they function ineffectively. The results as far as the subordinates are concerned will be that they tend to lose initiative with a stifling effect on creativity; any increase in skill or knowledge is likely to remain untapped or inhibited.

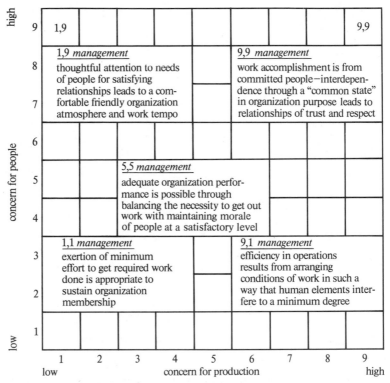

Figure 2.5: *The Blake Managerial Grid (From* The Managerial Grid *by Robert R. Blake and Jane Srygley Mouton. Houston: Gulf Publishing Company, 1964, p. 10. Reproduced by permission.)*

1,9: COUNTRY CLUB MANAGEMENT

The opposite of task management in which the emphasis is all on people. People always come first, whether or not production follows. Production will thus tend to suffer at the expense of harmonious personal relationships. Conflict will be buried rather than resolved.

1,1: IMPOVERISHED MANAGEMENT

Otherwise known as the WIB (weak ineffective bastard) style of management. As Mouton and Blake observe 'a business operated under 1.1. concepts would be unable to survive for long. The 1,1 style may be preserved in a country club or a bureaucracy. It is a situation of progressive and productive failure.'

5,5: DAMPENED PENDULUM MANAGEMENT

Swinging neither to 1,9 or 9,9, this is a situation of compromise. The manager may be aware of the compromise, but the *status quo* of concern for production and people is maintained. Although probably preferable to the 9,1, 1,1, and 1,9 styles, it does have its negative points. Again according to Mouton and Blake:

> '5,5 provides a poor basis for promoting innovation, creativity, discovery, and novelty. All of these are likely to be sacrificed by the adherence to tradition and "majority" standards of conduct. Long term, then, the 5,5 or *status quo*, results in a gradual slipping behind as more flexible, progressive organizations take advantage of new opportunities or better management practices.'

Management will thus seek and implement balanced solutions rather than the appropriate ones.

9,9: TEAM MANAGEMENT

'The needs of individuals to be engaged in meaningful interdependent effort mesh with the organization requirements for excellent performance.' This is, according to the premises stated earlier, the most desirable form of management, with an equal and earnest concern for both people and production. 'Production is from integration of task and human requirements.' In dealing with conflict, managers assume that agreement is possible.

The Managerial Grid is thus an effective tool for analysing management. It provides a means of structuring one's thinking about styles of management.

A modification of this tool makes it suitable for looking at systems development and design techniques. Let us now modify the original grid as shown in Figure 2.6(a). We are now measuring the bias, concern or attention given to the *machine* or computer based techniques on the one hand (replacing *production* on the original grid) and *user* or people on the other. Examples of what is included in the *machine* and *user* functions are shown in Figure 2.6(b).

It has long been realized that a conflict does exist between optimizing computer processing and associated operations (such as data preparation) and providing a user with an ideal system for people to operate. This can be seen from the following examples, based on the concern for *machine/user* shown in Figure 2.6(b). These examples include both major and minor points of conflict. The bias or extent of the conflict will be represented on the Systems Matrix.

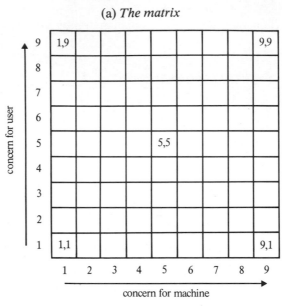

(a) *The matrix*

(b) *Examples of machine concern/user concern*

machine	user
—minimum program execution time —minimal core usage	—ease of data collection —free-form input
—use of complex codes for sorting/file access —data preparation method —document reading technique —minimum print time —file structures for machine efficiency —rigid data input rules —get the computer to do everything	—comprehensive, legible reports (minimizing abbreviations, legends, etc.) —flexible processing schedules —system solves business problems —aids user's primary function —human bias in codes

Figure 2.6: The Systems Matrix (1)

Example 1

Machine:

1. We must minimize print time.
2. One way we can do this is to pack as much information as we can on a line. (It takes as long to print five characters on a line as it does to print 132.)
3. The print time can be cut even further if we only use a limited character set.
4. Obviously we must reduce, as far as is possible, the amount to be printed.
5. One way we can do (4) is to cut down on headings, abbreviate and cut out all extraneous luxuries, like legends.

User:

1. We must have reports which are clear and easy to read.

2. We have our records at the moment on preprinted forms, index cards, etc. These we can read 'at a glance' because of good spacing and clear headings. This means wide margins, plenty of spaces between lines, horizontal and vertical column dividers, and using sometimes narrow paper (or standard A4 size paper) so we can run off a copy.

3. We might be able to refine the report in the future, but why should we have something inferior to start with?

Example 2

Machine:

1. To minimize data preparation errors and to get a high throughput, we must design an input document suitable for the key punch operators.

2. To do this, we must:

- —minimize page turning
- —use one side of the sheet only
- —eliminate key punch operator decisions as to what to punch
- —keep punching sequence from left to right, top to bottom
- —put data to be duplicated when keying on the left
- —put standard items on the left, optional entries on the right
- —not mix alpha and numeric data
- —highlight data to be keypunched
- —insist on clear, legible handwriting, using capitals, one character to a column box, etc.

3. This means we must redesign any user document to conform with this practice.

User:

1. We don't have time to print neatly. Most of us haven't printed in capitals regularly since we were at school—and since then only on tax returns. We just scribble on our sheets; the clerks know our handwriting and they know what we mean.

2. Of course our existing dockets are messy. Have you ever tried to fill in a form on the job, on a muddy construction site, without a good writing surface, in the open, in the wet and cold, with heavy equipment going?

3. The phone never stops with orders, requisitions, queries, and changes. We try to deal with as many calls as possible; get the details down as quick as we can, get off the line, push the note through for action and take the next call. The pressure is tremendous. We've all developed our own sort of shorthand.

4. When we do our job we fill the form in the sequence A, B, C, D, E. That's logical because that's the way we do our job. And A thru E is scattered over

the form, with our own special comments beside each entry. Now you want a sequence of A, C, D, E, B, all crammed on one line!

5. We don't use any of this preprinted form nonsense. We take a telephone call and just write out a note on a scrap of paper. And the system's worked well.

6. We've been using these forms for more than twenty years. Now we have to change just so your box of tricks will work.

Example 3

Machine:

1. For efficient file access we must have a unique key that clearly identifies each record. Each input transaction must carry that coded key.

2. For economy of file storage and ease of access, the coded key should reflect the way the file is stored. Preferably, the key should identify the record location on the disc file.

User:

1. We don't really use codes at the minute, just a short narrative. Everybody knows what the description means. The description can even vary and people still know. For example, $1\frac{1}{2}$ tons "spuds", "potatoes", "pots", "pts", "murphies", the clerks know it's potatoes we're after.

2. We get advice notes from our suppliers; to us, these are GRN's (goods received notes) which we use to update the stock ledger. Our suppliers don't put on our product codes. Neither do we. We know the products. But now we have to put a code on the GRN before it goes to the computer!

3. We used the old coding system for more than twenty years. We all knew it. And each code actually meant something. For example, P100BC meant a light bulb, pearl, 100 watts with a bayonet cap. C250S meant a light bulb, clear, 250 watts with a screw cap. Now we have a new range of codes, but it doesn't do anything for us down here.

Example 4

Machine:

1. The computer is a fast and powerful machine for handling data and calculating. It can do these things faster than humans.

2. It is also expensive and should therefore be used as much as possible.

3. Therefore, we should do as much on the computer as we can—preferably, the computer should do everything.

User:

1. We get orders by post at 09.00 hours. Each order has up to 200 lines. We use our knowledge and experience to go through and check the

order—product codes, pack sizes, reasonable quantities, contradictions in order patterns, and so on. If there was an error we could get straight on the telephone to check and correct it. The order processing system was a continuous manual process. If one line was in error and we couldn't immediately contact the customer, we would note what the error was and pass the order for processing. By the time the order was ready for the warehouse, we would have corrected the error on the 'phone and caught up with the order before delivery. Now its a batch computer system which can't use our knowledge and builds-in time delays with these correction runs.

2. We have 2500 monthly paid salaried staff and 12, weekly paid, hourly staff. It makes sense to do monthly payroll on the computer. But to do hourly paid is ridiculous. It takes one clerk less than an hour a week to do it.

3. We prepare the vehicle loading and routing schedule for 50 vehicles operating in Central London. There is little or no pattern in which customers will order in a day. The traffic pattern varies from hour-to-hour, day-to-day. There are a hundred-and-one things we take into account. No computer-produced schedule could replace our knowledge and experience. A massive computer system *might* be able to do it. Anything less than that must be inferior to the way we do it now, so why change?

4. The job of summarizing our sales figures takes us less than an hour on a Friday afternoon. It's an easy job. We like doing it; it shows us there and then how well we have done for the week. We can't make any sales calls at that time and it's a relaxing job. It's the only time in the week that we're all together in the office. A computer might be able to do it in five minutes. But why? It won't increase sales time or cut costs. We'd just sit around for an hour doing nothing—or take a longer lunch hour in the pub.

The Systems Matrix shows how the balance between *machine* and *user* is determined by the development technique and the aptitude and attitude of the person designing the system. The matrix in Figure 2.7 shows the situation of 1,9, 9,1, 1,1, 5,5, and 9,9 systems. (On in-house systems training courses given by the author, a battery of 20 questions has been given to a range of trainee analysts to attempt to place them on the matrix. The trainee analysts were invariably experienced programmers, users, organization and methods analysts, and first-job new employees. Although no formal follow-up was possible into their working environment, the results of systems designed in their case study work produced interesting results which are drawn upon in the following discussion.) The systems are discussed below. It must be remembered that we are not just considering the background of a single system designer on a system. The resultant system will be influenced by *all* the factors shown in Figure 2.4. In many companies, however, it is the systems analyst/designer who is a major factor in determining the quality of the new system.

Concern here is principally for the user—his methods, his people, and his problems. The emphasis on the machine aspects is negligible. This will mean in computer terms that the system is inelegant and inefficient. Run times will tend to be long, files large, and demand on core heavy. Processing programs will be complex and will require considerable effort to produce. Use will be

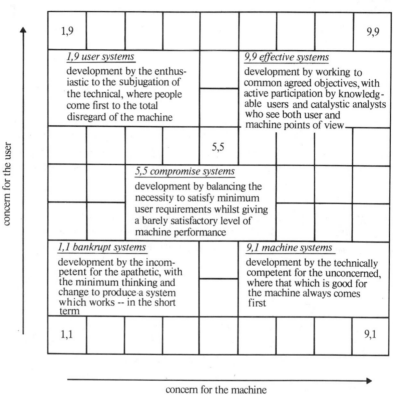

Figure 2.7:   The Systems Matrix (2)

made of free-form input and flexible file structures. The rationale is that it is still worth paying for a large computer configuration and incurring heavy development costs to give the user what he really wants. The problem is, of course, determining if what the user wants is the best for the business.

Typical causes for a 1,9 system can be:

1. Corporate policy that, in the long run, computers are cheaper than people.
2. A rush project in which there is insufficient time and effort available to refine methods on the computer. For example, computerizing an existing system with all the user data and methods transferred directly to the

computer; the only changes made are those which immediately give benefit to the majority of the users.

3. Inexperienced systems analysts and designers who do not have the knowledge to exploit the capabilities of the machine.

4. Systems analysts and designers with no programming background and little or no interest in the computer and its operation. For example, a system developed to the systems specification stage by *users* with the minimum of technical training.

5. Unbalanced project negotiations between users and data processing staff in which

(a) data processing staff were unable to present their case *or*

(b) users dominated the design decisions without adequate technical knowledge and experience.

1,9 systems are a rarity in the UK and are more prevalent in the USA.

1,1: SYSTEM DEVELOPMENT

A 1,1 system will be late in going live and by consensus should not have gone live at all. No objective criteria for making design decisions will have been agreed and the project will have proceeded under sufferance. A typical cause of a 1,1 system is a decision to go ahead taken from the top without prior consultation with lower-level user management or data processing personnel. The computer system will be inefficient and inelegant as described above. There will be no imaginative or innovative design of user procedures. This could be called design by the incompetent for the apathetic and is (luckily) a rarity. No company (which aims to stay in business) would support a computer development programme as bankrupt as this.

5,5: SYSTEM DEVELOPMENT

This can be categorized as survival by continual compromise. Both users and data processing are aware of the compromise, but the *status quo* is preserved. The quotation from Blake and Mouton on page 49 on 5,5 management is a perfect description of 5,5 systems and their long-term impact. The result of a typical 5,5 development will be to computerize the existing system with minimal changes. Methods which have worked reasonably well in one system will automatically be applied in future systems, irrespective of their relevance or suitability.

9,1: SYSTEM DEVELOPMENT

Machine-biased systems are prevalent in both commerce and government. The characteristics of 9,1 systems can be seen by reading the '*machine*' entries in the examples given previously. If a 9,1 designer were asked why a system used a particular technique, the answers would probably be:

'We *had* to do it that way to:
—minimize file storage and/or,
—keep program sizes to a minimum and/or,
—reduce execution time.'
'It's better for the machine that way.'
'It won't work on the machine unless it's done that way.'

Although no formal survey has been carried out as to the incidence of 9,1 developed systems, general indications are that this is the most common type. What, then, causes this situation? Again, there are several:

1. Restrictions on expenditure on hardware and software by corporate policy force the development process and system design towards 9,1. Even if there is concern for user requirements and people, this must take second place to the capability of the machine, because of its limited processing and file storage capacity.
2. User withdrawal, in which the user pays only lip service to the new system, means that design decisions are left completely to the systems analyst. There will probably be only passive acquiescence in the approval of specifications. Lack of user cooperation and involvement will be discussed in more detail later in this chapter.
3. Systems analysts and designers with a technical, computer-oriented background and with limited user exposure will tend to produce machine-biased systems. The systems analyst could be an ex-programmer. He may have spent two to five years programming, the most computer-oriented job in the organization. Without adequate training and time for adjustment, this means that his concern and expenditure of effort must be towards the machine. The computer will be the first consideration in any design decision.

This last point is a problem in organizations in which there is a natural career progression from programmer to analyst, based purely on seniority or programming job performance. This is not to say that there should be no migration from programming to systems analysis. Rather, the progression from programming to analysis should be based on *potential* for the analysis job.

Knowledge and experience of programming is important for the systems analyst who will be designing computer-based systems. Three to six months' programming can give the analyst the appropriate background in machine techniques. The quality of the programs produced during this time is not particularly important. Remember too, that part of the analyst's job will be to 'get a feel' for job content and people, and this can be applied to the programming function as well as user areas.

Some companies thus perpetuate the 9,1 approach by encouraging the development of computer-oriented analysts. Take, for example, the following career paths:

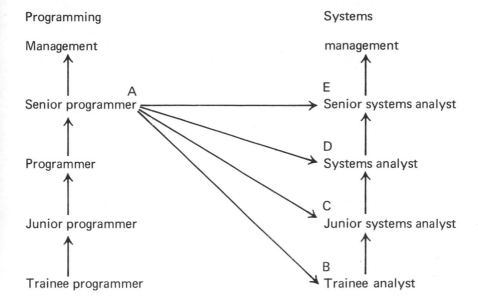

In this organization, systems analysts can be drawn from paths A+B,+C,+D or+E. (B upwards is the direct entry path.) Consider the case of a programmer going through to level A, senior programmer, then to E. It may take three years to reach senior programmer, and the man will be on a reasonable salary. To go to senior analyst would be an anomaly. This would imply that the man taking the A to E route would, to justify his new title and salary, become immediately productive. (Remember that a programmer in three years could work on 100 programs. In three years, the systems analyst taking path B could work on two or three complete systems projects from start to finish. A programmer may produce complete programs at a rate of one every two to three weeks. It would take at least a year to complete one systems project, i.e. all 11 steps in the system development cycle.) Path A+C or A+D will create salary, seniority, and job content anomalies.

9,1 systems are thus the result of corporate policy on limiting hardware/software expenditure, and lack of concern for user/people on the part of the systems analysts or users.

9,9: SYSTEM DEVELOPMENT

One of the basic premises upon which the Managerial Grid is based is, according to Blake and Mouton, that the best management is team management. 9,9 means that the 'needs of people to think, to apply mental effort in productive work and to establish sound and mature relationships ... with one another are utilized to accomplish organization requirements.'

By analogy, 9,9 systems development and systems design is the best form of development. It provides an answer to the question 'What is a good system?' *All* levels of user staff seek to discover the best and most effective solutions. Everyone, users and data processing staff alike, find their own sense of accomplishment. A prerequisite is that the objectives of user and data processing functions, *and of the system*, are clear to all. Conflict will occur, but problems are faced openly and not as personal disputes. Users recognize that the machine imposes certain restrictions, whilst data processing realize that it is the user who will be working with the system for many years.

Practically, it means there will be user involvement *at all levels* in systems development. It also means that the systems analyst is not constantly 'fighting for what is best for the machine'. The simplest way is to see the role of the analyst as follows:

1. Tells
2. Catalyst
3. Told.

The type 1 analyst is typical of 9,1 systems. The system is specified in terms of what is best for the computer and according to the analyst's understanding and interpretation of manager's job. The type 3 analyst is typical of 1,9 systems. He does not function as an analyst, rather he merely takes what he is told by users and constructs a system as best he can. The type 2 analyst is typical of the 9,9 situation, one who works with an integrated approach to machine and users. For this, he must have knowledge and experience of and *concern* for both. The catalytic analyst can only work where he has the opportunity to work closely with users, there is user interest and cooperation, and all parties work within or towards common, agreed objectives.

We have thus seen that systems approaching 9,9 on the matrix are good. 9,1 systems are the most common form of bad systems. A major aim in systems development is therefore to avoid machine orientation in the development approach and the system design. The easiest way to avoid this bias is by:

1. Defining and agreeing the objectives for the system in the organization as a whole.
2. Promoting user involvement at all stages of development and at all levels.
3. Providing a career structure and training programme for systems analysts which gives a balance of user and machine considerations.
4. Providing an adequate training programme for users in machine techniques (assuming that there is already a management training programme for users).
5. Ensuring that adequate time is allowed and attention given to a thorough investigation into the user area, thereby providing the analyst with a knowledge of the user area equal to that of his knowledge of the machine.

Finally, a question that the author has been asked many times on courses: is it possible to develop 9,9 systems in a 9,1, 1,9, 1,1, or 5,5 organization? The answer simply is *no*. As described in Chapter 1, the development of computer systems is a reflection of the management approach to running the organization. The analyst is working within the existing corporate environment.

Lack of user involvement

The impact of this problem on 9,1 systems was discussed above. The systems analyst working without user involvement will have no pressure to pull the emphasis away from machine to user business/people considerations. Not only will the system design tend to be machine-oriented; there will also be problems in running the new system. The system will always be *'their'* system (data processing), not *'ours'* (the user). In the worst case the system will be implemented and run under sufferance, if not with outright resistance and antagonism. An example of this is the user reaction to file conversion and user testing: 'Oh, *we* have to do that? Not likely, it's *your* system. You do it.' Other characteristics of the system are that it will only work as long as data processing staff are actively propping it up and that changes will be made informally to the system to adapt to user needs. An example of the latter is use of additional clerks recruited for 'system C' as described on page 44. (Note that in this example, the data processing staff were unaware of the system change because the new order form B was being received in the data control section in data processing operations.)

Figure 2.8 summarizes those factors which stimulate or inhibit user involvement. Some of these lie within the scope of the analyst and others lie outside his control and rest firmly with corporate policy and management climate. Part II of this book will deal with specific techniques for encouraging and promoting user involvement. Note, however, that user involvement must be controlled, otherwise the pendulum for systems development will swing towards the equally suspect 1,9 systems.

Insufficient investigation

Investigation (fact finding, data gathering, etc.) of the user area, its future growth and requirements, plays a major role in the development of a new system. An investigation will be necessary at many steps in the systems development cycle, e.g., steps 2, 3, and 11 in Figure 1.4. The major investigation will take place at step 3 in the cycle. If this investigation is incomplete or the results inaccurate or ambiguous, then this will be carried into the analysis and design tasks and, ultimately, into the operational system. This will be a major contributing factor to the operational system faults as listed in Figure 2.1.

Simply, if the analyst does not know or understand the reality of the organization (its structure, people, jobs, data, and procedures) then the system will be a failure. Lack of investigation will lead to unsatisfactory management reports, poor data collection procedures, and omissions of processing and data conditions in programs.

More generally, a poor investigation will pervade the whole design. It will tend to result in 9,1 systems, especially if there is little user involvement. There cannot be a 'concern for the user' to counter-balance the analysts' knowledge, interest, and experience of the machine. Techniques for investigation are thus of primary importance and are described in detail in Chapter 5.

Figure 2.8:   User involvement in system development

+   *Stimuli*
   +   Adequate time allowed in schedule for consultations and checkpoints.
   +   Reports, presentations are intelligible to non-technical users.
   +   Agreeing objectives as early as possible in project.
   +   Prior early warning given (i.e. in project plan) for time and effort required from users at each phase.
   +   User decisions are not pre-empted by data processing, i.e. users have a choice of action and are presented with objective information upon which the decision can be made.

−   *Inhibitors*
   −   Users blocked out of the project by not allowing adequate time for consultations and checkpoints, or imposing 'arbitrary' decisions from the top.
   −   Blocking lines of communication between analysts and users (e.g., not allowing analysts access to staff at the top or bottom of the organization).
   −   Countering all or most of the user suggestions or requirements with 'well, that's not possible on or good for the machine'.
   −   Presenting users with a *fait accompli*.
   −   There is a previous history of major system problems.

Lack of objectives

A system developed without specific, agreed objectives is rather like the old adage of Christopher Columbus' voyage of discovery: 'That he set out not really knowing where he was going, arrived not really knowing where he was, and came back not really knowing where he'd been.' Failure to set objectives for the system will have both short- and long-term implications. In the short term, lack of agreed objectives will directly work *against* 9,9 systems development. In the long term it will mean that the expenditure on the new system will be wasted because it will not make any meaningful contribution to the organization as a whole.

Note that objectives for a system is a statement of what the system should *achieve*, not what the system is to *do*. The latter is a product of the systems analysis and design stage. The setting of objectives is thus crucial to developing a system, for the benefits will come from meeting these objectives. There is also a secondary reason for clearly defining the objectives. This is that all staff can work towards a common goal, thus encouraging involvement at all levels.

Methods for setting objectives are described in detail in Chapter 6.

Inadequate people planning

The specifications produced as part of the feasibility study (step 2) and systems design (step 5) tend to be technical documents. They define, in different levels of detail, file contents and structures, processing requirements, impact on current hardware configuration, and so on. This technical data is necessary to produce the workload estimates, from which the essential timings and costings can be prepared, and so that the subsequent implementation phases of programming, testing, etc., can be carried out. It is interesting to note, however, that the amount of technical data in such specifications far outweighs the 'human' data. Sometimes this is the result of a reticence to commit ideas about people to paper. Sometimes it is because insufficient time and attention has been given to the impact of the system on people. We all tend to spend more time on those things with which we are more familiar. The technically oriented analyst will thus feel more at home with data and program specifications than with plans for people.

Throughout the project it is important to consider the impact of the system on people: how they will react to the change; the special training required, and how and when this can be given; the effect of the system on the work content and schedules. Failure to consider these aspects can cause serious problems at a time when they are least wanted: during the difficult phases of conversion and implementation. Examples of the requirements for planning for people will be given in Part II.

Summary

1. A system is a failure if it fails to meet the objectives set. A good system is one which, through meeting its objectives, makes a positive contribution to the continuing life of the organization. It must, however, do more than this: it must satisfy the individual needs of the members of the organization.

2. Typical system faults which will prevent a system from meeting its objectives are:

- unsatisfactory management reports (too long, too short, wrong format, timescale or accuracy) which do not aid the manager in planning and monitoring his resources
- low quality input data not submitted on schedule

- exceeded machine and people capacity
- failure to cater for all data types and processing conditions
- retention of the existing system (in whole or part) which operates in parallel with the new
- inflexibility because there are too many new rules and regulations which are (from the user's point of view) unrealistic

3. The systems analyst, the user, the systems development policy, and the methods standards all determine the quality of a system. The quality can be measured on the Systems Matrix (an adaptation of the Blake and Mouton Managerial Grid) which measures concern for user/people against concern for hardware/software. The analyst is aiming for 9,9 systems.

4. Such systems can only be attained if concern for hardware/software is matched by concern for user/people. This can be achieved if:

- the analyst does not take a machine-oriented approach to the job, despite possibly, a technical background
- there is user cooperation and involvement at all levels in systems development
- there is a thorough investigation of the user area
- specific, quantified objectives for the new system are defined, agreed and reviewed as development progresses
- there is adequate forward planning about the impact of the system on the individual.

5. Working within the existing environment of management climate, corporate computer policy, organization structure, development methods standards, etc., the analyst must strive to acquire knowledge and devise techniques which, in addition to his technical development, will enable him to achieve 4, above.

3

People at work—
Theory and practice

Everyone with whom the systems analyst comes into contact in the course of his work will react in some way both to him personally and to what he represents. What the reaction is will depend less on his own personality than on what he represents to those he meets, what their expectations are, and how they have been treated in the past. This is true whether the other person is a senior company executive, a clerical worker, or even a member of the analyst's own project team.

This chapter is devoted to providing the background for understanding how people are going to react to the systems analyst and to changes in their working lives that may be contemplated or proposed, whether the change is a rearrangement of their filing system, a new computer system, or reorganization of the whole company. Further, it will help the analyst to be able to predict what kinds of changes are going to be acceptable and what ones will never work because of the attitudes and expectations of management or workers. A chapter such as this can only provide a brief summary of tens of thousands of pages of ideas and findings, based on thousands of man-years of thought and research. This is provided as a basis for the techniques described in Part II of this book.

The thinking of psychologists, sociologists, and those who interpret and apply their theories and findings in the world of business management has changed drastically over the past 100 years. This thinking is still in the process of evolution. We will begin with a historical overview, tracing the change in management thinking from 'scientific management' through 'interpersonal relations' to today's vogue of 'organizational behaviour'. In doing so, we will meet some 'famous names' and important landmarks in the history of managerial psychology. They are:

F. W. Taylor and Scientific Management
E. Mayo and the Hawthorne Experiments
A. H. Maslow and the Hierarchy of Needs
D. M. McGregor and 'Theory X and Theory Y'
F. Herzberg and the Motivator/Hygiene Theory.

Taylorism

The concept of scientific management had its roots in the early industrial revolution. With machines replacing hand craftmanship and assembly line procedures replacing the cottage industry, all work came to be thought of as economic activity. Human beings were 'workers' rather than people, and could be manipulated just as machines and other resources were, to produce units of work.

This so-called scientific management is also called the 'machine theory' or Taylorism, after one of its prime exponents. (Frederick Winslow Taylor (1856–1917), an American, published his ideas in two books, *Shop Management* (1903) and *Principles of Scientific Management* (1911). In 1947 these two books, together with Taylor's testimony to a House of Representatives Special Committee, were published under the title of *Scientific Management* (Harper and Row). The testimony was given to the Committee after labour troubles developed at the Waterlow-Arsenal where his principles were applied.)

Taylor proposed four axiomatic principles of management:

- the development of a true science of work
- the scientific selection and progressive development of the workman
- the bringing together of the science of work and the scientifically selected and trained workmen
- the constant and ultimate cooperation of management and men.

Implicit in Taylorism is the assumption that people are by nature lazy, passive, and not at all ambitious. Close supervision of their work is always required, using the stick and the carrot, with emphasis on the stick.

This is not to say that nothing of value whatsoever came of the school of scientific management. On the contrary, application of its principles led to the establishment of work study as a discipline, and with it the first objective investigations of human beings in a working environment. From it came the use of psychological tests by the United States Army for selection of staff during the First World War, which was a notable contribution to the success of the Allied war effort.

It also led to the study of ways to improve productivity, reduce fatigue, and reduce accident rates, especially in British munitions factories. It was found, for example, that workers putting in a 12-hour day did not produce significantly more than when they were on a ten-hour day. Sunday rest-days and occasional holidays were restored and working hours were shortened, with the result that the rate of production went up and accident, sickness, and injury rates went down.

The effect of the worst excesses of Taylorism were pernicious, however, and are still being felt. This is especially true in Great Britain, and contributed directly to the rise of trade unionism as well as providing a fertile ground for the Marxist theories of class war and the continued struggle of the working classes against the oppression of capitalism and evil-minded managers.

The human relations school of management, which puts as much emphasis on personal job satisfaction as on productivity, was a direct reaction against Taylorism. The Hawthorne Experiments coming as they did on the flood tide of this reaction, gave strong impetus to the change in managerial thinking. Their effects are still being felt today and provided the theoretical basis for the human relations school.

The Hawthorne Experiments

The Hawthorne Experiments are so-called because they were carried out at the Hawthorne Works of the Western Electric Company, which was just outside Chicago. The researchers included personnel from the National Research Council, the Massachusetts Institute of Technology, and Harvard Business School. Among them were Elton Mayo (1880–1949) an Australian who spent most of his working life at Harvard University, eventually becoming Professor of Industrial Research at the Graduate School of Business Administration, and W. Lloyd Warner, the anthropologist. The experiments were paid for by the Western Electric Company and cost well over a million dollars. The experiments were begun in the mid-twenties and were continued into the early years of the thirties. There were four major phases to the experiments:

1. The Illumination Experiments
2. The Relay Assembly Test Room
3. The Interviewing Programme
4. The Bank Wiring Observation Room.

Of these, the relay assembly test room experiments are probably the most important, but we will consider each in turn.

The illumination experiments

This first group of experiments was designed along strictly Tayloristic (objective and scientific) lines. The researchers intended to test the effects of various levels of illumination on the productivity of workers on the assembly line. They confidently expected to find, as had happened with previous experiments carried out in the scientific management tradition, that there was a direct relationship between lighting and productivity, and that it would be possible to establish the ideal illumination for greatest productivity.

The workers were divided into two groups, one the experimental group and the other the control group. The control group worked with the conditions of illumination unchanged throughout. For the other group, the level of light intensity was varied.

The first results were disappointing to the researchers, for they found that there seemed to be no direct relationship between illumination and productivity. They thought that there must be 'contamination' from daylight coming through the windows. They therefore eliminated the natural light to make the experimental conditions more pure, but the results were unchanged. Worse, productivity in the control group *actually increased* while productivity in the test group varied, sometimes increasing and sometimes decreasing, with no apparent relationship to the illumination. In desperation, the experimenters began to reduce the level of light for the test group, and found to their consternation that the workers continued to produce more or less efficiently under conditions close to those of ordinary moonlight. A literal-minded, but obviously absurd, conclusion would have been that poor illumination was most desirable for increased production.

The researchers were forced to conclude, although reluctantly, that as a factor of the working environment the degree of illumination had no significance. This still did not explain, however, why the rate of productivity of the control group, whose lighting had remained unchanged throughout, had actually increased. Scientific method does not allow such embarrassing results to be swept under the carpet, and so it was hypothesized that some *other* but as yet unknown factors were influencing the performance of the workers.

The relay assembly test room

Assembling telephone relays at the Hawthorne plant was very boring, repetitive work. It required putting together 35 small parts with four screws. The parts were arranged in trays, in front of the worker, with the trays kept topped up all the time by a layout operator. An experienced operator could assemble 500 relays a day. Most of the workers were women, or 'female operatives', as they were called.

The women for the test group were chosen in an interesting way. The researchers selected two assemblers who were friends with each other. Those two chose three other assemblers and a layout operator, making six in all.

The experiment was divided into 13 periods lasting up to 12 weeks each, except for the final one, which lasted 31 weeks. During the first period, the operators' work was monitored on the assembly line so that, unknown to them, a base rate of production could be established for later comparison. The six then moved to a specially built test room. The only other person in the test room was an assistant to the research team, who acted as the supervisor. He kept records of the work, and a log of what happened. The environmental conditions of the test room were similar to those of the assembly line itself. During each of the subsequent periods, the working conditions were varied, principally by changing working hours and break durations and timing.

A summary of the 13 periods, and the results of each, are given in Figure

3.1. The increases in productivity in the earlier stages were easily explained by reference to the better method of payment and the rest breaks. But the increases in later periods, especially in period 12 when there were no rest breaks at all, were as baffling to the researchers as the results of the illumination experiments had been. *It seemed that no matter what changes were introduced, even ones that should have caused production to fall off, the output rate continued to go up.*

Figure 3.1:   Summary of the relay assembly test room study

Period	Length in weeks	Conditions	Results
1	2	records kept on assembly line work	base rate established
2	5	operators enter test room; no other changes	production up slightly
3	8	payment rate changed to give higher reward for individual effort	production up
4	5	two five minute rests, one morning and one afternoon	production up
5	4	rest breaks lengthened to ten minutes each	production up
6	4	six five-minute rest breaks	operators complain that too many breaks makes them lose the rhythm of the work; production up a little
7	11	15 minute morning break and ten-minute afternoon break; company provides refreshments	production up
8	7	work stops at 4:30 instead of 5:00; rest breaks as in period 7	production up
9	4	work stops at 4:00, rest breaks as in period 7	total daily production down slightly but hourly rate up
10	12	same as period 7	production up
11	9	Saturday work eliminated, rest breaks as in period 7	production up
12	12	same as period 3; no breaks	production drops slightly at first, then rises
13	31	same as period 7, but company supplies only coffee	production breaks all records

In the years since the Hawthorne Experiments, a number of explanations have been developed to give logical reasons for these results. Further experiments confirmed what was, in fact, happening in the relay assembly test room. The 'unknown' factor that influenced the results can be summarized as follows:

1. *Pleasant environment*: Although the physical surroundings of the test room were no better than those of the assembly line, the women said that they enjoyed the work in the test room more.
2. *Friendly supervision*: The women were, in fact, being supervised much

more closely in the test room than they had been on the assembly line. They felt, however, that the researcher was more friendly toward them than their regular supervisor had been.

3. *Feelings of importance*: The women were consulted about changes that were going to be made beforehand, and their feelings and opinions were solicited at the end of each period. What they were doing was important to the company; company management was interested in them, eminent scientists all but hung on their every word. The women felt that they were members of an elite group.

4. *Team spirit*: The women became a group rather than just workers on an assembly line. They became more friendly with each other, cared more about each other, and helped each other to work better.

5. *Common purpose*: A common objective or goal that is recognized as such by the group is an essential aspect of team spirit. In this case, the common purpose was an increase in the rate of output. Moreover, there was feedback on their success in reaching the goal, as the result of each week's work was given to the group.

To return for a moment to the illumination experiment, these factors also explain what was happening there. Remember that the control group, where lighting remained unchanged throughout the experiment, also increased their rate of production. This is accounted for by the fact that they too were singled out and given special attention; that group felt that they were members of an elite, that they were special in some way.

The interviewing programme

Although the total impact of the relay assembly test room experiment was still to be felt—indeed, is still being felt to this day—it provided the researchers with some ideas for the next phase of the experiments, the interviewing programme. The illumination experiments and especially the relay assembly test room had shown that the quality of the supervision was an important contributing factor to the workers' rate of output. It was therefore decided to interview a large number of workers to find out how they felt about their supervisors and work conditions generally. Among other things, the information collected was to be used to help design a training programme for supervisors.

Before the work was ended by the Depression in 1932, more than 20 000 Western Electric workers were interviewed. At first, the interviewers were armed with a set of prepared questions, mostly having to do with how the worker being interviewed felt about his job. It soon transpired, however, that the workers regarded some of the questions as irrelevant or silly, and also that they wanted to talk about more than just their bosses and the immediate working conditions. The interviews, therefore, were changed to become 'nondirective', i.e. there was no set list of questions and the worker was free to talk about anything he wanted to connected, even remotely, with his job.

The rules for the interviewer included the following:

1. Consult with the man's supervisor before taking him aside for the interview, and make sure that normal work was not disrupted.
2. The worker was to be paid his average earnings for the time spent on the interview.
3. Each interviewee was to have it made clear to him that everything he said was in strictest confidence, and although the interviewer took almost verbatim notes, the man's name or other identification would not be on the notes. His identity would never be revealed to management.
4. The interviewer was to be sympathetic and friendly. He would not, however, take sides or offer his opinion about who was right or wrong in any given situation. In an extreme case, he could tell the man about company benefit plans, and so on.

As a result of this non-judgemental approach, the researchers found out a lot more than just how the workers felt about their bosses and the company. They also gained valuable information about how individuals saw themselves in relation to their work groups, their families, and society as a whole. It turned out, for example, that in some cases apparent job dissatisfaction and low efficiency were in reality due to an unhappy home situation. In many cases, just having somebody to talk to about their problems and an opportunity to 'let off steam' helped significantly. As the relay assembly test room led to the birth of the modern coffee break, the interviewing programme resulted in the birth of the modern personnel counselling system.

Other interesting information came to light concerning the workers' attitudes toward company management. It is to be supposed that the Western Electric Company was no more nor less Tayloristic than any other large industrial employer of the day, and the workers were reacting accordingly. The researchers found evidence of an informal 'Mafia' among the shop floor workers, that existed to defend the workers' welfare against management. Features of the 'Mafia' system included the following:

1. The level of production was set by the 'Mafia', and no worker could exceed it with impunity. This was in response to the piecework incentive pay system, which the workers resented strongly. (Taylor's first published work was, incidentally, entitled *A Piece Rate System* read to the American Society of Mechanical Engineers in 1895!)
2. Those who went beyond the standard of the 'Mafia' were punished.
3. Each working group had its informal leaders who kept the group together and enforced the rules. Usually, there was one group leader who dealt with the supervisor and outsiders, and another who enforced the unofficial production standard.

It was to find out more about this 'Mafia' that the bank wiring observation room experiment was organized.

The bank wiring observation room

This experiment was not run in the same way as the relay assembly test room. All work factors were kept as closely as they could be to conditions that existed on the assembly line. A researcher acted as observer in the room, but he was not the workers' supervisor. Their usual boss was in charge. No changes were made to rates of pay, rules, or regulations.

The 14 workers were all male. The group comprised nine wiremen, three solderers, and two inspectors. Their job was to put together terminal banks used in telephone exchanges. There was a complex wage incentive plan, the objective of which was to encourage the workers to maximize their pay. The phenomenon being investigated was the fact that the wage incentive plan did not work at all, the group set the production rate, a rate that was far below what the men were capable of producing. Tests showed that there was no relationship between productivity and ability.

It took some time for the observer to gain the confidence of the men. Once he had done so, however, they were quite open with him. He found that there was a distinct difference between the way men acted when their supervisor was in the room—quiet, industrious—and their behaviour after he left—boisterous and relaxed. Each man produced what the group thought was a 'proper' amount of work, resulting in about two banks per day. Their reason for limiting the amount of work, and therefore limiting their own pay, was that if their output was higher the methods department would raise the piece rates, negating any extra pay they might have earned. Reading between the lines in reports of this and similar studies, it seems that this belief on the part of the men was not altogether unjustified.

These findings strengthened the framework of the human relations school, which sees workers as units in a group, and units within the business organization, reacting with peers and with management. It elevates interpersonal relations to take precedence over man as an economic creature. While this is a significant advance over Taylorism it also contains the seeds of its own failure, as we shall see later. Meantime, the glorification of the human relations school of management, with the impetus given to it by the Hawthorne Experiments, still has a long way to run. (Mayo and the Hawthorne Experiments are documented exhaustively in *Management and the Worker*, F. J. Roethlisberger and W. J. Dickson, Harvard University Press, 1949.)

Maslow's hierarchy of needs

A. H. Maslow (1908–70) was an industrial psychologist who has provided a major contribution to motivation theory in the working environment.

'Motivation' is a much abused term in business. In the *Concise Oxford Dictionary* the definition of motivation is 'to supply a motive', a motive being defined as 'tending to initiate movement'. In a detective novel, a motive is typically a reason for committing a crime. In the context of working, the motivation is variously used to describe a nebulous pressure as in 'they're a highly motivated group', implying some form of inspiration or dedication. A casual definition of motivation may also be 'the reason we do or don't do something—why we act in a particular way in a particular situation'. A far more precise definition is required in a more formal study of people at work. There is perhaps no better description of motivation than that shown in Figure 3.2.

Figure 3.2:   Motivation—a basic definition*

'Central to the concept of personality is the idea of motivation (i.e. behaviour instigated by needs and directed towards the goals that can satisfy these needs).

cause	generate	to reach	leads to

NEEDS———►DRIVES————►BEHAVIOUR———►GOALS————►REDUCTION OF OR RELEASE
OF TENSION

It is widely believed that when a person is motivated, he is in a state of tension and this generates energy. And further, when a person is in a state of tension, he feels impelled to take some kind of action. Motivation selectively organizes an individual's perception so that his learning is structured in a certain direction.'

---

* From Joe Kelly, *Organizational Behaviour*, Richard D. Irwin Inc., 1969, p. 175.

Maslow's theory of motivation is widely taught in American and British schools of business. Its basic postulate is that there are levels of needs that human beings strive to meet. When a lower level is fulfilled, the person will then and only then—go on to strive to satisfy higher levels.

The hierarchy of needs is illustrated in Figure 3.3. In more detail the levels are:

1. *Physiological*: These include homeostasis (bodily *status quo*, for example, the level of salt in the blood), satisfaction of hunger and thirst, sensory stimulation, and sleep. They are independent of other motivations and of each other. If these needs are unsatisfied, they will dominate the individual's thinking and behaviour until they are. For the man who is starving, there is no other interest but food. Only when the physiological needs can be satisfied can other needs operate as motivators of behaviour.

2. *Safety*: Safety needs include the need for bodily health, freedom from pain, and freedom from fear of physical attack. A man in imminent physical danger thinks of nothing else—although, to illustrate the concept of the

hierarchy, a starving man might deliberately put himself in physical danger in order to obtain food.

3. *Love*: Love needs include the need for affection, belonging, self-acceptance, and friendly relationships with other people. They include the love of a parent, sibling love, and the love of a husband and wife. Note that love is not synonymous with sex, which is a physical drive, not a need, and therefore does not appear in Maslow's hierarchy. Love may express itself through sex, however. In particular, love needs express themselves as the wish to be a member of a group, this includes both family groups and peer groups, e.g. clubs and *working teams*.

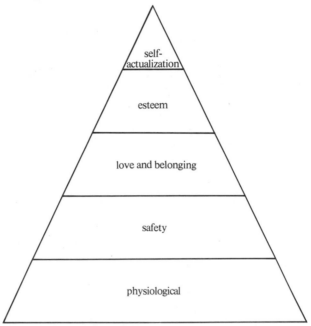

Figure 3.3:   Maslow's hierarchical theory of motivation

4. *Esteem*: If love needs express themselves through the desire to be a member of a group, esteem needs go on to the desire to be a special member of the group, such as *leader* of the group. This includes desire for status, recognition, attention, and appreciation. Esteem needs also include the need for self-esteem, including feelings of strength, achievement, confidence, and freedom.

5. *Self-actualization*: The self-actualization level assumes that the individual must do what he is fitted for, provided that lower level needs are satisfied. Self-actualization is becoming everything that one is capable of becoming. The form this will take varies tremendously from one individual to another, with abilities ranging from art to athletics to business. Maslow postulated that

many people never reach this level, either because they become 'stuck' at a lower level through deprivation or personality faults, or because society will not allow them to.

Some complementary features of Maslow's theory are that some people never rise above a certain level because of severe deprivation in early life, and that a person who has never been deprived can tolerate deprivation at that level more easily than someone who has. An obvious illustration of the first precept is members of the older generation who suffered during the Depression, especially among the working classes. They were deprived at the safety level, and always put a preference for job security, the *status quo*, and socialism above other needs. The proposition that one who has never been deprived can stand it better is less simple. Let us take this example: suppose two systems analysts are temporarily assigned to a project in an overseas branch of the company. They are not taking their families, and will be alone in a foreign country. Furthermore, their arrival is highly resented and they are given the cold shoulder by everyone in the branch office; in other words, they are completely (if temporarily) deprived of love and personal relationship satisfactions. Maslow's theory says that the systems analyst who comes from a happy family background and who has never been deprived at the love level will be able to stand this treatment better than the one who was as a child deprived of love. The first analyst may even be able to skip love needs altogether for a time, gaining his satisfaction at a higher level, with the feeling that he is doing a good job and will gain the esteem of management when the project is finished. The deprived analyst, on the other hand, might panic and devote all his efforts to trying to get those around him to like him, to the detriment of the project he is supposed to be working on.

There are other examples of reversing or skipping a level of the hierarchy. High-powered American business men are sometimes accused of reversing the love and esteem levels, neglecting their families in order to succeed at business. Saints and martyrs can suffer deprivation at *all* the lower levels in order to achieve self-actualization.

Maslow's theory lends considerable support to the human relations school of management. Firstly, it is assumed that most people in our society, especially those who are employed, are satisfied at the physiological and safety levels. This is particularly true in peacetime in a welfare state, where even the unemployed do not have to worry about starving. Motivating workers therefore becomes a problem at the levels of belonging, esteem, and self-actualization. This leads to labour—management bargaining, personnel programmes geared to the needs of the employees, training of supervisors to increase their sensitivity and understanding of workers' motivations, and therapy and manipulation as the prime tools for fostering management—worker relations.

Two other important human relations theorists have based their work on

Maslow's hierarchy of needs. They are McGregor and Herzberg. Each will be discussed in turn.

McGregor's Theory X and Theory Y

Douglas McGregor (1906–64) was an American social psychologist; for ten years he was Professor of Management at the Massachusetts Institute of Technology. He analysed various approaches to managers under the general heading of Theory X and Theory Y *(The Human Side of Enterprise,* McGraw-Hill, 1960).

Theory X and Theory Y are two different ways of viewing management's work. Theory X is the traditional Tayloristic approach, while Theory Y is oriented toward human relations.

Theory X has three basic propositions, as held by conventional managers:

1. Company management is charged with the duty of organizing the 'four Ms':

> money
> material
> men
> machines.

Their task is to maximize company profits through manipulation of these four resources.
2. In order to do this, people can and must be manipulated through their economic nature.
3. This implies that workers are passive, dislike work, and will avoid it if they can; they need to be coerced, threatened, and punished in order to put forth the adequate effort, and prefer to avoid all responsibility.

In contrast, Theory Y is based on Maslow's hierarchy, and makes the following assumptions:

1. Management is responsible for organizing the four Ms in pursuit of economic objectives.
2. If people are passive and dislike work, it is because of their previous work experience.
3. Management should understand human motivation and give individuals the chance to direct their own behaviour.
4. Management's primary goal must be to arrange things so that staff can set and meet their own objectives, achieving self-actualization while also directing their efforts towards the economic goals of the company.

Within a team of professional scientists or data processing technicians, it may be not only possible but also highly desirable to adopt Theory Y as a management philosophy. Where McGregor fails is in not realizing how difficult it is to implement Theory Y management in the industrial worker/management climate as it exists today. Nevertheless, this view of management is widely taught, and has helped to bring about such things as job enrichment programmes and performance appraisal systems.

Herzberg's motivation/hygiene theory

Frederick Herzberg is Professor and Chairman of Psychology at Western Reserve University, Cleveland. Herzberg's theory is based on many years of research which, indeed, is still going on. His basic method is the interview, and his work has been with such diverse groups as engineers, accountants, supervisors, agricultural workers, elderly executives, scientists, technicians, nurses, and unskilled hospital workers.

The types of questions asked in the interviews were related to things that the individual liked about his job and those he did not like. He is asked to think of incidents and events on the job that made him feel particularly good or especially bad, and to describe them. Herzberg divides the situations described into 'long-range' and 'short-range' experiences, depending on how long the feeling lasted. He identified a large number of types of experiences in each of the 'good' and 'bad' categories, but by far the largest number of stories fell into one of ten groups, five for each of the major categories. These will be described briefly.

The motivators

The good experiences that led to increased job satisfaction are called *the motivators*. The five major ones are:

Achievement   Equalling pride in doing a job.
Recognition   Especially praise.
Work   The actual performance of the job, especially when it is interesting and challenging.
Responsibility   Not necessarily a promotion or advancement but being given extra authority and the responsibility for carrying out tasks independently.
Advancement   This means an actual change in status, such as a new title and a rise in pay.

In other words, the motivators are the kinds of things that lead to self-actualization within a working environment. They are all connected with the actual conduct of the job itself, and—an important point for managers and supervisors—they are under the direct control of the individual's immediate superiors, even at a fairly low level in the organization.

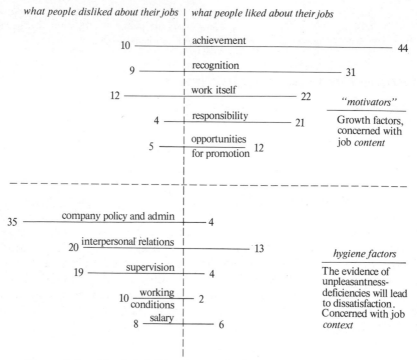

Figure 3.4: Frederick Herzberg—the hygiene theory of motivation: example of motivator and hygiene factors

The hygiene factors

The negative factors, called *hygiene factors*, also number five. These are the kinds of things that make a person feel unhappy and dissatisfied with his job and with the organization that employs him. Removal of dissatisfiers does not alone create job satisfaction; it only removes sources of dissatisfaction. This is why Herzberg calls these things hygiene factors, in an analogy to the removal of trash to keep the environment clean. The hygiene factors:

Company policy This includes poor organization structures that make it difficult to communicate, not knowing what the job responsibilities are, and so on.

Technical supervision Working for a boss who is incompetent.

Salary Especially a salary level that is seen as unfair.

Interpersonal relations Dislike of a boss; note that this is not the same as a boss who is incompetent.

Working conditions Inconvenient location, poor safety measures, uncomfortable surroundings, lack of proper tools to do the job assigned.

Now, an interesting feature of the hygiene factors is that they are not really connected with the individual's job itself but with the organization and the environment. This is in striking contrast to the motivators, all of which have to do with the actual conduct of one's job. It should also be evident that the hygiene factors are almost entirely out of the direct control of a supervisor, of a team leader, or of any middle management executive. They stem from the overall company policy, the organization structure of the company, and top management's philosophy of business life.

A further interesting aspect of Herzberg's findings is that there is no connection between the motivators and the hygiene factors. Presence of the hygiene factors leads to dissatisfaction, presence of the motivators leads to satisfaction and the will to work harder. But *removal* of the hygiene factors does nothing to increase job satisfaction; it merely lessens dissatisfaction. Both sets of factors can be operating at the same time entirely independently of each other. This gives a ray of hope to the low-level supervisor who has control only over the motivators but not over the hygiene factors.

Herzberg's work has had an enormous impact on management thinking and has advanced the human relations school tremendously ('you've got to treat your staff as if they were human beings', etc.), and has wider implications for our understanding of our industrialized society as a whole.

Herzberg is in one way profoundly pessimistic about the meaning of his findings. One reason for this, as has been implied earlier, is that the way our society is organized very few people can achieve self-actualization through their jobs. As long as this is true, there must be a sharp division between how one views one's work as opposed to 'real' interests in life. Work has no real meaning; true satisfaction is found in hobbies, in pigeon racing, gardening, stamp collecting, or other 'leisure' activities unconnected with work.

Herzberg says:

> 'What does this mean for society? It poses a real danger of an inflexible and uncreative society that will be unable to react adequately to the stresses posed by an always demanding world. If the major rewards in our society are hygienic, if conditions not related to the actual conduct of work are the major sources of satisfaction, there is little motivation for the fulfilment of the highest potential in the work of the individual. When such a society has to cease living off the fat of earlier creativity, it may well suffer the fate undergone by earlier societies now no longer in existence. The world is full of the dusty ruins of empires that were not resilient enough to cope with barbarian invaders' (Frederick Herzberg, Bernard Mausner, and Barbara Block Sayderman, *The Motivation to Work*, 2nd edn, p. 131, John Wiley and Sons, 1959).

Barbarian invaders to the contrary notwithstanding, Herzberg's theory has generated an enormous volume of further research. In recent years, a number of studies have been published that attempt to refute his findings. These have not been entirely successful, although any really great theory will survive only if it can be modified and expanded; Einstein and Freud are two examples that spring easily to mind. Herzberg's work has made valuable contributions both to management training and to mental health research and will no doubt continue to do so.

From human relations to organizational behaviour

The death knell of the human relations school of management has been sounded, although the corpse will continue to twitch for a long time to come, just as Taylorism still finds expression from time to time.

The major criticisms of the human relations school are that it is insufficiently scientific and that it takes too narrow a view. The first may be somewhat unfair, because this field is so large that enough scientific research to satisfy the purists would take centuries to carry out, by which time the whole fabric of society might have changed to such a point that the original findings were meaningless anyway! The second point is much more telling.

The school of human relations considers individuals in small working groups. In recent years, this has come to mean more and more, groups of working men, as opposed to managers and executives. It ignores the roles of the organization itself as a factor in how our society operates. It became obvious after the Hawthorne Experiments that workers could no longer be viewed as mechanical objects responding to economic stimuli; the concepts of 'morality' and the 'conscience of the organization' became popular. But the reaction went too far, and the underlying thesis was not comprehensive enough.

Organizational behaviour as a discipline attempts to take a wider view. It purports to study the relationships between individuals and between groups in the organization, and the interactions of the individuals and of the organization in society as a whole. It points to the failure of human relations to solve the management–worker conflict in Britain, and proposes a long road of change. As with any new discipline, its research findings are inconclusive and contradictory. As yet, it has had no Hawthorne. There are a number of general features of organizational behaviour which can be identified and are of interest in our present context, however. These are as follows:

1. Modern organizations have failed to give the individual an adequate outlet for his creative and self-actualizing tendencies, and thus created alienation and undesirable conflict.
2. Conflict and tension *per se*, however, are not necessarily undesirable. We need to understand more about the nature of conflict and to utilize it to improve business organization structures.
3. It is possible to design an organization that does allow its individual

workers full scope for self-actualization, while at the same time the workers are helping to further the economic aims of the organization.

4. It must be recognized that different individuals have different levels of skills and ambitions. Managers must be able to manage if the organization is to fulfil its economic objectives. A shop floor worker may have neither the ability nor the experience to make management decisions, just as a senior executive may have neither the ability nor experience to operate a machine.

5. Modern management has become too democratic; we must return to more authoritarian attitudes of management without going so far as to invoke the excesses of Taylorism.

The aims of organizational behaviour as a discipline have been summarized as follows:

'The demanding standards of a technologically sophisticated society lead to the development of ingenious and powerful management techniques which have the effect of dehumanizing the employee. The student of organizational behaviour accepts that the impact of the organization on the individual warrants constant study. The aim of organizational behaviour must be the fulfilment of the need for better achievement of the organization's objectives through the integration of the aspirations of its members' (Joe Kelly, *Organizational Behaviour*, pp. 55–6, Richard D. Irwin Inc., 1969).

Before leaving this review of people at work, as a basis for discussion of systems techniques in the next part, it is useful to review a further, computer-oriented research project. This is the work of Enid Mumford and Olive Banks in their book *The Computer and the Clerk* (in *The British Library of Business Studies* series, Routledge and Kegan Paul, London, 1967).

This book is essential reading for all systems analysts concerned with computerization of clerically based systems.

Briefly, the book describes the work of Mumford and Banks (colleagues on the staff of the Liverpool University Department of Social Science) in studying the effects on clerical staff of computerization in two companies between 1960 and 1965. (A study of a third firm was started in 1957 and abandoned when computer work was discontinued some eight months after it was installed.) The two companies studied in detail were a bank and a local manufacturing company. In each case an interview programme was carried out on user clerical staff, divided into two major phases—pre-change survey (i.e. before computer) and a post-change survey (after computer). In the bank, discussions were also held with branch managers, senior staff, computer staff, the O & M department, and unions.

The bank planned to computerize the work in nine branches and interviewing began in the branches in August. Shortly after the interviewing began, the bank revised its plans and the number of branches to be computerized was reduced to five. Interviewing for the pre-change survey was completed in April 1962. Post-change interviews took place from April 1963 to June 1964. During this time, plans to transfer the work of the largest of the five branches were dropped. The results of post-change survey were thus based on four computerized branches and one on non-computerized branch, for comparative purposes. In the local manufacturing company, the surveys were conducted from 1960 to 1963.

Remember that this research work was in conjunction with limited, first and second generation computers, with low-level languages. Interestingly enough, several technical problems endangered the systems development in all three companies. In one, the computer was found to be unsuitable for the requirements and was returned to the manufacturer, not to be replaced. In another, the firm decided to scrap its first computer and replace it with a larger and more reliable model during the post-change survey. In the third, the computer was delivered several months late, was in the hands of commissioning engineers for four months and 'progress now began continually to be held up by machine breakdowns'. With the advances of hardware and software technology and system design techniques in the past decade, these technical problems, although still in evidence today, have mostly been overcome. There is no reason to suspect, however, that the people-oriented findings of the study have been invalidated by time.

What, then, were the major findings of the study? The authors identified three practical points. There is no better way to document these than to reproduce the writers' own telling words as a summary to this chapter.

> 1. That introducing a computer is not merely a simple change from one system to another. It is something much more fundamental and far reaching, which can affect the structure of a firm and the organization of departments, the nature of the work, and the attitudes and behaviour of employees. Technical change is like a bomb explosion. If no precautions are taken, there may be widespread panic and confusion. However, if the area of impact is known in advance with some precision, precautions can be taken that will do much more to cushion the shock.
>
> 2. That office automation has quite different implications for different individuals and groups within a firm and in consequence, people will react to it in different ways according to their own particular needs, values, and interests. Some will welcome a computer, others will be neutral and others again will be hostile or afraid, seeing the new system as a personal threat. It follows that because people react differently they will need to be treated differently and any blanket policy for change is likely to have only a limited success.
>
> 3. That the introduction of any major technical change must involve the formulation of policies and strategies which are based on a careful

preliminary analysis of all the variables operating in the change situation. This is perhaps our most fundamental point. We believe that adequate prediction, planning, and the successful execution of plans, can only be achieved if a situation is looked at as a totality and analysed in this way. In order to do this, a management must take into account technical, organizational, and human relations factors' (op. cit., pp. 16–17).

Implications for the people side of systems

We have in this chapter summarized the history of research into how human beings behave at work and why, drawing a variety of conclusions. What implications does this have for the systems analyst and his projects in his own organization? Three general points will be made here.

1. The systems analyst should be familiar with the history of human relations and organizational behaviour, and should keep himself abreast of significant new developments in this field. He who is intellectually curious and serious about professionalism in his job will have no difficulty in doing this through regular reading of the technical literature that probably passes his desk daily.
2. The systems analyst should see individuals in the organization not as cogs in a machine, nor yet solely as persons within the working environment. There is more to it than that, including the distinct and separate role of the organization itself.
3. The systems analyst should try to understand the motivation and reactions of those for whom he is building new systems. If the theories of motivation presented here help in this task, then they have served their purpose. *The test of a psychological theory is whether it helps one to understand other people and to predict how they will react to a given set of circumstances.* Psychology as a science has a long way to go in this area, and none of its theories is perfect or complete: but one or more of the theories presented here should help in explaining why people act as they do. More specific examples of the application of this material will be given throughout the remaining sections of this book.

Part II

Project techniques

4

Acceptance of the system

Change in computer systems development

The systems analyst's job is concerned primarily with change. This concern is not only with designing changes, but he is himself *part* of the change itself. To many user staff he may personify the elements of change itself. He is also seen as an advisor about change, recommending and suggesting timescales and methods of change to management. If we accept that the systems analyst is not just a designer of machine-based systems, then he must understand the nature of change, its short- and long-term implications and how to deal with specific situations.

As described on page 80, the changes associated with the introduction of a computer-based system are wide-ranging. They can go deep into the structure of an organization, the job content, and working conditions, as well as the simple mechanics of new documents and machines. The analogy used by Mumford and Banks is an excellent one:

> 'Technical change is like a bomb explosion. If no precautions are taken then there may be widespread panic and confusion. However, if the area of impact is known in advance with some precision, precautions can be taken that will do much to cushion the shock.'

In this chapter, we will restrict the discussion to those changes which are directly related to the introduction of a computer system. The basic principles do, of course, apply to any change in an organization.

> A large plant hire contractor was organized into some 20 local depots scattered throughout the country. Each branch was an autonomous unit, a profit centre, with its own management, staffing, procedures, and plant. The company had grown by acquisition in accordance with local building demand. Depot management attitudes were very parochial; a manager was interested only in what went on in *his* depot with *his* resources. Senior management decided that the financial performance of the company would be improved if the autonomous control of plant

by a depot was replaced by the concept of 'a national pool'. Plant would be transferred as required between depots and large contracts would be satisfied by drawing on the plant in many depots. The national pool of equipment would be implemented by an on-line system network, with all record keeping on a computer at one point, i.e. by having one computerized plant register, accessed and updated by all depots.

Regardless of the validity of the decision to go for a 'national equipment pool', there were two distinct change problems in this example. The first was the general change from heavily decentralized operating methods and control to a heavily centralized organization. The impact of this change on the role and style of depot management would be considerable, and the problems immense. The other facet of change will be the introduction of new equipment and procedures within depots, such as the installation of VDUs, complete revision of documentation, and modified job content and working conditions. It is with the latter type of change that this chapter is principally concerned although, as has been stated, the principles of handling change are as valid for major organizational restructuring as for dealing with technical innovation at a local level.

With the wide range of system techniques currently being applied in many different applications in many organizations, it is difficult to place types of change into neat, self-contained categories. It is possible, however, to group the most common types of changes into five categories:

1. Revised procedures/and work content
2. New equipment
3. New documentation
4. Revised work direction
5. Staffing and organization changes.

Examples of these types of changes are shown in Figure 4.1. They will be a trigger to a variety of reactions in all the user staff, which can be expressed as a series of questions. These questions (probably not articulated) and the answers assumed or given will determine how an individual behaves during systems development and implementation, and in operating the system thereafter. Twelve such questions are shown in Figure 4.2.

Users will become aware of change both formally and informally during the project; formally, in discussion and consultation, investigation interviews, training sessions, etc; informally via gossip and rumour. Formal user contact with change is shown in Figure 4.3. How the user reacts during this work depends on the change, on the questions he formulates, and on the answers he gets or assumes.

In all of the following discussion it must be remembered that the reactions to change by users on any one systems development project must be seen

Figure 4.1: Typical system changes

1. *Revised procedures/ work content*	—lack of immediate visual records. —different, tighter work schedules. —work fragmentation among staff and more functions, —different, tighter procedures, with more formalized, rigorous, standards. —reduction in immediate personal control (e.g. less discretionary powers dealing with a supplier/customer, formalized, impersonal approach dealing with member of public, etc.).
2. *New equipment*	—visual display unit or keyboard printers introduced in office. —data collection terminals (e.g. badge readers) introduced in plant. —microfilm/microfiche readers introduced for use with COM output. —new office equipment to deal with filing, etc., of computer input and output.
3. *New documentation*	—introduction of machine-readable documents (OCR, mark reading, mark sense cards, MICR, etc.). —change in forms to make them suitable for transcription-type data preparation. —new/changed output reports—different content, format, timing and accuracy. —use of modified coding and numbering systems on documents,
4. *Revised work direction*	—computer-produced information is used to monitor or direct work done: e.g., computer directed: production scheduling and control sales call schedules transport loading, routing scheduling account chase lists
5. *Staffing/organization changes*	—elimination of some jobs or combining jobs —introduction of more staff or a different type of staff. —change in organizational hierarchy. —holding staffing levels but expecting greater throughput.

Figure 4.2: 12 example user reactions—questions raised

1. Will it affect my *earnings*?
2. Will it block my *promotion* prospects?
3. Will it limit my *freedom* of action?
4. Will it mean I *lose* my job?
5. Will it 'take the *fun*' out of the job?
6. Will it mean more *supervision*?
7. Will it *cut* the number of my staff?
8. Will I just become a '*new boy*'
9. Will it erode my *authority*?
10. Will it increase my *work-load*?
11. Will I be able to *cope* with everything?
12. Is this just the first step—*what will it lead to next*?

against the long-term past and future management climate as a whole. Similarly, we are considering the relatively 'independent' role of the systems analyst, who does not have the same immediate involvement with the staff as do the user supervisors and management.

Figure 4.3: Formal user contact with change

General discussions	Throughout project, but specifically with management during user request and feasibility study, and with most staff in design decision consultations later in the project.
Fact-finding interviews	The more formal interviews during the feasibility study, and detailed investigation (step 3).
Study specifications, reviews and approvals	The formal review of major development documentation such as the feasibility study and system specification, as well as documentation produced at intermediate checkpoints.
Pre-implementation training	Introductory and training sessions for all staff on the functions of the system and specific operational procedures.
Conversion and implementation	First contact with the introduction with new equipment, documentation, and procedures, and work on file creation, output vetting during parallel running, etc.

First and subsequent periods of live running

The nature of change

There are three important elements in any change situation as shown in Figure 4.4: the reason for the change, the change itself, and the way change is presented to those concerned.

Why: The objectives as laid down in the user request and validated in feasibility study; problem identification in systems analysis (step 4 in system development cycle).

What: The design as postulated initially in the feasibility study, as detailed in the systems specification, as documented in procedure manuals, operating instructions, etc.

How and when: Early discussions in the user request and feasibility study, the initial announcement of the project, conduct and timing of fact-finding interviews during the investigation, method of documenting and promulgating specifications at checkpoints, method of 'launch' of new system, conduct and timing of training sessions.

A reaction to a new system can vary from enthusiastic cooperation and support to deliberate sabotage, with a wide range of intermediate reactions as shown in Figure 4.5. Management is, of course, trying to maximize acceptance, and to minimize resistance.

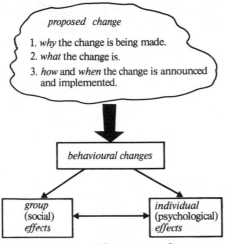

proposed change

1. *why* the change is being made.
2. *what* the change is.
3. *how* and *when* the change is announced and implemented.

behavioural changes

group (social) effects ↔ individual (psychological) effects

Figure 4.4: Elements in change

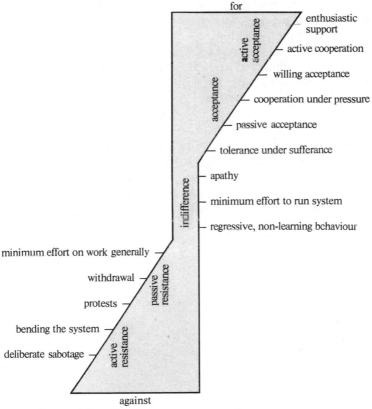

Figure 4.5: The system acceptance/rejection spectrum

As Mumford and Blake demonstrated in *The Computer and The Clerk*, problems of change exist in clerical and administrative areas as well as with manual workers. In fact, they suggest that change may present a number of difficulties in the office not found on the shop floor. These include the fact that manufacturing processes (methods and machines) have in the past been subject to a greater rate of change than clerical procedures in the office. As a result, production managers have acquired more experience of change. They had to proceed with caution because of the countervailing pressures of organized trade unions, less evident in offices. Mumford and Blake suggest that shop-floor workers have become more accustomed to change, as opposed to the 'secure and sheltered environment' of the office. Both these points, however, are becoming less and less true, with rise in trade union representation in offices, the introduction of more and more equipment-based systems, procedural changes caused by fluctuations in the economic situation, legislative changes, and the modified working conditions like 'flexitime.' Problems of change thus affect both office and manual workers. As any experienced systems analyst will tell, problems of change go further than this—to the reactions of both line *and* senior management, where reactions can be more 'against' a change than at the lower levels!

The reactions as shown in Figure 4.5 will manifest themselves in many ways. Some of these were discussed in Chapter 1. The system faults in Figure 2.1 were attributed to failing to gear the system to the aptitude and attitude of the staff. A negative attitude can be engendered by an unfavourable response to a *change*, i.e. to all three of the interlocking elements shown in Figure 4.4. A 'don't care' attitude will lead to high input errors, no action on reports, missed schedules, and so on. A more hostile attitude of resistance can lead to the retention of exisiting system in protest, beating or abusing the system to prove it doesn't work or, at the extreme, trying to demolish whole or part of the system.

Remember also that some of the faults in Figure 2.1 (such as not providing for all processing or error conditions) can be the result of user attitudes during development, which again is a direct result of acceptance or rejection of the project during development. For example:

- Project slips in time and cost because checkpoint reviews are extended (users delay in signing off reports).
- User misleads the analyst or tells outright lies during investigation.
- Users become 'unavailable' for interview during the fact-finding phases.

Employees faced with the same change situation will react in different ways. Each employee's perception of the new system will not necessarily be the same, as shown in Figure 4.6. The feelings of A, B, C, D, and E could be totally different in the same situation, and the behaviour of the individuals can be different as well. Further, two individuals, A and B, may have, on the surface, the same feelings towards change, but may behave in two different ways. Or again, A may feel very strongly about the change, would *like* to act in a particular way, but behaves in a different way because of the *group's* reaction to the change.

As a basis for formulating some guidelines in dealing with change we must first investigate what is meant by 'group' and 'individual' effects as shown in Figure 4.4.

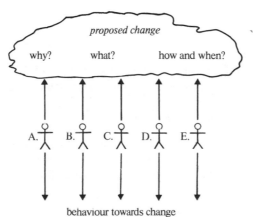

behaviour towards change

Figure 4.6: Perception of change

The individual and the group

We all have predisposed feelings about change—not about any particular change—but about change *per se*. A psychologist may argue that man has a natural predisposition against change, not automatic hostility, so much as a cautious and uncomfortable reluctance to accept it. He could develop this by pointing to the changes which occur in early infancy.

The changes which we all go through are birth, weaning, toilet training, and (in our society at least) going to school. These changes are imposed upon us without consultation or choice and could be seen as adverse changes or unpleasant experiences; leaving the warm womb for the cold world, leaving the secure nipple for a mechanistic bottle, leaving freedom for the discipline of toilet training, leaving the security and freedom of the family for strangers in the school room. The more unpleasant the changes were, the more we might be suspicious of future change situations. Whatever our predisposed feelings towards change are, they lie deep within us. One can say that these feelings towards change lie so deep, they are difficult to establish, impossible to articulate.

In an individual, these inherent predispositions to change will be there to a lesser or greater extent. As Arnold Judson says (*A Manager's Guide to Making Changes*, John Wiley and Sons Ltd, London, 1966):

> 'From an adult's childhood experiences with changes he retains a legacy in the form of a residue of faint but persistent memories. These memories from the past can exert a pervasive influence on his attitudes when he faces changes in the present. For many, the prospect of an unknown or uncertain future stimulates primarily doubts and fears. A measure of courage and self-assurance is required to enter into any new situation. It is a rare person who can undergo changes with comfort and confidence.'

Note that these feelings do not, in the well-balanced personality, lead to outright hostility and rejection of *all* change. 'He (*man*) is by nature resistant to change' is a proposition in the Theory X approach (as described on page 74) which has little credence nowadays. To quote Peter Drucker (*The Effective Executive*, World Press, 1962):

> 'It is not true, as a good many psychologists assert, that human nature resists change. On the contrary, no being in heaven or earth is greedier for new things. But there are conditions for man's psychological readiness to change.'

Let us now turn from something within the individual to something within society: our cultural beliefs. Culture, custom, and convention influence how we react to many situations. Consider the following quotations:

> 'No man ever looks at the world with pristine eyes. He sees it edited by a definite set of customs and institutions and ways of thinking. Even in his philosophical probings he cannot go behind these stereotypes; his very concepts of the true and false will still have reference to his particular traditional customs' (Ruth Benedick, *Patterns of Culture*, Houghton Mifflin Company, 1934).

> 'Culture shapes personality chiefly because it provides ready made, pre-tested solutions to many of life's problems. Out of his own life experience a child could hardly be expected to invent a language or a scheme of medical treatment; he could not evolve a science, an ethic, or an embracing religion. He must rely on the experience of his race. Culture offers him stored up solutions—not always accurate but at least available. Culture has an answer (sometimes merely rough and ready) to every question that can be asked. It is a prearranged design for living' (Gordon W. Allport, *Pattern and Growth in Personality*, Holt, Rinehart and Winston, New York, 1961).

A psychologist would draw the difference between a *real culture* and a *culture construct*. (As in the work of R. Linton, *The Cultural Background of*

Personality, Appleton–Century–Crofts, New York, 1945.) Real culture provides a framework with limits of acceptable behaviour, but considerable limits of freedom exist within this framework. Within real culture it is possible to draw only broad or approximate resemblances among individuals in the same culture. The culture construct on the other hand ignores the *range* of acceptable behaviour, it deals with the norm—the usual, common practice. It is thus a generalized pattern based on a majority pattern. (To a certain extent McGregor's work in *The Human Side of Enterprise* presents two culture constructs: Theory X and Theory Y.)

In the working environment, a culture construct could be used to describe basic beliefs of management, clerical workers, and manual workers. But this wouldn't be of much use in describing or dealing with a *specific* person in a change situation. An individual is influenced by real culture, not the construct abstraction. In terms of dealing with change in the working environment, we must recognize that there will be basic beliefs and accepted conventions in each person which will influence his attitude to change.

A culture construct for workers might have the following basic assumptions:

- computers are complex machines run by a technological elite
- computers equal machines, their introduction equals automation, automation equals redundancy
- in all cases of redundancy, staff should be released on a 'last in—first out' basis.

And:

- promotion should be primarily based on length of service
- an organization should retain staff for as long as possible, because long, loyal service is intrinsically desirable
- management is out to exploit the workers, to get the most out of them at the minimum cost.

Culture, custom, and convention in the world of business and government are thus those basic axioms which are not easily challenged or given up. They can be viewed on a national level, regional level (even to a specific location), type of worker, type of industry, and so on.

If a change runs contrary to the basic beliefs and accepted conventions, then it challenges something fundamental to the employees' way of life. The problem is thus to modify these beliefs if the change is to be implemented—no mean task for any manager or analyst.

We are now building up a picture of an individual's reaction to change. Figure 4.7 is a diagrammatic representation of an individual facing a proposed change. The individual is reacting by asking questions, as shown at the top (a summary of the list shown in Figure 4.2). The two boxes shown in Figure 4.7 illustrate the factors influencing the individual's reaction to the change: the questions framed, the desire for certain answers, and the action taken.

So far we have considered two factors: the deep-rooted feelings towards change that lie within the individual, probably stemming from early childhood, and the operation of the customs and conventions determined by, and operated within, a group. Let us explore the other factors shown.

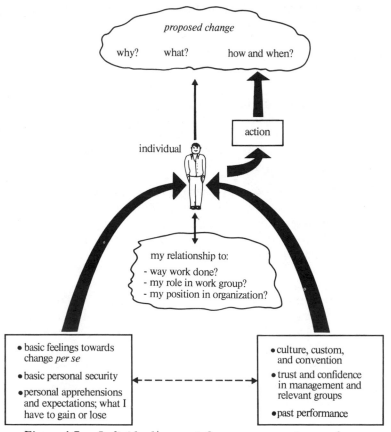

Figure 4.7: Individual/group influences on reaction to change

'**Trust.** Firm belief in the honesty, veracity, justice, strength, etc., of a person or thing. . . .'

Concise Oxford Dictionary

Trust and confidence will play a major role in an individual's reaction to any change. We must consider the individual's trust in a number of groups.

Trust is a function of how a group has lived up to the expectations of the individual, of how the group has supported him or looked after his welfare in the past. This will include the promises made, the promises kept and the promises broken. Note the diagram below shows that the individual looks for support from several sources: his management, the organization as a whole, his fellow workers, and his staff association or trade union.

Trust in the management, fellow workers, etc., is probably founded in culture, custom, and convention, but it is the personalities that count in any specific situation. The role of trust in influencing basic attitudes to change will be demonstrated in the example system changes given later in this chapter.

Let us trace through the possible steps in a change situation, Figure 4.8. This is a typical situation in a computer systems development project and, as we shall see later, it is not necessarily a desirable sequence of events. A working example is given below.

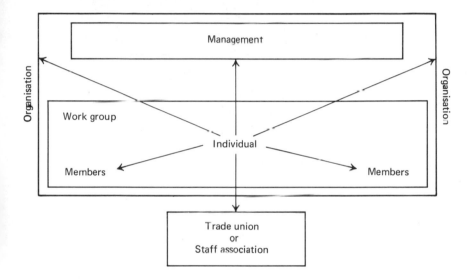

There are 12 stock clerks reporting to a supervisor. They receive orders for the issue of goods from a warehouse and goods received notes for the receipt of goods into the warehouse. All their work is concerned with maintaining a stock ledger: updating the stock balance, processing part orders (where there is insufficient stock), adjusting for stock discrepancies, and raising requisitions for more stock when the balance falls below a pre-set minimum. A summary diagram is shown in Figure 4.9(a). The stock control section had been formed more than 15 years ago, and the methods had changed little during that time.

The staffing of the department is shown in Figure 4.9(b). The staff fell into two broad groups—the old hands and the newcomers. The supervisor was a fiery Welshman who had joined the company five years ago; he left his previous company when he was 'made redundant' with the introduction of a computer system.

The senior management of the company was worried that the staff of the stock control section would continue to grow at the same rate as the business

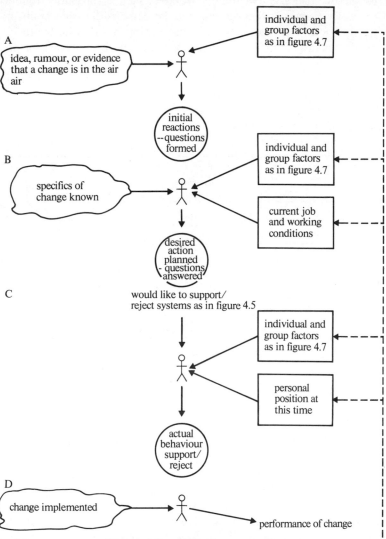

Figure 4.8:   The change cycle

expanded, but with the service provided deteriorating. It took an average of eight days to turn an order round (i.e. from receiving an order from a customer to the customer receiving the goods). The general manager of the company had said that 'They're a necessary evil, I suppose, but I don't like

Figure 4.9: Example change situation

(a) Summary of inputs/outputs/files

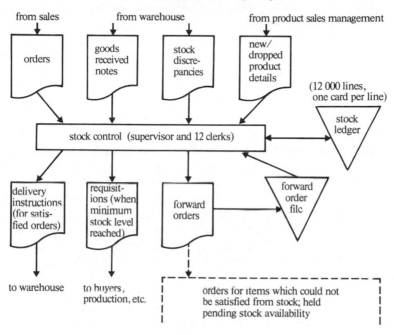

(b) Summary of staffing

Employee	Sex	Age	Length of service in company	Time in stock control section
Supervisor	M	45	5	5
Clerk 1	M	52	22	15
Clerk 2	M	48	18	15
Clerk 3	M	40	15	15
Clerk 4	F	40	14	12
Clerk 5	M	32	12	12
Clerk 6	M	30	8	8
Clerk 7	M	37	4	3
Clerk 8	M	30	3	3
Clerk 9	F	27	2	2
Clerk 10	M	19	1	1
Clerk 11	F	18	1	1
Clerk 12	F	18	2	1

spending money on paper-shufflers—all they do is juggle papers; that section is a fire risk.' Finally, the manual methods meant that stock control (setting minimum stock levels and re-order quantities) was rather a haphazard affair.

For all these reasons, the general manager wanted to computerize the whole of the stock control section's work. The project was started with complete secrecy, but soon became known to all of the stock control section. Referring to Figure 4.8, the supervisor became aware of something in the air (point A) when he was visited by a systems analyst for 'a half-hour chat' during the feasibility study. (He never, in fact, saw the feasibility study). The clerks were not visited, but they knew of the visit. The clerks were interviewed during the detailed investigation. The project was not announced, in any way, to the staff. The analyst simply arrived saying he was charged to 'look at computerizing the stock ledger because the general manager says so'. The stock control staff were not only concerned about what would happen to them in the future—they were absolutely lost about how the project would develop. (A) was thus a very unsettling time in which the questions were formed, based on the individual and group action. There was a delay of about six weeks before a design was finalized. This was discussed with the general manager and the order processing manager to whom the stock control supervisor reported. The stock control staff were not consulted. During this time clerks 8, 10, and 12 left, and clerks 3 and 4 sought transfers, unsuccessfully, to other departments. An edited form of the system specification was finally sent to the stock control supervisor, who reviewed it, added his own (sarcastic) comments and circulated it to the remaining staff. The system design lived up to their worst fears and expectations. This was stage (B). Each clerk evaluated the system against his hopes and fears, based on his existing position. Reactions varied considerably. Clerks 1 and 2 were sad that the manual stock ledger carefully maintained for 15 years would disappear. Clerks 4, 6, 7, and 11 were keen to see the radical improvements. The supervisor and principal clerks 1, 3, and 5 were thinking militantly in their rejection of the system. Not only were the results of (C) different among the staff for different reasons (B), the action taken at (D) was different from the initial desired action (C).

As a united group, they resisted the introduction of the new system. File conversion slipped, test data supplied by the clerks contained totally unrealistic data conditions, the shortcomings in the processing logic were identified in great detail by the clerks and used as excuses for all delays. Batch totals were invariably wrong, and data errors detected by the data vet rose to an astounding 20 per cent +. It was interesting, however, that the individual action at (D) did not necessarily correspond with the initial reactions (B) and (C).

The intensity of the acceptance of or resistance to the change at (B) and (C) will depend, as we have seen, on many factors. An effective way of showing the relationship between the factors *is the change equation*. Figure 4.10 shows the change equation (Arnold S. Judson, *A Manager's Guide to Making Changes*, John Wiley and Sons, London, 1966)—that resistant feelings are a function of constant and variable attitudes and feelings. As Judson says:

- 'Resistant feelings will be intense when the factors appearing in the numerator of the expression are great and the factors appearing in the denominator are small.
- Resistant feelings will be reduced by strong feelings of personnel security and trust, even though the magnitude of the factors in the numerator might be large.'

By definition, management can do little to influence the constants, and can have only minimal impact on trust, past events, and so on. The equation also shows that there is more to evaluating the change than the change itself: there is the manner of change.

Another way of viewing change is to apply the 'How much do I have to lose?' test. First, on the basis that the greater the privilege or status of the individual in the current system, the more he has to lose—and if threatened will react very strongly indeed.

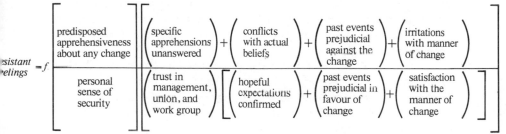

Figure 4.10:   The change equation

Referring again to Figure 4.9, clerk 1 enjoyed a privileged position. He had his work organized so that it could be completed in the minimum of time. He did not look for any other work, but he did take long lunch-hours, and arrive late and leave early. He had an elaborate series of covers. His knowledge of the existing procedures, his good personal contacts with all staff in the company (and suppliers) meant he was a respected source of information. He rated highly on the informal hierarchy. With so much to lose under the old regime, it was a case of maximum resistance to preserve his position. Clerk 9 was a case of offering the minimum resistance—with little power, influence, or status under the old regime, he had little to lose and much to gain in comparison with clerk 1. Clerk 1 would be pleased, perhaps, to gain the experience of working with a computer.

Finally, we may summarize the individual's reaction to change by looking at the concept of *psychological advantage*. This is the individual's private notions of what constitutes 'his own best interests'. The individual is striving to *be* a type of person according to his own personal values and standards; his 'best interests' aim to satisfy what the person wants to be. These best interests, as we have seen, are not necessarily job security or financial;

indeed, they may make little sense to the other members of the group. Few people, therefore, are bloody-minded just for the sake of it. Resistance to a change will decrease if the change is seen as favouring the psychological advantage of the individual concerned.

Dealing with change

Earlier in this chapter it was stressed that the analyst was an agent of change and that he was the third point in the eternal triangle of management–worker–analyst. This situation creates special problems. The analyst becomes involved in many change situations: during the various investigations and reviews, presentations of interim results at checkpoints, formal documentation and dissemination of design, training sessions, conversion and implementation procedures, and so on. We are therefore primarily concerned with those situations in which *both user management and the analyst* will give time and attention to the people side of change. If the attitude of management is that people are cogs in a machine, with no feelings, who will do what they are told to do, there is little the analyst can do to ameliorate such a situation.

It is difficult (if not totally unrealistic) to say to an analyst 'think about the type of change and manner of change' without a specific framework to aid his thinking. One practical method of viewing a change situation is the *balance sheet approach*. This has been advocated by a number of writers on management, and has been used by the author on a number of projects. It is one way of clarifying thoughts about the problems of change presented in a specific situation. A sheet of paper is divided into two columns; personal gains are recorded on the left-hand side and personal losses are recorded on the right-hand side. An example is shown in Figure 4.11. (The conventional book-keeping balance sheet or 'statement of affairs' lists the liabilities on the left and assets on the right, equivalent to the losses and gains in change respectively. Simon Stevin of Bruges in the early part of the sixteenth century produced a statement of affairs with liabilities = left, assets = right. This was incorporated in British law in the middle of the nineteenth century (Companies Act 1856). It is now recognized that the *logical* approach is assets = left, liabilities = right, as in many European countries and the USA. This convention is used in this book.)

During the entire project, from user request through design to implementation, the analyst estimates the gains and the losses on the sheet. These can be summarized for a group as a whole. Wherever possible the analyst should review the balance sheets with the appropriate management, who will be able to help in their interpretation. The analyst, on the other hand, will be able to bring his objectivity to bear on the situation, to counter the subjective, possibly distorted view of management. (Such consultation will serve little use if the manager takes a distinctly Theory X approach!)

Needless to say, the balance sheets should be regarded in their original form as personal data and should be treated with confidentiality and security measures taken to protect them.

The balance sheet is thus a means of anticipating possible reactions, updated as the project proceeds; a means of clarifying ideas about the people involved in the project. It is, of course, no more than a documentation technique as the basis for planning. To deal actually with the change situation, user management, analyst and staff will interact in face-to-face personal meetings and discussions.

Figure 4.11: The balance sheet approach to change

Acceptance (estimated gains)	Resistance (estimated losses)
financial +	financial −
security	insecurity
convenience	inconvenience
job satisfaction	job dissatisfaction
social	anti-social
manner of change	manner of change
general	general

The exact entries made on the sheet will depend on the people and the project. *Example* losses and gains are shown in Figures 4.12 through 4.17. In these tables, the feelings are expressed as statements in the first person singular. On the actual balance sheets they should be expressed as succinct phrases.

A balance sheet can be produced for an individual or for a group. As a means of testing one's understanding of the individual's point of view, each of the entries can be weighted to show strength of feeling. One example rating system is to use a three-point scoring system:

3   very strong, very important
2   strong
1   somewhat
0   insignificant (should not really appear in the table at all).

Note that it is the *relative* award of points that is important, rather than the absolute values. The ratings will invariably change as the project progresses and as the design of the system is developed and modified. If the value of a gain is given a plus and that of a loss a minus the absolute difference between the sum of the two columns will be a *general indicator* of how the individual/group feels about the project. This can be compared to the analyst's general impression and force the analyst to become more critical in his

Figure 4.12:   Gains/losses—financial

Gains	Losses
My *current* earnings will be increased because I think that:	My *current* earnings will be decreased because I think that:
—in effect I'm being asked to do less work for the same money	—in effect I'm being asked to do more work for same money
—I will do more work and get more money	—I will do less work and therefore get less money
—I will do more lucrative overtime	—I will do less lucrative overtime
My *future* earnings will be increased because:	My *future* earnings will be decreased because:
—my job will be upgraded, using new skills and applying my experience and I will be suitably rewarded	—my job will be down-graded because the skills used and experience gained will no longer be valid
—my earnings are related to rate of promotion in the company and the rate of advancement will be faster	—my earnings are related to rate of promotion in the company and the rate of advancement will be slower
—if I leave the company, I will be more attractive to a new employer and my earnings will therefore be improved	—if I leave the company with a downgraded job, my potential earnings in a new company will be affected
—there will be fewer staff and more money to go around	—bonuses, etc. will be decreased based on a higher throughput
	—there will be more staff and less money to go around
Generally:	*Generally:*
—the computer will produce information which shows how good/valuable I am to the company, I will be suitably financially rewarded	—the computer will monitor my work and produce information to show that I've made mistakes, not producing enough, etc., and I will be penalized for this via my earnings
—I am being exploited by the management	—I'm being exploited by the management

Figure 4.13:   Gains/losses—security

Gains	Losses
If the computer system goes right, it will improve the company's trading position and my job will become more secure. My security of tenure in the job will increase because I think that: —I will be able to deal with the new techniques, procedures and equipment, thus demonstrating my value to the company —I will become more essential to operations in the future, and will therefore be more insulated against any redundancy —I will have more responsibility for the work done in the future The investigation will show what a splendid job I've done in the past, and this will make my value to the company become known and increase my security.	My job—and me with it—will disappear because I do the sort of things that computers do better. If this computer system goes wrong, it will damage our trading position and my job can be laid on the line. My security of tenure in the job will decrease because I think that: —I will not be able to learn and adapt to the new procedures —I will not be able to cope with the new techniques and equipment —I will become less essential to operations in future and will therefore become more exposed to redundancy if there's a cut-back —I will be held responsible for some work on the computer over which I have no direct control—and if things go wrong, it'll come back on me —the computer will produce information that will show all my errors and mistakes, and allow easy comparison between my productivity and other people's An investigation is going to show that my section is in a mess and I am worried that when it comes out I'll be for the high-jump.

Figure 4.14: Gains/losses—convenience

Gains	*Losses*
This system will be convenient because I think that: —I will have to work less hard —I have more freedom in the hours I attend the office and more flexibility for time-off —It will be a help in the conduct of my life personally (less travel and more sociable hours, etc.) —working conditions will become more pleasant—break timings, hours, physical environment, talking, making personal calls, etc.	This system will be inconvenient because I think that: —I will have to work harder —I will have to attend the office more regularly with inflexibility for time off —it will interfere with my personal life (more travelling, more unsocial hours, etc.) —working conditions will be unpleasant—break timings, hours, physical environment, taking, making personal calls, etc. —I will have to give-up my own methods, shortcuts, and work rhythm built up over the years

Figure 4.15: Gains/losses—job satisfaction

Gains	Losses
The content of my job will be upgraded because I think the new system will make it: —more interesting —more of a challenge —less restrictive —more enjoyable	The content of my job will be degraded because I think that the new system will make it: —less interesting —less of a challenge —more restrictive —less enjoyable
In this upgraded job I will have: —more authority —more responsibility —more chance to exploit my knowledge and skills —more influence —more/less pressure	In this degraded job I will have: —less authority —less responsibility —no chance to exploit my knowledge and skills —less influence —more/less pressure
The new job furthers my immediate corporate and/or long-term career plans.	The new job does not fit into my immediate corporate and/or long-term career plans.

Figure 4.16: Gains/losses—social

Gains	Losses
My relationships with other people I like will be improved because I think the system will: —increase my personal contact with my fellows in the work group —maintain the pleasant atmosphere of the work group I'm in now, giving us more time —increase my personal contact with other people I like dealing with (other groups in the company, suppliers, customers, etc.) —I'll be working with Mr Y who I like and respect as a manager	My relationships with other people I like will be damaged because I think the system will: —reduce my personal contact with my fellows in the work group —break up the pleasant work group I'm in now —reduce my personal contact with other people I like dealing with (other groups in the company, suppliers, customers, etc.) —I won't be working for Mr X any longer
My standing in the group will be increased—I will have enhanced status because I think the new system will: —really use my skills, knowledge, and experience, far more so than at present —increase my authority and responsibility —increase the number of staff reporting to me	My standing in the group will be damaged—I will lose status, I think the new system will: —invalidate my previous knowledge and experience —reduce or limit my authority or responsibility —reduce the number of staff reporting to me
I don't like working in a team and this system means I will work by myself in the future.	I will be forced to work with/for people I don't like.
My association with a sophisticated computer system will raise my status in the community.	If I cooperate on the new system I could/would contribute to making other people redundant.
	I like working by myself and this will force me into a team.
	I will have to work with new people and I don't like making new friends.

Figure 4.17: Gains/losses—manner of change

Gains	Losses
This has been an opportunity to get all the things that have built up off my chest.	Someone has been complaining that I haven't been doing my job properly.
I like being part of a modern technological change, pioneering the use of terminals, computer-based control techniques, and so on.	I haven't seen any good reason for the change—the system we've got is good enough. It's just one of those hair-brained schemes to make management look good.
I feel special—flattered—that I'm being consulted on this project, with these highly qualified, expensive technicians spending so much time with me.	'*They*' don't know really what's going on or what our problems are—*I* was never asked.
I feel proud, part of a select group, that is getting special attention.	I don't like having things sprung on me—there has been insufficient time for thought.
I'm satisfied and pleased that management and analyst are seeking my views.	This sort of thing is typical—we're kept almost in the dark and things drag on and on—then suddenly everything becomes an urgent rush.
I like talking about what I'm doing and the analyst has provided a good listening post.	I resent the criticism implied in the change, especially when the criticism comes from computer backroom boys who don't know what happens here.
It feels good to make suggestions which are listened to and used	I've been told to change—no consultation. All the reports have told me *what* to do—all the decisions have been made by '*them*'.
I'm pleased that I'm participating on this project, because it affects what I will be doing over the future years.	I've got to live with the new system—'*they*' haven't.

appraisal. Examples of the use of this approach will be given in the case studies later in this chapter.

The balance sheet approach—A warning

It has been stressed above that the balance sheet approach is a simple documentation technique to help the analyst focus his attention on the problems of change of a specific project. Ideally, it is used in conjunction with talks with user management; without the cooperation of user management; its validity is in doubt. Few analysts have either the psychological training or intimate knowledge of user personnel. Its use can be criticized as an abuse of 'scientific management', in which assumptions are made and applied in the manipulation of people as 'cogs in a machine'. Remember that the reasoning is:

- dealing with change is an important aspect of systems development
- the analyst must consider this aspect of the work
- analyst and user management must consider the problems of change together
- the balance sheet approach helps analyst and user management to concentrate their attention on various staff reactions
- just as an individual's perception of a change is different from another's, so the perception of the individual's reaction to change by the analyst or managers can vary.

The ethics of documenting one's feelings about other people's reactions depends on the honesty, knowledge, and intelligence with which it is done, the privacy of the record, and the use to which the information is put.

Participation—Good or evil?

Study after study has shown that participation of all levels of staff is essential for a constructive acceptance of a change and for the subsequent increase in work done, throughput, accuracy, and so on. But is participation the panacea for all system development ills? How should it be organized? Is participation always practicable?

First, let us review briefly the work of some research studies on participation. From the early work of Mayo *et al.* in the Hawthorne Experiments, it became apparent that productivity and acceptance of change was a product of group dynamics and the way the group interacts with supervisors and management. Many research projects have been conducted into how participation in decision making by a group affects later productivity of the group. Many experiments used three comparable groups with different methods of implementing changed methods. The three groups would be, typically:

1. *Control group*: no alteration in method, i.e. exisiting group/supervisor interaction retained.
2. *Zero or minimal participative group*: with no prior consultation, decision making held by management with *de facto* announcements of change.
3. *Maximum participation*: with many consultations with the group, and some decision making given to the group.

Some experimenters went further to explore different grades of participation between the extremes of minimal and maximum participation.

Take, for example, the experiments at the Harwood Corporation, a manufacturer of pyjamas in Marion, Virginia, USA, conducted by L. Coch and J. R. P. French, Jr (*Overcoming Resistance to Change*, Human Relations, vol. 1, no. 1, 1948). The company employed approximately 600 people, mainly manual workers. The company had good labour relations, with the exception of extreme resistance by workers to the many changes (based on the nature of the business) in its products and production methods. It was the increase in labour turnover, fall in production, and hostility towards management during these periods of frequent changes that Coch and French investigated. The experiment involved four groups of workers, as shown in Figure 4.18.

The results speak for themselves. They are supported by a further experiment when 13 members of the initial control group were subsequently given the opportunity of full participation on methods changes. This gave similar results to the original groups 3 and 4 (i.e. a rise to about 70 units per hour after change). There was also a considerable drop in labour turnover and less hostility to management.

Contrast these results with the work of Morse and Reimer. Their experiment took place over a period of two years in a clerical department of an insurance company. The experiment involved some 500 people, divided into four divisions, each division performing exactly the same type of work. A summary is given in Figure 4.19.

Note that average productivity increased *more* in the hierarchical programme with *less* participation, than in the autonomy programme, a surprising result. Further, *rate of increase* was greater under the hierarchical programme than under the autonomy programme. There were also interesting differences in the interpersonal relations of staff within the two programmes, with better, more positive relationships developing in the autonomy programme. What, then, accounted for the results? The authors suggest the following:

Hierarchical programme—less participation. Productivity up because management *ordered* a reduction in the number of staff assigned to tasks. Clerks *had to* increase productivity.

Autonomy programme—some participation. Productivity up because of

Pre-change production level for all groups = 60 units per hour

Group 1: control group

Method: existing procedures for making changes.
Description: new or modified jobs timed, rates set by time study: results announced to workers.
Results after change: drop to 50 units per hour.

Group 2: participation

Method: participation through representation.
Description: Reason or need for change presented forcefully to group, followed by acceptance by group for change. Selected group members work on the design of new jobs with management, time-study, etc. Suggestions are incorporated into new methods. The selected operators are timed and rates set, and they explain to and train the other members of the group.
Result after change: initial drop followed by return to 60 units per hour, thence slowly to 70 units per hour.

Groups 3 and 4: full participation

Method: participation of all members.
Description: as for group 2, but smaller groups, with *all* members participating in design and timing.
Results after change: 60 units per hour, thence rapidly to more than 70 units per hour.

Figure 4.19:   Autonomy versus hierarchial programmes Nancy Morse and E. Reimer, 'The Experimental Change of a Major Organizational Variable', *Journal of Abnormal Social Psychology*, 1956 **52,** 120–29

Group 1: two divisions—autonomy programme

Description: greater delegation to lower levels, control placed further in the hands of clerks who have group meetings on their working conditions (break times, holiday schedules, etc.). Training given at lower levels in human relations.
Results: productivity up some 20 per cent.

Group 2: two divisions—hierarchical programme

Description: control held mainly by higher levels of management, with minimal delegation to lower levels. Most decision making at higher levels and passed down to lower levels.
Result: productivity up some 25 per cent.

---

increased motivation of staff, with a *voluntary* reduction in the number of staff assigned to tasks (e.g. not replacing staff who left).

Clerks *wanted to* increase productivity.

The authors did, however, express reservations about the durability of the hierarchical programme production increases.

From all the research work that has been done, we may draw three practical conclusions for the systems analyst:

1. For long-lasting acceptance of change and sustained increase in productivity, participation of all employees is essential.

2. The participation has to be based on and directed towards an agreed aim.

3. Genuine participation is only possible if there is common ground and accepted objectives.

This last point is very important, and draws a distinction between *pseudo-consultation* and *genuine participation*. For example, suppose the stock control clerks as in the example in Figure 4.9 opposed the use of computers; the general manager is in favour. With this situation, what would be the value of participation? Consider the following quotation by H. A. Simon ('Authority', in *Research in Industrial Human Relations—A Critical Appraisal*, C. Arensberg, S. Barkin, *et al.* (eds.), Harper, New York, 1957):

> '*The manager* can tolerate genuine participation in decision making only when he believes that reasonable men, knowing the relevant facts and thinking through the problem will reach a decision that is generally consistent with *his* goals and interests in the situation.'

In the stock control example, manager and employees have prejudged the issues. With the current climate, the general manager would probably be loath to permit active participation because, with all the facts, etc., the stock control section would not reach a decision which was generally considered with his (the general manager's) goals and interests. The views of the system analyst add a third dimension to the problem. The analyst might be loath to permit too much participation by management because they could decide on an off-line batch system, while the analyst (for his reasons) favours an on-line system.

Herzberg, for example, puts a strong case against full participation of workers in the job content aspects of design ('One more time: how do you motivate employees?', *Harvard Business Review*, January—February, 1968, pp. 53–62). He believes that it is the redesigned job which motivates employees, not their attitudes about involvement. Decisions on job content must be made by management. Lower level supervisors may well worry about too much participation, that it represents some weakness or loss of control on their part. Certainly the ground rules for participation must be clearly laid down at the start of the project.

We can therefore say that true participation can only take place if the climate is right, and if it is directed towards the agreed common aim. Note that in the Harwood experiment there were in effect five phases:

—present and accept reason for change
—agree method for developing change
—design change

—train workers in change
—operate change

The first two steps are of primary importance.

Pseudo-participation in systems development has been applied in many organizations. The general form is:

1. User management and data processing agree the objectives and design for the new system.
2. Discussions are then held with users; any suggestion which is contrary to the initial design is suppressed, those which agree with the initial design are encouraged.
3. User staff are sold on the system, gently and indirectly, during these conversations.
4. The system is launched as 'a product of our joint ideas and labours'.

The acceptability of the ethics of this approach is left to the reader to decide.

Some companies have found that it is difficult if not impossible to sustain what is, in essence, a deception. When staff discover that only lip-service is paid to their views, that their suggestions are not sincerely sought or evaluated, and that an insidious sales campaign has been mounted, considerable hostility and rejection are generated, calling the validity of the system into question.

The antithesis of participation is development in total secrecy and silence, with no consultations at lower levels. This can mean that the system is based on inadequate investigation, as discussed in Chapter 5. By the time the system is announced, all the design decisions have been made. User staff, faced with *fait accompli* would, perhaps understandably, fight the apparently arbitrary introduction of the new system. If they cannot have any influence on the design, the users' only course of action is block the system or make changes informally.

There are two reasons that are given to justify silence and secrecy. The first is that there can be delays in a project between the various steps in the system development cycle. The longer the period of uncertainty, the more rumour can take a hand, and unrealistic hopes and fears can escalate. Not only will the change questions form, but the most pessimistic answers will be assumed. The second reason is based on management's lack of confidence in how the staff will react to the impending change; the staff will quit at the rumour of a change, or organize resistance to hamper system development.

In the first case, it is the lack of *communication* which feeds the uncertainty. Management sees a trade-off between secrecy and its problems, against the time and effort of telling staff what is happening, trying to stem the rumour and answer the change questions. The second way of thinking is indicative of poor management–worker relations in the past. The cumulative mistrust based on previous performance will not be overcome in the life of a single project.

There are some projects that have to be initiated and progressed in secrecy because public knowledge would damage the company's trading position, such as the release of new products or services, new marketing methods, new pricing policies, and so on. Indeed it may be a legal requirement to limit knowledge of the project, as in the case of a system in preparation for a company merger in the future. Generally, on computer-based system development projects, the problem lies in balancing uncertainty against early consultations, and keeping the project cloaked in secrecy. Specific techniques will be presented in subsequent chapters:

Chapter 5: conducting an investiation.
Chapter 6: seeking user involvement in checkpoints and in systems conversion and implementation.
Chapter 7: designing the new system.

Case studies

We end this chapter with two case studies which illustrate some problems of introducing change in computer systems development. They involve sales and order processing, but the principles apply to all applications.

Study 1: Order entry by salesmen

The company produced and sold paper products. Sales representatives brought in new customers, i.e. they served a promotion function, and advised prospects on how to tackle very difficult or large printing jobs. The salesmen, on the other hand, took orders mainly by telephone but also by post from established customers. This was no straightforward clerical operation.

The company sold a wide range of products with many variables (size, finish, weight, cut, etc.). The salesmen were experts in the range of products, their production *and* their use. Further, there were very complex rules for determining conditions of sale such as pricing, discounts and delivery. In the existing system, they took telephone calls, armed with various catalogues, discussed the customer's problem and his order, and noted down an order.

The order would then go to clerks who would add some additional coded data and produce a neat copy. The copy went to data preparation where it was punched onto cards, and thence to the computer. The computer suite did much of the order processing work, the detail of which does not concern us here. Salesmen were paid commission. They were friendly with the clerical staff.

An on-line system was being considered, in which the salesman would build-up the order on a VDU while talking to the customer on the telephone. This would eliminate the costs and delays of clerks and data preparation. Additionally, the product catalogues would, in effect, be computerized to provide a faster reference look-up system and instant validation of input. By having immediate access to stock figures, the salesman could advise on the availability of stock and thus delivery time.

The company had several regional offices, with the largest office in London. The plan was to introduce the system first in the London office, and it was thus developed with strong representation and influence from the London office. There was rigorous investigation in the London office, together with meaningful consultations with the salesmen. As the systems design evolved, the salesmen expressed the following apprehensions about the change.

- Would the new system reduce them to mere copy typists, where they would spend more time banging away at keyboards?
- Could they cope with the volume of typing, since none of them had any experience or training?
- Would the computer take over their product and pricing decisions?
- Would their career prospects be blocked? (A salesman's ambition was to become a sales representative. What did typing have to do with the sales rep's job and how did it further their training and career prospects?)

An example balance sheet for a salesman as he saw it at the initial design stage is shown in Figure 4.20. Note that this shows the typical answers that a salesman would put to these questions, and the implications in other areas.

Because these hopes and fears were recognized early in the project, management could deal with them. They stated as a matter of policy that career progression would not be hindered, that training would be given in keyboard operation as required, that the volume of typing would be strictly limited in message design, and that visits could be arranged to see similar systems being used in other companies to demonstrate the simplicity of VDU operation. They also said that the salesman's experience and knowledge of the products would in no way be automated; the system was there as an aid.

Two further reactions came to light as the project progressed. The first was that salesmen were worried that the clerical group would be disbanded. The salesmen liked the support of this group, who were also used for general 'fetching and carrying'. Management agreed to investigate the total work load of the eight woman clerical group and, if necessary, retain one or two for general duties. The other reaction was a salesman's argument that went: 'We *are* doing more work; the company should take some or all of the clerical section's wage bill and divide it amongst us.' Management countered with an argument that the operational cost of the new system, even offsetting the wage earnings of the clerical group, would be slightly more expensive than the existing system. The benefit would be a better service to the customer and, ultimately, this would be reflected in increased sales, which would show in

Figure 4.20: Case study 1—saleman's balance sheet

Gains

Financial +
Outside possibility that more orders will go through and my commission up.

Security:
No enhancement.

Convenience:
Cutting down mass of paper in office, easier to find copy orders, price changes, etc.

Job satisfaction:
I will be totally responsible for getting my customers' order into the system, and keeping an eye on delivery.
I can give more information to the customer when processing an order.

Social:
No enhancement.

Manner of change:
I'm glad I'm being consulted because I can make sure my interests are guarded. I'm pleased management is consulting me and using my experience.

Losses

Financial –
I'm doing the work of more people (e.g. clerical group, punching) for the same money.

Insecurity:
I won't be able to cope with typing quickly and accurately, and with operating VDU.
Computerization of all product data will invalidate my experience; I could in the future be replaced by a (cheaper) clerk.

Inconvenience:
Noisy 'machinery' in office.
More work because of lack of clerical support.
More work because of careful keyboard operation (versus jotted note).

Job dissatisfaction:
My knowledge and skills will be inhibited by inflexible, automated techniques.
A copy typist's job is boring.
New work load in no way prepares me or is relevant to my promotion to sales rep.

Anti-social:
No loss.

Manner of change:
No loss.

the salesmen's commission. No increase in base salary was agreed for the salesmen.

This brief study shows the wide range of reactions when staff are faced with change, and how these can be dealt with if they are considered early in the project.

Study 2: Sales ordering

The company sold a range of confectionery products. Salesmen paid regular calls to small shops and supermarkets. They took orders that would be delivered by the distribution service up to two weeks later. The order form used by the salesmen had been introduced some three years before when a computer-based order processing system had been implemented.

The existing batch computer system was unpopular. It had been developed without proper investigation and with minimal cooperation from the staff. It was a top management order: 'This system will be used as from the third quarter.' Further, the system had generated more work for the salesmen because the order form required extra codes and tighter data entry standards. Many salesmen worked unpaid overtime transcribing the rough orders taken on site to the preprinted order forms for data preparation. The turnaround period to deliver had *increased* when the new system was introduced.

Both management and salesmen pushed for a better computer system. Learning from the previous project, management insisted that the analyst should carry out a detailed investigation, and that salesmen and order processing clerks would be consulted. The new system design was acclaimed enthusiastically by all the staff.

The new system was based on a pre-printed, easy-to-complete mark reading document. Additional sales coding was eliminated. The form also *aided* the sales process by providing an easy-to-use catalogue. (It thus had the potential to increase sales, by 'pressuring' the customer into placing an order, by being so quick and simple to complete.) The basic data collection procedure was thus operationally practical and effective.

A major snag, however, developed when the time came for conversion. After the design had been accepted in outline, the analyst suggested some enhancements. His case was that the modified order form and the revised customer file could provide additional valuable management information and increased control. He presented two ideas. The first was that the order forms could be analysed not only to show sales by salesman but also *calls* by salesman; this could be used to raise the number of calls (and thus sales) still higher. The second idea was that the computer could produce call lists (in fact, order forms with the name and address pre-printed) based on time since last call, geographic location, and so on.

The result was that the salesmen found out about the call analysis report and objected vehemently—they had always been assessed on sales revenue, never calls. The call list was discarded as being irrelevant and unworkable. For example, one salesman pointed out:

'The computer in its logical way would say visit Mrs Jones' shop in Bloggs Road today. Wednesday is never a good time to call. It's early closing, and Mrs Jones probably won't be there because that's when she visits an aunt in hospital the other side of London. Her son minds the shop and he isn't allowed to place orders.

Just prior to going live, therefore, the saleman's general feelings about change are shown in Figure 4.21.

Most of the gains refer to the consultation-derived procedures, the losses to the subsequent designs. The call list system would probably have been very much revised—but at least more useful. The call analysis was a complete waste of time. The number of recorded calls shot up—most of them classed as unsuccessful, such as 'owner not present'. The recorded calls, needless to say, were merely entries to beat the system. The quality of input data of the OCR documents was far lower than had been anticipated and indicated in test runs—which had taken place *before* the two changes had been announced. The system was subsequently modified along the lines suggested above. But the after-taste left by, as the salesmen put it, slipping the late changes in and springing the decisions on them, remained.

Summary

1. In this chapter, the importance of understanding and dealing with change has been discussed and explained. The analyst is often called upon as an adviser on how to deal with change. He must generally work within the existing management climate.

2. A computer-based system means not only procedural and local staffing changes (as in Figure 4.1), it can also have an impact on the fundamental nature and structure of the organization.

3. A change can be reviewed in terms of three elements: *why* is the change being made, *what* the change is, *how* and *when* the change is announced and implemented. The change will require that people behave differently, and this is influenced by both group and individual feelings. The *why*, *what*, *when* and *how* of change can be perceived differently by members of the same group.

4. An individual's feelings towards change are deeply rooted within his personality and depend on his predisposed feelings towards change, his basic feelings of personal security, and his apprehensions and expectations. Closely related are custom and conventions, trust, and past experiences.

5. A change cycle was presented, starting with the individual's initial reaction to change when change is in the offing. This was explained in terms of

Figure 4.21: Case study 2—salesman's balance sheet

Gains	Losses
Financial+ Very probably my earnings will increase because sales would go up because of a better delivery service and the order form acting as sales aid. My commission will increase because there is opportunity for more sales calls to be made (because of less clerical work).	*Financial —* No losses.
Security: No enhancement.	*Insecurity:* 'Big brother' type of spying on me via the call analysis report.
Convenience: I will spend less time in the evening, etc., tidying-up order forms—more time on personal things.	*Inconvenience:* I don't necessarily want to be in that part of London when the computer says I should be there. I like to tie in business with shopping, visiting friends, etc.
Job satisfaction: The clerical work load is lifted from me, and I have an easier, far more aggressive approach.	*Job dissatisfaction:* I resent being watched, with the number of calls being monitored. I could treble the number of calls but only get an additional pittance for it; I am evaluated on volume of sales. I don't like being told what to do by a machine—especially when the system is unrealistic. I don't like being involved with a half-baked idea.
Social: No enhancement.	*Anti-social:* No loss.
Manner of change: I'm pleased that management asked my advice about the new ordering system, getting the benefit of my experience. They obviously learnt from the results of the last mess.	*Manner of change:* Why, oh why, did management muck the whole thing up? I bitterly resent the backdoor method whereby the system was changed, with no consultation. The sly method of putting in the call analysis system means that they must be going to do something with it that will do us down.

'questions' being raised in the mind of the individual. When the specifics of the change are known, the individual reacts to the answers to the change questions, and desired actions are formulated. The actual behaviour will not necessarily be the same as desired action. There are, again, individual and group influences to modify the action taken.

6. A change can be viewed by means of a change equation as in Figure 4.10. A practical balance sheet approach to considering change was discussed (Figures 4.11 to 4.17), in which the individual and group reactions to system changes are mapped out as gains and losses. This is a planning tool which focuses the attention of both analyst *and* management to change.

7. Participation is recognized as generally the most effective way of dealing with change, but this is not always the case, as when there are diametrically opposed cultural beliefs and objectives. The participation must be controlled and covered equally: *why, what, how* and *when*. Participation, however, takes time and effort, and might be precluded by the need for confidentiality about the change. Secrecy and silence may be expedient in time, money, and management effort, but severe problems can be generated in the future.

5

Investigation versus inquisition

The importance of an investigation and its objectives

The consequences of insufficient investigation were described in Chapter 2. An investigation is necessary at several stages in systems development. For example, an analyst can be required to carry out an investigation at the following steps:

1. *User request*: To help determine objectives, to review the environment and to identify problems.
2. *Feasibility study*: To collect information prior to verifying the user request and to proposing outline systems designs (with development plans and cost/benefit analysis, etc.).
3. *Hardware/software selection*: To gather information about suppliers and their products, prior to providing decision-making information to management.
4. *Investigation*: To collect detailed information for analysis and design, leading to the system specification. The investigation will include people, procedures, data, jobs, organization structure, and future growth requirements.
5. *Evaluation*: To gather information about the operation of the system for post-implementation audit.

The basic techniques for investigation apply to all these, with minor variations depending on when and why the investigation is being carried out. For example, the investigation for the feasibility study is intentionally brief because *outline* solutions are being prepared. The analyst will concentrate his effort in discussing the new system's requirements with senior and line management, with *selective* sorties down the organization to gather key items of information in detail. The investigation at step 3, however, is far more rigorous and detailed, in which all relevant functions and levels are consulted.

Investigation is thus the foundation upon which the subsequent tasks of analysis and design are based. If the foundation is unsound, the analysis will be invalid and the design decisions will be incorrect. The interdependence of these three steps is shown in Figure 5.1. Ideally, each step is completed before the following step is commenced. In practice, however, this rarely happens. The analysis step usually leads to more investigation; the design step requires further analysis to be done, and this in turn may require further investigation. The *aim* must be to complete one step before progressing to the next. If there is excessive backtracking—from design, back to analysis, back to investigation—the development process becomes inefficient.

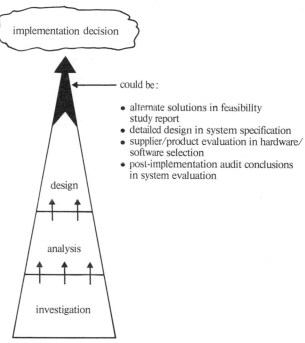

Figure 5.1:   The interdependence of investigation, analysis, and design

The objectives of an investigation can be summed-up as follows:

> *To collect the maximum of correct, relevant information in the minimum of time, whilst performing the necessary 'public relations' functions.*

This does not mean that the investigation is an impersonal, bulldozing inquisition. The analyst is going to collect information about the existing environment and how it may change. He should do this in an organized, disciplined manner. At the same time, he must not alienate staff, rather he must seek their active support and cooperation. In some cases, the users will be helpful and enthusiastic; in others they may be sullen and obstructive. The public relations aspect of the analyst's job is thus to leave people thinking that they have had a 'fair hearing'. At best it is to gain the cooperation of the antagonistic, at worst, not to alienate further the obstructive.

Carrying out an investigation is a people-oriented job. On the one hand there is the analyst's knowledge of *the data* he must collect if a successful system is to be designed. On the other is the analyst's skill in *getting the data*. This chapter is principally concerned with the latter. It presents a series of tried and tested techniques. Intelligent application of these techniques will give a successful investigation; they must be modified and adapted to suit particular local circumstances. The blind application of these techniques without taking into account the local conditions is as dangerous as implementing a standard system or software package without understanding the environment in which it will work.

Golden rules

Basic rules for any investigation are shown in Figure 5.2. These six golden rules are so important that if any is broken then the investigation will not meet the objectives as defined above. Some vital facts will be missed, some information will be unreliable, users will be unhappy, and progress will be slow. It is therefore important to review these rules and to formulate techniques to ensure that they will not be broken.

First the rules:

Figure 5.2:   Golden rules for investigation

- be objective
- validate
- be professional
- don't give up
- follow through
- be diplomatic

Be objective

Objectivity in this case is 'seeing the existing situation as it really is, not as you or anyone else would like it to be'. This means distinguishing between fact and opinion. It is the hardest rule for an analyst to follow.

Loss of objectivity from the user's point of view is a problem which always faces the systems analyst. Consider the example shown in Figure 5.3. The analyst visits three users: line manager A, supervisor B, and worker C. He asks them each 'What happens in this part of the company?' Note the range of possible answers. Each user can give a range of different answers, some fact, some opinion. Nobody has actually lied, all perhaps have tried to be helpful.

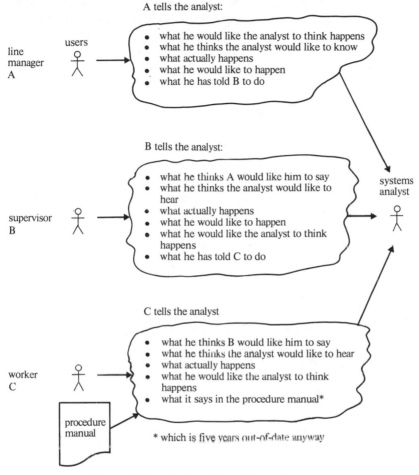

A tells the analyst:

line manager A — users

- what he would like the analyst to think happens
- what he thinks the analyst would like to know
- what actually happens
- what he would like to happen
- what he has told B to do

B tells the analyst:

supervisor B

- what he thinks A would like him to say
- what he thinks the analyst would like to hear
- what actually happens
- what he would like to happen
- what he would like the analyst to think happens
- what he has told C to do

systems analyst

C tells the analyst

worker C

- what he thinks B would like him to say
- what he thinks the analyst would like to hear
- what actually happens
- what he would like the analyst to think happens
- what it says in the procedure manual*

procedure manual

* which is five years out-of-date anyway

Figure 5.3: Losing objectivity—the users

Three specific examples are given below:

Systems analyst A: 'Some years ago, I was doing an investigation in a distribution organization. I went to see the Order Processing Manager. It was about 10 o'clock in the morning. The manager thumped the table and went on for about half an hour about the importance of a late delivery report; it seemed, from what he was saying and the way he was saying it, that the report was vital. So I built it into the system. About three months later, I presented the new system to the users. When it came to the late delivery report, the Order Processing Manager shuffled, frowned, and finally said 'Rubbish! What's that report all about?' It was a difficult ten minutes!

A couple of days later I found out what happened. Just before I'd spoken to him three months before, the Sales Director had yelled at him about a delivery for an important customer going astray. It had happened perhaps once or twice in ten years. The unpleasant session he'd just had with his boss was uppermost in his mind. The result: lack of objectivity.'

Systems analyst B: 'On my last project we were looking at the computerization of the accounts payable system. The project schedule was ridiculous; we had to cut back on the investigation. This meant we had to rely on a description of the existing system from one or two key users, mostly the Accounts Receivable Manager. I spent three days with this man. His explanation was a dream: clear, concise and comprehensive. We were well into programming when I was browsing through some papers that came to light in an office move. I found a report that was seven years old. It had been written by the Accounts Receivable Manager when he was an ordinary clerk, describing a proposed new manual system. It was word-for-word the same as the description of the system he had given to me. But there was a stack of correspondence attached which turned the system down; it was never implemented. So there we were, basing a new system on a rejected idea that was seven years old. He had been pushing for this new system all these years and used the computer to finally get it. If we had gone on with the system, it would have been a disaster. We scrapped it and started again.'

Systems analyst C: 'We were putting in computerized production control in a medium-sized engineering company. The company, let's call it X, was formed about ten years before as the result of the merging of two companies, A and B. On paper it looked as though the two companies were integrated. But people still thought of themselves as company A men or as company B men. The materials department used the ex-A procedures, but had a hard core of B people. For example, we were told about the B procedures, data, and problems as though they were in use.

The progress chasing section was, to put it mildly, in a hopeless mess. The manager knew it, the staff knew it, we'd heard rumours of it. I don't think there was any formal conspiracy but we were given a really distorted view of what went on. Nobody lied; they just changed the context of the answers. The whole project was like the drunken mate and the captain. The mate was habitually drunk. The captain was getting fed up with this so one day he made an entry in the ship's log: 'The mate was drunk today.' The captain went off duty and the mate took over, reasonably sober. He read the previous day's entry in the log and was angry. So he made an entry for that day "The captain was sober today."

Cases of users lying intentionally do happen, but they are rare. Simply, a user can explain the system as *he* sees it. He may have lost touch with what actually happens but is trying to be helpful. He may be taking advantage of the investigation to talk or relieve himself of all the frustration he has had over the past years. He may think that his work does not bear too close an examination. Or he may be worried about potential changes in the new system.

The systems analyst can also be the one to blame for losing objectivity, asking the wrong questions or misinterpreting the answers.

Figure 5.4 summarizes the major causes of losing objectivity, which are described below.

Figure 5.4: Losing objectivity—the systems analyst

- the 'halo effect'
- done it before
- personal reaction to user as an individual
- design in detail too early
- withdrawal in confusion
- frustration with progress
- too close association with user area

THE 'HALO' EFFECT

One 'good' or 'expected' answer distorts the interviewer's subsequent questioning or his interpretation of the responses. Or, one or two unfavourable answers colour what questions he asks in the rest of the interview. For example:

> Interviewer (who believes decision tables are great and has developed local standards for their use):
> 'Tell me, Mr X, what do you think of decision tables?'

> Interviewee: 'I love using them; everyone should. With good standards, of course.'

The interviewer goes on to ask about the interviewee's practical experience of file conversion, prior to a system going live. It turns out that the interviewee has never actually finished a project. The halo effect from the previous answer colours the interviewer's questioning on this point to where the interviewer thinks to himself 'Well, that isn't so important' or 'He's probably had some experience of it—enough anyway'. No matter what the interviewee says from now on, he can do no wrong in the eyes of the interviewer.

The same pattern can occur in fact finding. The analyst has a preconceived notion of what happens. The user explains that the system doesn't work that way. The halo effect takes over—this means that the analyst must rethink his ideas and do more work on that subject. Or again, if the user says that a new computer system will be great, the analyst may not bother to check facts and figures or apply critical thinking to the stated management reporting requirements.

The halo effect can also be caused by attraction/repulsion based on non-verbal behaviour. This is discussed in 'Personal reaction to the user' below.

DONE IT BEFORE

This means that the analyst has previously worked on a similar project elsewhere in the company or in another company. To save time and effort, he bases this system on the previous one, seeing only similarities, not differences. He thus forces this project into the image of the last.

PERSONAL REACTION TO THE USER

This is a variation of the halo effect. The personality or attitude of the user colours the analyst's interpretation of the information given. For example, an actual case was quoted as follows:

> 'As a junior analyst I investigated the procedures in a large department store. There were two main users I had to deal with—let's say Mr R and Mr Q. Mr R was enthusiastic but bombastic. He answered any question immediately and positively, in a shout. Mr Q was a homosexual. I must admit I dislike homosexuals. His answers were very slow, hesitant, and quiet. I believed everything that R told me, and dismissed what Q told me without even checking. As it turned out, R didn't really know what was going on, but Q did.'

The impact of an interviewer's personal bias on the responses of the interviewee has long been appreciated by experienced personnel interviewers. There is a real danger that the interviewer's biases may be transmitted unconsciously to the interviewee; this can distort the latter's responses and reactions. Consider the following:

> 'What are some of these biases? To answer this question in a general way, several persons were asked to list ten traits, habits, or other characteristics which they considered objectionable and which would influence adversely their judgements of persons possessing them. Three of the lists obtained are given below:
> A. People who:
>   1. Bite their fingernails
>   2. Talk with a cigarette in the mouth
>   3. Interrupt you
>   4. Play with articles on their person
>   5. Smoke chain-fashion
>   6. Are pretentious or braggarts
>   7. Use 'I' continuously
>   8. Are inconsiderate

9. Avoid looking you in the eye
10. 'Alibi'
B. People who:
1. Chew and snap gum
2. Are jittery or fidgety
3. Are non-stop talkers
4. Are too aggressive
5. Wear loud clothing
6. Are not meticulous about personal hygiene
7. Are mousy and bashful
8. Are fresh and 'smart-alecky'
9. Make gestures with their hands
10. Are foreign-looking
C. People who:
1. Have short arms
2. Have bad breath
3. Are shifty-eyed
4. Are too well groomed
5. Are sloppy
6. Jiggle their legs continuously
7. Tap
8. Doodle
9. Have acne
10. Are ugly

It would have been just as simple to elicit from these same persons lists of characteristics which they consider particularly desirable' (Frances S. Drake, 'The interviewer and his art', in *The Personnel Man and his Job*, pp. 134 and 135, American Management Association, New York, 1962).

Although this is addressed to personnel selection interviewing, personal bias can influence the systems analyst in an investigation interview. As Drake goes on to say, the good interviewer tries to understand his personal biases (his attitudes and beliefs) and tries to compensate for them, if not to change them. Note that the above lists include non-verbal behaviour as well as verbal.

DESIGN IN DETAIL TOO EARLY

This is a common fault, especially when there is a commitment to a design in the feasibility study. It is human nature to collect that data which supports the hypothesis and to miss or discount that data which destroys or undermines the hypothesis. Returning to the example of the department store:

'Mr R's staff kept a card index of "hot credit cards", which were lost or stolen. When a card was presented in the store for a purchase of greater than £20, the sales assistant telephoned the clerks who kept the hot list. As R explained what happened, I could see in detail the new system: an index-sequential disc file of stopped card numbers, with the index held in core, and the record size kept to a minimum so that the whole index was stored on one cylinder. I got everything to confirm this idea. What I missed was half a dozen key points which, subsequently, disproved the idea. Additional information that had to be stored: recycled cards, overseas usage, and so on.'

WITHDRAWAL IN CONFUSION

This happens when the analyst takes an undisciplined approach to investigation or when control is taken over by the user. Faced with a mass of information, the analyst withdraws. He fails to follow-up and understand exactly what happens, and objectivity is lost. Closely allied to this is:

FRUSTRATION WITH PROGRESS

Each step forward seems to move the horizon further back with more and more procedures and data revealed at each session. Because of his desire to get on with the design work, the analyst takes too many short cuts and ceases to be critical of the information he is given.

TOO CLOSE ASSOCIATION WITH THE USER AREA

Familiarity can lead to complacency and assumptions that previous knowledge and experience are still applicable when they may not be. Possibly the analyst's previous association was with only part of the user area and inferences have been made on hearsay or even gossip. This does not mean that an analyst should not specialize in a particular area, but it does mean that previous knowledge and experience must not be allowed to colour the analyst's critical faculty.

One hundred per cent objectivity is rarely obtainable, but this is no reason for not making it a goal. Closely allied to retaining objectivity is the need for validation.

Validate

Validation can be summed up as 'never assume that any information is complete or correct until all reasonable steps have been taken to check it'. Here are some practical examples of the results of failing to validate:

Systems analyst A: 'I was looking at the sales ledger and sales statistics procedures in a pharmaceutical company. I discussed the product sales statistics with the Marketing people. They wanted them broken down by *territories*. This was a geographical area—north, west, south-east, south central, and so on. Production and Finance also wanted sales statistics by territory. Programming was almost finished when, almost as an accident, the definition of territory was defined. For Marketing it was a geographical area, but for Finance it meant a *salesman* (for commission, etc.) and for Production it meant *type of customer*, such as research laboratories, private practitioners, hospital pharmacies, chemist shops (for pack-sizes, etc.). This meant a complete revision of file content, coding structures—*and* processing programs. The mistake was obvious—we *all* assumed. There was no validation, no double checking.'

Systems analyst B: 'On my first and largest system—it was daily order processing—we had to validate. Conflicting stories were given by users. The existing system had been great ten years ago, but had been far outstripped by the success of the company. Most users probably admitted to themselves that the system was certainly creaking, if not crumbling. But nobody would agree exactly where the problems lay. There was also buck-passing: 'The goods aren't getting out as quickly as they should, but that's so-and-so's fault—go and see him.' Investigation in the order processing department which did all the paper work showed that the average daily throughput of orders was about 200 per day, about 80 per cent of orders received. We then validated this, checking the average number of orders received at the warehouse each day; 280 per day. A massive discrepancy! The answer was simple; the OPD received about 250 orders and 200 were cleared on the average. The backlog was cleared on a quiet day. A typical order consisted of about 50 items. If stock wasn't available, OPD raised a 'forward order' and stuck it in a file until stock was received and the order could be satisfied. This forward ordering system was a real mess, hopelessly inefficient. The users had, initially, done a marvellous job in covering it up—hiding it from us. The maths of the situation were:

new orders received each day $= 250$
forward orders generated in a day $= 80$
forward orders released in a day $= 80$
orders cleared by OPD in a day $= 200$
orders to warehouse in a day $= 200+80$

If we hadn't validated, I don't think we would have discovered the magnitude of the problem, or the incredible procedures for dealing with forward orders.'

Validation does not mean repeatedly asking the same question in the same form. It does mean changing the form of a question, asking a number of people the same question and taking samples. No matter how straightforward and obvious a fact appears to be, it must be evaluated and *checked*. But the checking must be discreet, not with an attitude of overt suspicion, creating an air of mistrust with the users.

Be professional

Given sufficient time, any analyst may eventually complete a satisfactory investigation. The professional analyst is one who collects the maximum correct and relevant information in the minimum time. An amateur, on the other hand, relies completely on user cooperation, on his previous knowledge, or on close personal and working relationships built up over a period of years. What will happen if he is assigned to a totally new application area or moves to another company? The professional does not rely solely on the active cooperation of the users, nor on his previous knowledge of the area, nor on drawing upon long-standing relationships. He realizes that there will be instances, perhaps many, in which he is faced with a situation of going in cold. The analyst must thus have a range of investigation styles and techniques upon which he can draw depending on the circumstances. It means that the analyst does not amble through the organization, indulging in casual chats and gleaning information at random. The professional will take a disciplined and orderly approach, determining the information required from the investigation and deciding how best to get it *before* approaching users.

There is certainly a place for the analyst who has worked exclusively in one user area, has been trained in systems work, and spends his time on projects associated with that area. He will be a valuable asset to any company, but his limitations must be realized by himself—and his employer.

Don't give up

This can be described as polite tenacity. The analyst will not give up until he has gathered *and understood* the data he needs. He will get his questions answered; he will review, analyse, and clarify until he understands what the answers mean. This does not mean that the user is subjected to an inquistion, nor does it mean imposing management pressure from above to force cooperation. If the analyst is not getting the information he requires, he will think the situation through and try a different approach. Similarly, if he is confused by a mass of data, he will reorganize the data and re-examine it, probing to fill in the gaps, until he does understand. He should never give up totally: 'Well, I don't understand how or why this works, but I suppose it will all come out in the wash.' It won't!

Follow through

This is a technical requirement. The analyst must trace each document, file, or oral message from its source to its ultimate destination. To do this, he may have to go outside the boundaries defined in the terms of reference (e.g., the user request). Remember that these boundaries defined the limits of the solution; they cannot be applied blindly to the investigation. On the other hand, this does not mean that the analyst has *carte blanche* to investigate the entire organization for every project. If each development project included a complete investigation of all the whole organization, timescales would be ludicrously long, users would soon be bored and irritated by so many visits and much of the information gathered would be irrelevant to the project in hand. The analyst makes *selective* excursions outside the prescribed boundaries to trace the source and final destination of all data used in the system.

Be diplomatic

Considerable space will be devoted to this later in the chapter. According to the *Concise Oxford Dictionary*:

> 'diplomacy, n. Management of, skill in managing, international relations . . . adroitness, artful management, tact.'
> 'diplomatist, n. One officially engaged in diplomacy; adroit negotiator.'

Changing the context from international relations to industrial relations, and applying it to the activities within an organization, these are definitions relevant to the systems analyst. From time to time the following quotations also apply:

> 'Diplomacy is to do and say the nastiest thing in the nicest way' (*The Reflex*, Isaac Goldberg, 1877–1930).

and:

> 'In a diplomat's role you may find iron ore, but it is usually oil—and in a whale of a diplomat you'll find the whole equipment—the blubber of charity, the whalebone of flexibility, the oil of commodity. A great diplomat is a regular Moby Dick' (Review of Roser B. Merriman's *Suleman the Magnificent*, Francis Mackett, *The New York Times*, 1945).

The analyst must pursue the investigation with tenacity and firmness. He has a job to do. But he cannot steamroller through the organization, ignoring the reactions of the user staff. The major requirement for diplomacy is a negative one: not to upset staff or alienate them. The positive side is to engage and encourage the interest and enthusiasm of the user staff. Listed below are four situations in which diplomacy is critical.

1. *Antagonism to the analyst and project as an extension or manifestation of poor worker/user management relations which has built up over the years.* Staff have the attitude: 'There's *us* the workers and *them*, the management. Any management idea is for them, against us. The computer is a management idea, and thus against us. You (the analyst) are therefore a representative of them, but are not one of them. Because you don't have the authority or seniority *of them*, we can reject management's idea by rejecting you.'

This is a very unpleasant situation; finding a solution is difficult. Nothing the analyst can do in the short term will improve the situation, but a lack of diplomacy can make it worse.

> *Approach 1*: Adopt the staff's attitude. Use the poor management–worker relationship as a lever: 'We both know that your management are unsympathetic, incompetent, and ineffective. So work with me on this project and we'll use it to right all the past wrongs.'

This may appear to be the easiest short-term solution to complete the project in the simplest way. One of two problems will probably be caused. The staff may see the analyst as a friend, an ally or even a messiah. If the analyst doesn't take the side of the staff against the management (remembering that a state of conflict exists already), he will be seen as a traitor and the system will, eventually, be operated by default. Alternatively, the analyst may be seen as the champion of the staff against the management. Experience has shown that systems developed with such an attitude will only be implemented and function satisfactorily as long as the analyst is participating in running the system. As one user manager described this situation: 'It's like a marriage going wrong. And it's a case of the co-respondent alienating affection. The divorce never goes through but we've got to live with each other after the affair.'

> *Approach 2*: Adopt the management's attitude. If the management dosen't consult or communicate, nor will the analyst. If the manager takes the Theory X attitude approach, so will the analyst.

This approach may in some ways be more acceptable than the one described above. But it has its problems. Diplomacy is first recognizing that the situation exists, second making a conscious decision about the course of action to be taken, and the third is consistently applying it. There can never be a happy short-term solution to this situation, but the damage that the analyst can cause by blindly going into the situation can be considerable.

2. *Group satisfaction with the current methods, supported by the immediate (line) management.* This is typical of a system being imposed from the top without adequate prior consultations. Consultations are left by senior management to the analyst. The analyst is introduced as an outsider and, as such, is seen as a threat to the group. This is a situation in which there is no outright antagonism between management and worker. Rather, it is one of complacency which covers a basic clash of objectives. This is a situation in which the analyst must tread very carefully. For the long-term good of the organization, the analyst cannot ignore the shortcomings of the present system, nor can he act as an arbitrator in industrial relations. It is dangerous for him to bring the situation to an outright confrontation at least without prior agreement. Again, diplomacy is pursuing the policies of the company

without causing a war. An ambassador is a representative of his government, not a campaigner for his own dogma and ideals. Both government and ambassador should be in accord. If they are not, the ambassador should be a radical party worker to change the government. Remember that an ambassador rarely has to live with his decisions and actions.

3. *Personal rejection of or objection to the analyst as an outsider—a purveyor of change for the sake of change, because that is his job.* This is a reaction to the way the analyst has projected himself to the user. The following are three quotations from users who had been visited by one inept analyst and who complained to the project leader.

> 'I resent someone coming in here with three years' experience in business and asking me what I do. I've been here for over 24 years. I know what I'm doing and why I'm doing it. He hasn't been through what I have. How can he *really* understand what happens?'

> 'Look mate, I've got 'phones going all day long, and a group of good but very tough blokes. How do I give your analyst the real *flavour* of what happens here? How can I give him 30 years' experience in 30 minutes?'

> 'We (actuaries in an insurance company) have had intensive and expensive training for our professional qualifications. How could a systems analyst not qualified as an actuary really understand either our procedures or our problems?'

These reactions will be caused in all or in part by the prejudices of the user, aggravated by the attitude of the analyst. Let us again turn to our analogy of the ambassador. The professional ambassador can negotiate with any sophisticated or unsophisticated government. With only a short time for orientation to local personalities and conditions, he must become effective quickly within his relatively short term of office. (This applies regardless of the support given by professional civil servants who are familiar with local circumstances!)

Diplomacy in this case is being able to adapt to the attitude of the user. The analyst will *never* have the knowledge and experience that the user has and should acknowledge that to himself. He might have, finally, a greater knowledge of the user's *systems and procedures*. Most users will react favourably to the diplomatic analyst who uses professional techniques: 'I might not agree with the project, what it's trying to achieve or the way it's going. But this analyst knows what he's doing. He's asking sensible questions, he seems to understand what I'm talking about.'

4. *Suspicion.* What *is* the analyst doing there? Why is he asking these questions? What will the outcome be? In practical terms:

> 'What are you doing here? Somebody must have been complaining about the way I do my job. If they hadn't you wouldn't be here.'

'What I say now reflects what I have done in the past and what will happen in the future. What *is* going to happen in the future?'

'Are you work study? Are you here to cut staff?'

'Computers equal automation. Automation equals redundancy. The only cost saving you'll get here is cutting staff. Does that mean I'm on my way out?'

Without too much cunning, without dishonesty, and false promises, these reactions have to be dealt with by both the systems analyst and *user management*.

Perhaps the responses to the practical situations listed above are tested in Goldberg's definition of diplomacy ... 'to do and say the nastiest thing in the nicest way'.

The attitudes and reactions discussed above have essentially been negative. This is because it is in those situations that diplomacy is most important. Remember, however, that diplomacy is also required in situations where users are over enthusiastic: where a user sees his own VDU on his desk, where complex and costly reports are required, where the computer is seen as the panacea for all ills.

The basic methods

The classic way of conducting an investigation is for the analyst to go out into the user area to gather the required information. Various alternative methods have been tried: getting users to do the investigation themselves and to pass over a comprehensive report or appointing user liaison staff who act as intermediaries between user and data processing, for example. In some organizations these methods have worked well; in others they have failed. In this chapter we shall assume that the traditional method of investigation is used.

The structure of a full investigation project, as at step 3 in the system development cycle, is shown in Figure 5.5. Sources of information are:

- general background reading
- study of existing documentation
- observation
- interviews
- questionnaires.

Many projects will involve most of these methods, with the possible exception of questionnaires.

The design of a good questionnaire which will be sent directly to users is a time-consuming and difficult job. As someone once wrote of job application forms:

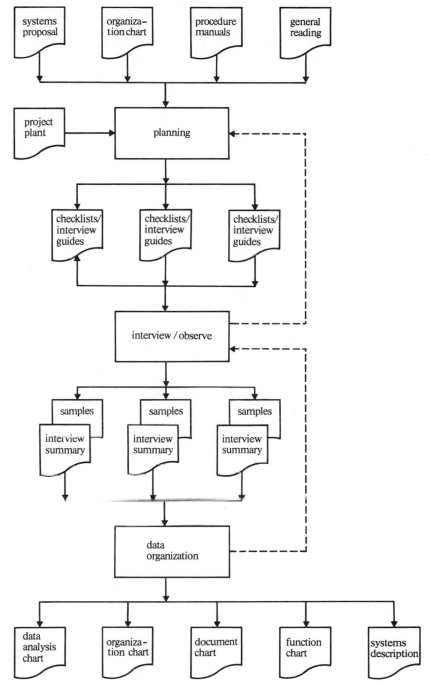

Figure 5.5:   The investigation process

'Primitive man buried his hair and nail clippings, lest an enemy should find them, and use them to cast a spell on him. Traces of the attavistic lurk within us all, and even if we do not care what the barber does with our trimmings, we may still feel reluctant to give away more of ourselves than we need when filling in a form' (Martin Higham, '*The ABC of application forms*', *Personnel Management*, October, 1967).

The same is true of the fact-finding questionnaires. For a successful questionnaire, *all* the implications of the questions need to be considered, together with user aptitudes and attitudes to the answers. Pilot screening of the form is invariably required before it is released. Selective follow-up interviews will be required to test the validity and reliability of the answers.

Too much reliance on the study of existing documentation (organization charts, job descriptions, procedure manuals) can also be dangerous. Very rarely will these give a complete and realistic picture of what goes on in the organization. Many job descriptions and procedure manuals are out of date before the ink is dry. Such documentation may be useful background, *but all such material must be validated.*

It is possible also to rely too much on observation. One quotation from an experienced systems analyst will illustrate this:

'I found out about relying on observation the hard way. It was on my first investigation and design job; the billing system. I was an ex-programmer, with no formal training in systems work. I decided that the very best way to find out what went on was to go and work in the department. So this I did for about three months and then I designed a new computerized billing system. Thank heavens the users went over the proposal with a fine tooth comb. It was really terrible. You could've driven a horse and cart through the holes in the system. For a start, I never saw the special year-end procedures in operation, only what led up to them. So I had made a whole set of assumptions about what happened—most of them wrong. Then, in the time that I'd spent there, I saw perhaps 30 per cent of the possible errors and exceptions that could happen. I'd catered for the 30 per cent I knew about but not for the other 70 per cent. I know I could have done a better job in a fraction of the time by asking a series of sensible questions about what happened, why and when.'

Interviewing is therefore the most important investigation method and one on which the analyst will expend most time and effort. We must define very clearly the meaning of the term 'interview' in this context. An interview is a meeting between analyst and user, preferably *one* analyst and *one* user. The term interview has, over the years, come to mean a very formal meeting. This approach is obviously out of the question where the analyst and users have built a close working relationship. A good interview can be defined as formal in that it has been very carefully planned in advance but informal in that at the meeting there is the atmosphere of a 'chat'. Some analysts feel strongly that the formal element is important in the interview, no matter how close a personal friendship has been established. One analyst working in a large engineering company put it this way:

'Take, for example, a session with Freddie Young, Production Co-ordinator. I've known him pretty well for about 10 years. But when I go to see him during an investigation, I try to create as formal an atmosphere as possible. I believe that a fact-finding interview is so important that I ought to make it special. So I say: "Look, Freddie, it's vital that I get some things straight. I've done some homework, and I'd like to spend the next 45 minutes going over these points. No *idle* chat." '

The checklist/interview guide approach

The key to good interviewing is preparation. The greater the preparation in advance of the interview, the greater the time and attention can be devoted to the user during the interview. One method for organizing the preparation is shown in Figure 5.5. Initially, the analyst studies existing documentation and plans what information will be needed for the subsequent analysis and design work. This is a *checklist*, a guide to the type of information to be collected. The *interview guide* is used to conduct the interview. An interview guide is thus developed from the generalized checklist. It is a questionnaire used to control the interview, to ensure that all points to be covered are covered, and to give a framework upon which the analyst can work.

The checklist is developed by the analyst based on his experience of what is usually required for the analysis and design steps, and from background knowledge of the organization and the application area. Many analysts prefer to start with a very generalized checklist (as in Figure 5.6) and then to refine this to a greater level of detail. Again, it is emphasized that these are not questions, they are topics to be discussed, information to be gathered. When the checklist is matched against a particular man in the organization, the topics are expanded to form specific questions for that man. The generalized checklists shown in Figure 5.6 are for senior and intermediate (line) management. (Note that the differences between senior and line management checklists are minor. The senior management checklist takes a broad, long-term view, whereas the line management checklist becomes more specific to what happens over a shorter timescale.)

Checklists for investigation of how the system works at the lower levels of the organization can take the form similar to that shown in Figure 5.7. Questions at the lower level are prefixed with one of the following:

- how
- what

Figure 5.6:   Example checklist

Checklist

Senior management		Line management
		↑
1. Job title		
2. Job responsibilities		As
3. Organization		for
4. Staffing		senior
5. Overview		management
6. Philosophy of operation		
7. Current reports		
— Timelines		
— Accuracy		
— Scope		
8. Future reports		
— Timelines		
— Accuracy		
— Scope		↓
9. Objectives (long term)		9. Objectives (medium term)
10. Growth		10. Growth
11. Policy		11. Tactics
12. Strategy		12. Scope and overall approval—operational
13. Business methods base data		

Systems Proposal
His attitude
His solutions

- why
- when
- where
- who.

It is at the operational level of the organization that there is a mass of detail. To prevent confusion, the analyst must use a disciplined approach to both preparation and interviews.

Figure 5.7: Example checklist/interview guide

Checklist for document receipt

1. *Identify (what)*
   —name?
   —sample?
   —number of types?
2. What is entered—when received?
3. When is it received—cycle? (daily, weekly, monthly, etc.)
4. When is it received—time? (continuously, 09.00 hours and 14.00 hours, etc.)
5. *How many* are received
   —against timescale of cycle?
   —'average' and maximum?
   —peaks and troughs?
6. Where does it come from?
7. Who does it come from?
8. How is it delivered?
9. Who delivers it?
10. Where is it received?
11. Who receives it?
12. What happens to it?
    (lead into procedure)

Items 1 and 2
    5 to 7
    apply to *content* as well as document.

An operational system can be seen as a series of interlocking procedures, each procedure having the form shown in Figure 5.8(a). (Note that a computerized procedure can be represented in the same way with a program and its associated inputs, outputs and files.) An output from one procedure can be the input to another and so on giving a cascade of inputs/outputs (Figure 5.8(b)) which make up the whole system. Identification of these procedures on a 'divide and rule' basis will enable the analyst to conduct a series of self-contained interviews to build up the complete picture. A series of checklists is prepared that can be used for *any* input, *any* output, and *any* file.

Figure 5.7 is one example of such a checklist. It can be used to collect all

(a) *schema*

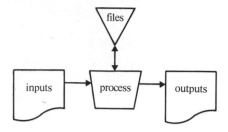

(b) *example linked procedures*

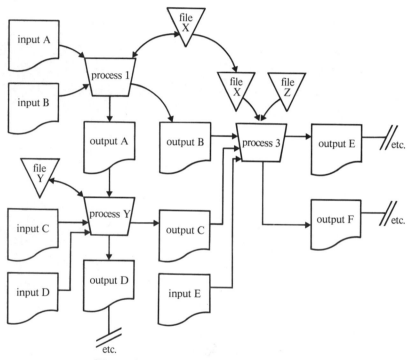

Figure 5.8: Operational level procedures

the information about any input document. By inverting the questions it can also be used to investigate any *output* document. This type of detailed checklist is approaching the level of an interview guide.

The interview guide does not contain all the questions, word for word, as they will be asked at the interview. Such a list would make no provision for the reactions of the interviewee, and would take too long to prepare. The interview guide contains thoughts and ideas for use during the interview. For example, it is necessary to know how the volume of data will grow and the workload increase. One heading on the management checklist will therefore be 'growth'. Let us suppose that the new system will be concerned with order processing. The analyst could ask at the management interview: 'Tell me about future growth of sales.' Such a question is extremely dangerous. It means that the analyst is relying on the user's definition of 'sales' and 'growth', as well as the user's knowledge of what growth figures are relevant to a computerized order processing system! The analyst is being lazy by not preparing in advance. On the interview guide, therefore, the analyst provides a list of what *specific* growth figures he needs. For example, in the checklist 'Growth—sales', in the interview guide, this becomes *more specific*:

'Sales—growth, per year, five-year period.
Increase/decrease in value of orders (price rises incl.)

„	volume sales (i.e. goods)
„	number of orders
„	number of lines
„	number of customers
„	number of products
„	number of salesmen.'

At the interview:

'As you know, Mr X, any new system in this company must have an effective life of five years. So we must make an allowance in the design for any increase in workload. I would like to review sales growth projections with you. If we could think of an annual increase, per year, over five years. First value of orders   increase in sales revenue—' etc.

In summary, the importance of the interview guide is as follows:

1. It enables the analyst to become a positive gatherer of data, not relying on the user's knowledge (if any) of the types of information required. It also minimizes the number of additional sessions required for clarification.
2. The interview question–answer cycle is shown in Figure 5.9. A well-prepared interview guide enables the analyst to concentrate on steps 2, 3, 4 and 6, minimizing effort on steps 1 and 5, establishing a rapport and an interesting conversation.
3. It enables the analyst to pursue the information he requires despite the personal reaction of the interviewee, over-enthusiasm, reluctance, or hostility, and so on.
4. It presents the analyst as a professional; he knows what he is doing. The user might criticize the project but he cannot criticize the man.

Hints for the preparation of the guide are given in Figure 5.10. The length and format of the interview guide are important. If it is spread out over many pages, then there will be too much fumbling and turning of pages. If it is crammed into too little space, then the analyst will compress and abbreviate the questions so that they are difficult to read, and there will be little room left for notes.

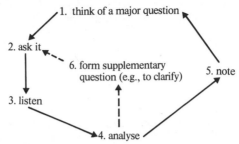

Figure 5.9:   The interview question–answer cycle

Figure 5.10:   Interview guide—do's and don'ts

Do

1. Keep phrasing simple
2. Keep a logical sequence
3. Leave room for notes
4. Keep questions relevant to the man being interviewed
5. Have back-up checklists for documents, files, and procedures, and a simple referencing for their use.

Don't

1. Be vague in phrasing
2. Cram for space or be untidy
3. Be parochial—prepare for lower level, later interviews

A format used by the author is three columns: on the left of the page, the questions; in the middle, space for notes; on the right-hand side a small ($\frac{1}{2}''$) column for special notes. The latter is used to control the progress of interviews. A simple code for this would be:

✓ = satisfactorily answered
? = not satisfactorily answered, but this point can be returned to later
* = break point: there was an interruption at this point and must be covered when the interview is resumed
● = something that the interviewee has agreed to do (check a figure, provide a sample document, etc.)
× = point apparently irrelevant and not pursued at this interview

A good way of constructing the guide is to list all the points, in rough, as they occur to the analyst. The final copy of the guide is prepared from these notes. As the questions are listed, the analyst asks himself four questions:

1. What do I mean by this question; what am I trying to get at with this question?
2. Is this question clear, concise and *simple*?
3. Is this question in the right place?
4. Is this question relevant to the man being interviewed?

Using key-words, there is no need to write out the questions word for word, but the analyst must ensure that it can be phrased simply when it is asked.

The sequence of questions is also important. The ideal sequence is one which is a natural progression. Because the next question logically follows the previous one, the analyst need only glance at his notes as a reminder. It may become obvious during the interview that a complete set of a dozen or so questions on a particular topic is irrelevant; in which case, the entire block of *adjacent* questions can be skipped.

Where the analyst has only a scant background knowledge of the application area, it is difficult to decide exactly what is relevant. One does not obviously ask the managing director what happens on the shop floor. Nor does one ask the man on the shop floor for the five-year plans of the company. The analyst should make his best approximation of relevance. This will be checked during the interview. For example, does this subject matter lie directly within this user's responsibility, knowledge, *and* experience? (In one case, a user gave a very comprehensive account of one subject which was officially his responsibility and implied he had knowledge of it. It turned out later, much later, that the man had only been in the job for less than three weeks. His answers were theoretical ones; how he thought logically it should be done.) The analyst's initial assessment of relevance will improve as the investigation progresses.

Preparing for lower level interviews (*don't* 3 in Figure 5.10) is important in improving the analyst's assessment of relevance. Consider the following case:

Department X

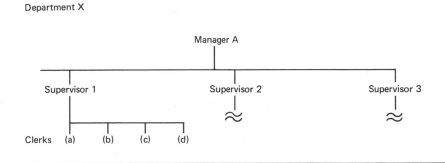

If the analyst asked manager A only about *his* job, and the general role of department X, he (the analyst) would be going in 'blind' when he interviews supervisors 1, 2, and 3. Similarly, it will only be after he has interviewed all three supervisors that he can see their responses to his questions in context. It is vital, therefore, that the analyst does not take a parochial attitude in his questions to A. He should ask those questions which will enable him to prepare specific interview guides for 1, 2, and 3. A similar case exists in asking questions of supervisor 1 which will enable him to validate and structure a guide for the clerks (a) to (d).

The analyst should also have to hand standard checklists (as in Figure 5.7) which can be used when any document or file is encountered. A simple cross-referencing system can be used to relate the checklist-to-notes-to-sample-to-interview.

The introduction at the interview is very important. The whole tone or progress of the interview will be determined by the first few opening minutes. It must therefore be planned as part of the interview guide. The analyst must explain:

- who he is
- why he is there
- what he is going to do
- how long it will probably take.

Ideally, this should all be covered by user management who introduce the analyst to their staff. At all but the senior levels, intermediate or line level management and supervisors might need to be told this themselves.

The principle of all analyst–user contact is: *management and staff relations are the responsibility of user management.* The analyst will sooner or later be faced with the questions or reactions from users as shown on page 134; 'Where will I stand in the new system?', 'Has someone been complaining about the way I do my job?'. The analyst will be the man on the spot: he will be the one to face the questions. This does not mean, however, that the analyst presents his own philosophy of handling management–staff relations. He *must* put management's point of view in a suitable form. *This means that it is incumbent upon him to check his introductory remarks with user management.* He is therefore, within reason, merely representing management's views in his introduction. One effective way of checking the introduction is to pose management the types of questions which could be encountered.

Interview technique

We now turn from the pre-interview preparation to the face-to-face meeting of analyst and user. The general structure of the interview is shown in Figure 5.11.

Review and introduction

Just prior to the interview, the interviewer should review the guide and wind-up his concentration. The best way to explain this practically is by this example: there may be 60 points on the guide, and each of them lies just below the analyst's awareness. When any point in the interview is raised out of sequence, the analyst can go more or less directly to the relevant question.

The introduction should proceed as previously planned. Introducing the interview guide at the beginning of the session can be very useful. It demonstrates that the analyst has done his homework, that the interview is important and that the analyst knows what he is looking for.

Figure 5.11:   Summary of interview format

- prepare interview guide
- review guide
- introduction
- ask questions
- analyse and put supplementary questions
- note
- conclude
- leave and *immediately review notes*

Phrasing the questions

The interview can be either *directive* or *non-directive*, or possibly a mixture. A directive interview is one in which the analyst guides the course of the interview from beginning to end. In the non-directive interview, the user is encouraged to talk whatever he considers important. Fact-finding interviews at the senior level tend to be non-directive, as do interviews forming part of user request and feasibility study. Directive interviews are used mainly in the detailed investigation. But note that both approaches can be used in the same interview.

The interview will consist of a number of questions and answers in the cycle shown in Figure 5.9. The types of questions can be categorized as follows:

- direct
- leading
- ambiguous
- partly answered
- non-directive.

These are described briefly below.

Direct questions define precisely the data required and seek a specific response.

'How many pages in the X file?'
'Where do you send the Z docket when you've finished with it?'

Leading questions direct the type of response that the user will make. Often the user is encouraged to say something which he has not already said or admitted.

'You do get delays?'
'Where are the bottlenecks?'

Ambiguous questions do not give any indication of a desirable or undesirable response. Often the questions require the user to make one of two extreme responses. Sometimes a term is used in the question which is left to the user to define, as in 'excessive' and 'major' in the following examples.

'Is the backlog of document X's waiting to be processed excessive?'
'What do you consider to be the major problems in the system?'

Partly answered questions give examples or particulars to be confirmed, qualified or denied by the user. The user's response tends to be determined by that part of the question already answered.

'What are the major problems in the procedure? The time delay is, of course, important.'
'What are the main functions of the A document? Distribution recording must be a major one.'

Non-directive questions are general ones to which the user can respond in many different ways.

'What do you do in the A system?'
'What happens to the X docket?'
'What are your views on the project?'

One effective way of phrasing a non-directive question is to take the last few words of the previous response and to turn this into a question by an inflection in the voice: for example:

User: '. . . then we file the X document in the Y file.'
Analyst: 'The Y file?'

There is a role for all these types of questions in a fact-finding interview. The direct question is used to elicit facts and will therefore be the most common type used. The other types of questions will be used to discuss general problems and requirements, to put the user at ease, and to get the reticent user to talk.

An interview is a meeting of two people and the interaction of their personalities. The selection of the types of questions and the style and pace of the interview must therefore be adapted to the interviewee. Take, for example, the 'difficult' interviewee:

'The inarticulate

The voluble

The person who has been 25 years in a job and is so familiar with it that he cannot explain it

The automaton

The empire builder

The obstructionist or deceiver

The person with the attitude 'what can you find out in half an hour about a job that has taken me ten years to learn?'

The extremely diffident or shy

The person with the 'no time to waste on you, too much work already' attitude

The sick or hypochondriac

The person with an outlook limited to his one job

The man with a grievance

The user of technical and unintelligible jargon' (G. E. Milward (ed.), *Organization and Methods*, p. 172, Macmillan, 1962).

Elton Mayo, for example, said that interviewing had two values: one therapeutic and the other a method of enquiry!

The pace and style of the interview will depend very much on the reactions of the interviewee. The good interviewer is flexible: he will adopt the approach best suited to the interviewee. For a quiet interviewee, the analyst will use the occasional easy, open-ended question (one which cannot be answered in a monosyllable), the use of reinforcement gestures (such as head-nods and 'yes, yes' noises) and the interviewer himself will be careful not to talk too much when the user is in full flow. For the voluble (or even the bombastic) interviewee, a totally different approach will probably be used. This will include the use of compact, closed questions, limiting the answers. To give the analyst time to make notes, he will probably use suppression techniques: the restraining hand and pleasant smile, 'I'd like to make a special note of that', and so on.

Figure 5.12 is a checklist for dealing with the question–answer cycle, and is discussed below.

The phrasing of questions should be as simple as possible. It is possible to cover the most complex document or procedure in a series of simply phrased questions. Multiple questions should never be used. These are questions of the form: 'Tell me Mr X, do you cross total the values on the (A) document and note them, or pass the (A) document on to the sales department, or do you file it in the dead file?' These questions are normally indictive of too many assumptions on the part of the analyst, coupled with woolly thinking.

At one interview observed by the author, a trainee analyst asked a storeman the following question:

'I would like an approximation of the cyclical peak–trough workload over a typical working day, taking hourly loads as a basic reference point.'

The grunt and facial expression of bewilderment and wonderment in the storeman's face was a joy to behold. It changed in a second to hostility. 'Nah, mate, we don't do that sort of fing dahn 'ere.' The analyst tried to recover the situation, but to the storeman the analyst was a young, precocious college kid who could never understand what his job or his real problems were. The

Figure 5.12:   Interview do's and don'ts—questions and answers

---

Do
1. Keep phrasing simple
2. Talk to an operational man in his terms (not systems and procedures)
3. Be polite, interested, and enthusiastic
4. Keep eye contact (but don't fix the user with a beady glare)
5. Get samples—completed samples
6. Get permission before seeing subordinates
7. Always listen and pay attention
8. Be fluid

Don't
1. Argue, lose your cool, appear superior
2. Criticize, conjecture, or lecture
3. Use technical jargon
4. Move on until you understand the current point
5. Be inflexible

---

analyst would probably have got a very much warmer response if he had asked the question: 'Do you have any times when you're really pushed with too much work?' Again, if it had been very important to get a picture of the workload over a day, the analyst could have taken the following approach (compressed in the narrative):

'Mr X, let's divide your working day into four parts (*scribbles on pad that Mr X can see*)

—when you arrive at 09.00 to your coffee break 10.30.
—from 10.30 to your lunch at about 12.30.
—from 12.30 to when you go at 5.30.

Is that a fair division of the day?'
'Yes.'
'Now, when would be your busiest period?'

Using the *practical* time-slots agreed (which will probably mean more to the user than just clock hours) the analyst can probe the workload. This is what is meant by talking to an operational man in his terms, rather than systems and procedures (*do* 2 in Figure 5.12).

On another occasion, an experienced analyst was interviewing a very down-to-earth transport manager. Most of the questions asked by the analyst were oriented towards the paperwork involved. 'How many X dockets do you receive?' 'Where do you file the Z docket?' And so on. The gulf between analyst and user widened to a rift, to open hostility. To the transport manager, paper was a nuisance. He would grudgingly admit that some of it was necessary. But it was incidental to what he did; he wasn't paid to shuffle paper. The analyst needed the information he asked for, but he went about it the wrong way. He should have concentrated on the manager's job: 'How many runs, drops, misdeliveries, confirmation of deliveries, etc.', introducing the paperwork at each step and reconciling it with the description of the job.

The best attitude to take is polite, interested, and enthusiastic, but impersonal, projecting a rather neutral image. Enthusiasm is important, but must not be taken to the extreme. For example, an analyst may, as an expression of enthusiasm, compliment the interviewee on the way he does part of his job. At the later design phase, the way in which the job is done is changed for several reasons. How do you think the user would react to such a situation? Again, the analyst may interview a clerk with a very boring, repetitive job. A burst of enthusiasm on the part of the analyst would be out of place. The clerk probably knows he has a very boring job and the false patronizing show of interest will merely cause antagonism.

It must not be inferred from the above that the analyst projects a neutered personality or is emotionally emasculated. A user who is antagonistic to or wary of the project may attempt to browbeat the analyst: to test him out, to see if he can be dominated or put off. The analyst must be firm; he cannot afford to be intimidated. A strong stand that the investigation is necessary must be made. But the analyst does not invite conflict or begin the argument.

Taking notes

This is an important task in the interview (see checklist in Figure 5.13). The analyst may receive 90 per cent of the required information during the interview, but this is pointless if it is not recorded for further use. The information gathered during an interview may be used two or three months after the event. On the other hand, the note taking must not be allowed to interfere with the flow of the dialogue. The balance of holding a conversation *and* note taking is acquired through confidence and experience.

The interview guide will be a great aid to taking notes; short answers can be noted beside the questions. *That is, provided the questions are asked as they are written on the guide, otherwise the answers will be totally misleading.*

The interviewee may sometimes give what both parties feel is an unfavourable answer. For example, the user doesn't know why he's doing a job, two copies of a form are produced when one is obviously unnecessary, or staff are grossly under-utilized. It is dangerous in these situations to pause

149

and there and then note the response. This will be most disconcerting to the user. Similarly, the analyst will never establish a rapport if he buries his head in his notes. Some analysts have an unnerving habit of fixing the user with a beady stare, never looking at their notes but writing all the same!

The use of a tape-recorder during an interview is a controversial topic, but generally they are best avoided. A tape recorder must never be used surreptitiously (a Nixon-type situation could well result). A tape recorder on the table can have a very inhibiting effect on the user. It can also cause the analyst to be lazy, especially in analysis. If he does not understand the current point, he takes the approach 'Well, it's on tape, I'll listen to it *later*'. And later means another session with the user. The background noise of the

Figure 5.13: Interview do's and don'ts—notes and review

Do
1. Make meaningful notes
2. Take notes you can read
3. Watch timing and eye contact
4. Ask if the interviewee has any objective
5. Immediately review and rewrite notes after the interview

Don't
1. Be too surreptitious
2. Make notes on samples before getting permission—they may be the master or only copies
3. Rely on remembering
4. Take down everything the interviewee says—analyse first

---

interviewer (shuffling papers, etc.) can obscure many key responses. As one senior analyst summed it up:

> 'The first, and last time, I used a tape recorder during an interview was a disaster afterwards. I relied on it, but it was impossible to understand afterwards. For example, there would be things on the tape like: 'I add up these figures *here*, add them to the total *there*, file the completed form *there* after removing this point. . . .' Because it was on tape, I didn't take notes. I wasn't certain what he was referring to, so I made assumptions—mostly wrong.'

(A tape recorder can be a very useful tool *after* the interview, when notes are reviewed. Dictating using a tape recorder is a speedy and efficient method of recording comprehensive notes.)

Concluding the interview

At the conclusion of the interview the analyst must get permission to see any required subordinates, agree introductions for subsequent interviews, and ascertain the availability of subordinates, e.g., when staff are on leave or completely occupied with peak business periods. The latter is important; the project can be seriously delayed if the analyst does not arrange his interviews around staff availability.

The analyst should also review with the interviewee the list of what he has agreed to do; checking figures, obtaining samples of documents, effecting introductions, and so on. After the interview, the analyst should make a note to follow-up all these requests. Users are understandably angry when, after taking time and trouble to get the data, nothing more is heard from the analyst.

The analyst makes another appointment, if necessary, thanks the user for his time and cooperation, and leaves.

Reviewing notes

Immediately after the interview, the notes must be reviewed and rewritten. For every hour that the notes are left without a review, some of the information gathered will be lost or distorted.

Rewriting notes into narrative form and sending them back to the interviewee for confirmation is useful. The use of a narrative, impersonal form of the interview summary is important. In a highly charged political environment, the straight question and answer format of an interview guide can be provocative. In such an atmosphere the user may well assume that the notes are a statement 'which should be signed in blood, and may be used in evidence'.

Special points

Figure 5.14 lists situations which require special consideration. They are prefixed by the term 'beware of'.

POLITICS

Realistically, if a user wishes to embroil the analyst in a political battle, there is little or nothing he can do to prevent it. The warning here is not to jump in with both feet, to be circumspect about using corporate politics with the short-term aim of aiding user cooperation during the investigation. Otherwise, enormous problems can be created during and after the implementation of the new system.

'YOU'

The term 'you' used during an interview can be very misleading to both parties. For example, from the analyst: 'Tell me, Mr X, do *you* do a credit check?' What does this mean and how will it be interpreted? It can be interpreted as:

'Do you, Mr X, do a credit check personally?'
'Does your department do a credit check?'
'To your knowledge, is a credit check done somewhere in the organization?'

CONFIDENCES

An analyst, when faced with a barrier, is sometimes tempted to break it by taking the approach: 'Well, tell me *in confidence*, what is the problem here?' The analyst's sources of information are not privileged. If an answer is given and incorporated into the analysis and design work, the analyst may be called upon to explain why something is done—and what was the source of the information. An answer will break the confidence; not to answer is unrealistic in business terms. Similarly, confidences volunteered by a user can

Figure 5.14: Interviewing—bewares

Beware of:
1. Politics
2. 'You'
3. Confidences
4. Procedure manuals
5. Statistics
6. The new system

---

be equally dangerous. The following is a practical example drawn from the author's own experience:

'The job was stock recording and control system. In one interview in a warehouse, a stock clerk volunteered the following: "You shouldn't be worrying about this paperwork problem. The biggest problem down here is leakage—pilfering. At three o'clock every Friday afternoon, old Fred drives a small van up to the third window on the left. Old Henry passes the stuff out through the window." This was not directly relevant to the project. At a subsequent presentation the Director of Distribution asked the question: "The system looks fine. But while you were in the warehouse did you, as a by-product of your investigation, find out anything about our leakage problems?'

The answer poses a series of interesting ethical questions about loyalty to project, users, company, etc. The practical solution is to avoid confidences in the first place!

PROCEDURE MANUALS

The danger of relying on existing documentation which purports to describe the current system has been described previously. An existing write-up of the system, people, or organization may seem like an expedient short-cut. The problems of documentation reflecting the actual system are known to every computer man! All documentation should be validated in interviews.

STATISTICS AND FIGURES

The danger here is taking any figure at its face value. For example, 'The increase in sales will be 10 per cent per year.' What does this mean? Is it volume of sales or revenue (including price increases)? Is it increasing the volume of paperwork because more customers are ordering a wider range of goods? Is it that the same range of customers are ordering the same goods at the same price, but in larger quantities? All terms need to be defined, all figures qualified, no matter how self-evident the interpretation seems to be.

THE NEW SYSTEM

Although users are to be encouraged to give their views on problems and their ideas on solutions, detailed discussions on the new system are best avoided during an investigation. The new system cannot be designed until the detailed investigation and analysis are completed. Promises cannot therefore be given or commitments made. Neither is the interview the place for a summary 'introduction to computers' course.

Data Organization

As the investigation progresses, so the analyst accumulates interview summaries and samples. The summaries may be validated by the users after the interviews. The next step shown in Figure 5.5 is data organization, essentially a documentation process, in which the results of the interviews are consolidated to show the system as a whole. (The documentation techniques at this step are described in detail in Keith R. London, *Documentation Standards*, 2nd edn, Petrocelli Books, 1973.) This is similar to assembling a jig-saw puzzle in which pieces may be mis-shaped or missing, and further interviews will need to be done to clarify these points.

If the existing system has been in operation for many years, is complex, and has never been fully documented, a formal checkpoint is useful after data organization is completed. The documentation is sent to the key users for review. The question asked of the users is: 'Before any more time or money is spent on analysis and design, do you agree that this is a complete and accurate description of the existing situation and growth?' If the answer is yes, then the analyst can proceed to analysis and design with the knowledge that he is building a sound base. But a few words of caution about the data organization phase from two senior analysts:

> 'It's very dangerous to go back at this stage and do a *complete* re-interview. The type of question asked at this stage should make the user sit back in his chair and say, "That's a good question, I've never

153

thought of that." Going back to real basics will probably make users very unhappy, especially after all the time they've given on the previous interviews.'

'The formal checkpoint is very good in theory, but you have to be very careful in practice. The documentation which the users get at the checkpoint must be 99 per cent right. Otherwise you can have some very upset users with the reaction: "You guys have spent two months with my staff and you *still* haven't got it right!" Or: "These are the people who are going to design the new system and they can't even understand what goes on now!" '

Summary

1. An investigation is *always* required in the development of a new system. There will usually be two levels of investigation: an outline review as part of the feasibility study (step 2) and a detailed investigation (step 3).

2. The major investigation will be into the people, the organization and jobs, the procedures and the data. The analyst must understand the current situation and how this will change in the future.

3. An inadequate investigation (at step 3) will result in invalid analysis and poor design. The specific objectives for the investigation are to collect the maximum of correct, relevant information in the minimum of time, whilst performing the necessary 'public relations' function.

4. The techniques used by the analyst must satisfy the objectives in 3 above and ensure the cardinal rules in Figure 5.2 are not broken.

5. Of the cardinal rules in Figure 5.2, retaining objectivity is the most important. Reasons for losing objectivity on the part of both users and analyst are shown in Figures 5.3 and 5.4.

6. Of the investigation methods available, interviewing is the most important. This requires careful planning, as in the checklist/interview guide approach shown in Figure 5.5.

7. The analyst must have a flexible interviewing style, which can be adapted to the level and attitude of staff being interviewed. Hints for interviewing are given in Figures 5.10 to 5.14.

6
The importance of user involvement

The nature of user involvement

Throughout this book, the importance of user involvement has been stressed. The impact of *not* having user involvement was shown in Chapter 2 and the relevance of user participation in the acceptance of change was described in Chapter 4. Techniques for investigation, involving all levels of user staff, were described in Chapter 5. In this chapter, specific methods are discussed for user involvement in the following areas:

the importance of defining and agreeing the aims of the project
the use of liaison officers
decision making at checkpoints
staff training during systems conversion and implementation
staff participation during implementation.

As described in Chapter 2, development of a computer-based system should be a joint effort of systems staff and user staff. Too little participation on the part of the user will generate a host of problems, from machine-biased system design, to resistance to the new system. On the other hand, too much uncontrolled user participation can cause delays and insufficient attention to the technical aspects of design.

Agreeing the aims of the system—the user request

A recurring theme in discussing reactions to change in Chapter 4 was the necessity for agreeing the *reason* for the change. User involvement on all levels is encouraged if the aims of the system are known and agreed. The aims of the new system are initially defined in the user request (at step 1 in the systems development cycle), and modified as necessary as the project progresses. This can be done during the feasibility study (step 2), analysis (step 4), and design (step 5).

The initial definition of the aims of the system in the user request is therefore important and deserves discussion here. Many systems development projects start in a rather casual or informal manner, but the user request must be a formal output from this phase. The thinking and methodology that goes into this phase is often imprecise and unanalytical. The justification for this is sometimes the nebulous nature of work involved. Nevertheless it is possible to lay down guidelines for this important phase. One method for preparing a user request is the 'problem-oriented' approach, described below.

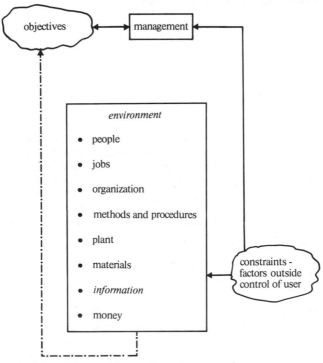

Figure 6.1:   The problem-oriented approach to a user request

How does a user or analyst identify the need for a computer-based system? The first step is to identify the problems to be solved. The second is to evaluate the impact of solving these problems. The final step is to look for a solution, to establish whether or not a computer can help, and if so at what cost. The problem is now to provide some answer to the question 'What is a problem?' The diagram in Figure 6.1 gives a basis for an answer.

The major functions of a manager can be summarized as follows:

- defining and refining his objectives—what he must achieve through the application of his resources, and agreeing this with his management
- creating an environment to meet these objectives.

The term 'environment' is used here to mean that part of the organization under the control of the manager. For a managing director, the environment would be the company, for the sales manager it is the sales department, for a foreman it is his shift or gang. A problem is defined as follows:

1. *If the environment is geared up to meet the objectives (short- or long-term), then the user has not identified a problem.*
2. *If the user sees, now or in the future, that the environment does not meet the objectives, then there is a problem.*
3. *If the user can say* what *is wrong with the environment that is preventing him reaching the objective, then he has* identified a problem.

Step 3 is the basis for seeking a solution.

How, then, do problems arise under the definition 2? There can be a number of reasons:

1. The user manager is under constant pressure to refine and improve his objectives (see Figure 6.2(a)). This pressure can come from a tightening in trading conditions (from the economy generally or from specific competition), as directives from superiors, or as stimuli from some other source. An example of the latter is the data processing manager *suggesting* that performance could be improved by the use of computer. This may in turn lead to a modification of objectives. At one point in time there may be no problem (i.e. environment = objectives), but the objectives are then modified and this means that the environment must be changed so that it meets the new objectives. This change to the environment may involve the use of a computer.
2. The next case where problems arise is the corollary of 1 (Figure 6.2(b)): the objectives remain the same, but the environment changes. For example, people of a certain grade leave and become difficult to replace, materials become harder to obtain, plant has to be replaced, budgets are cut, workloads increase.
3. In the two instances given above there was a planned revision of objectives and/or a foreseen change in the environment. The third case can be called 'creeping crises' (Figure 6.2(c)). Perhaps the objectives were never clearly defined and a review is carried out which clarifies the objectives and dormant problems are thus identified. A more likely situation is that the performance of the environment has slowly deteriorated over the years and a point has been suddenly reached at which inefficiency and ineffectiveness becomes blatantly obvious. A typical reaction when the problems are exposed is 'How did we get into this mess?'

The difference between the first two and the last case is, of course, forward planning; in the first two instances, problems are seen in advance and steps can be taken to solve them before they occur.

- problem exists when environment $\neq$ objectives

- problem identified when reason for environment $\neq$ objectives is known

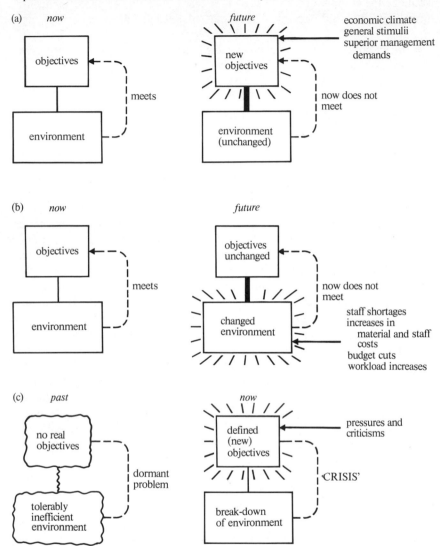

Figure 6.2:   How problems arise

There are three important axioms to this approach. These are:

- quantified objectives
- complementary objectives
- rational management.

Quantified objectives

Statements such as:

> 'Computerize stock control'
> 'Perform credit checking by matching value of new order against customer's outstanding balance and credit limit.'

are worse than useless as objectives. They do not explicitly say *why*. Consider the following:

> 'Develop a new system for stock control. The new system must:
> 1. Reduce capital tied up in stock.
> 2. Provide a better level of service in satisfying customer orders.
> 3. Provide a better check on stock levels in cases of pilfering, unauthorized write-offs, etc.
> 4. Reduce clerical processing costs.'

This is certainly preferable to the statement 'computerize stock control' but is still inadequate for proceeding with development. The statements are still unquantified. For each statement we must ask the question: 'By how much?'

The best way to test objectives is to imagine the new system in and running. A formal evaluation is to be done—step 11 in Figure 1.4. The test is whether it is possible to answer the question: 'Have we succeeded in meeting the objective?' Suppose we find that the stock holding has gone down by 0.01 per cent, representing a decrease in capital of £5000. Is this success? Suppose we find that the cost in processing an order has gone down from 75p to 74p, or that we satisfy 80 out of 100 orders as opposed to 79 per 100 in the old system. Again, the answer is 'yes' we have met the objectives. But this is not a meaningful answer because the objectives were originally unquantified. If the objectives were re-expressed in specific quantified terms, then this provides targets for *all* staff to work towards. Three examples are given in Figure 6.3.

It is important to recognize that some objectives are objective, others are political (with a small 'p'!) or subjective. Those that are objective can be easily quantified, because they can be deducted from available data and the impact of meeting the objectives can be readily seen. For example: 'Reduce the £1 million capital tied-up stocks by 10 per cent' is an objective statement. By taking into account inflation and interest rates it could be reasoned that this means a saving of £2 million over the life of the system. This can be weighed against the financial objectives and forward position of the company.

The subjective or political objectives cannot be directly proved; they depend on different interpretations of available data. The data itself is incomplete, and management induces conclusions from the data based on intuitive feeling and experience. For example: 'Reduce the time taken to fulfil a customer's order from 48 hours to 24 hours.'

Upon what will this decision to reduce order turnaround be based? On what basis is the 48 hours considered unsatisfactory? Who is to say that 36 hours would not be satisfactory? Or, in the extreme, that 60 hours would be satisfactory? The target of 24 hours may be derived from a knowledge of what the competition is doing, what customers have specifically demanded, what is now an accepted level of service, and so on. Sometimes, the intangibility of the objective is used as an excuse *not* to quantify it. Most objectives are quantifiable, even though the basis of quantification is

Figure 6.3: *Quantified versus unquantified objectives*

Unquantified	Quantified
1. Provide a better customer service.	1(a) Reduce order-turnaround time from 48 hours to 24 hours. 1(b) Reduce the number of out-of-stock instances in fulfilling an order from 25 per cent to 5 per cent. 1(c) Reduce the number of mis-deliveries and breakage complaints from 50 a day (average) to no more than five a day.
2. Improve invoicing.	2(a) Average delay for submitting invoice from delivery goods is at present eight days. Reduce this delay to one day for approximately 80 per cent of invoices, three days for the remaining 20 per cent. 2(b) Reduce the correspondence and excuses for late payment by improving the accuracy of invoices from 85 per cent to at least 95 per cent. 2(c) Reduce the cost per invoice from an average of £1.50 to no more than 70p.
3. Improve ordering process.	3(a) Reduce number of errors on orders from 12 per cent to no more than 1 per cent. 3(b) Reduce time spent on order preparation and reconciliation from 30 per cent of saleman's time to no more than 5 per cent. 3(c) Ensure that at least 75 per cent of orders taken in a day are received for processing by 09.00 the next day. The remaining 25 per cent to be received not later than 17.00 the next day.

subjective. The same reasoning described for objectives can be applied to setting project boundaries, constraints, and timescales. The setting of objectives should take place at step 1, the user request/problem definition, and reviewed at all subsequent stages to step 5, systems design.

It is dangerous to assume or to create the impression that the objectives set in the user request are fixed and inviolate. Detailed investigations and analysis may mean that the objectives are modified. Similarly, consideration of hardware/software may result in objectives being refined. The analyst can perform a valuable function acting as a catalyst in defining and refining quantified objectives.

Complementary objectives

Some objectives may appear to be contradictory. That it is impossible to fulfil two objectives because they are mutually exclusive. For example:

Objective 1: reduce capital tied up in stocks by 10 per cent (currently £1 million)
Objective 2: raise the level of order satisfaction to 95 per cent (currently 80 per cent).

There is, of course, a conflict. If stock levels were uniformly increased, then Objective 2 could be easily met. But this would be against Objective 1. The system will *attempt* to satisfy both requirements but there will be occasions when this is impossible. In this case it is essential that priorities for objectives are clearly stated, thus making them complementary. Setting these priorities is a management function, not a technical design function. Failure to agree and specify priorities will result in compromise, conflict, and confusion throughout the project.

Another example of conflict is where two departments are apparently working to two different, contradictory objectives. For example, a medium-sized engineering company produced a limited range of domestic electrical appliances. The company was divided into two major divisions: Sales and Production. The specific objective in Production was, over a two-year period, to *reduce* cost per unit of production by at least 20 per cent. Although there was a limited range of appliances, there was a wide range of options—colour, styling, finish, and so on. The only way in which significant cost reductions could be made was by standardizing on models, i.e. reducing the number of options. As far as Production was concerned, they wanted to produce one version of each appliance—matt black or white finish, with round knobs, two voltage options only, and so on. Sales, on the other hand, had the objective of increasing volume sales by at least 30 per cent over the two-year period. The only way they could achieve this was to sell anything to anybody. If a chain store wanted to buy a large quantity of red units, with octagonal knobs, etc., Sales would agree. They then had the job of persuading Production to make it. The result was a continual state of civil war between Sales and Production. (This finally came to a head when Sales obtained a very large, lucrative export order for an outrageously non-standard model. Production refused point-blank to make it, and the entire contract was sub-contracted, at a loss, to the company's biggest competitor. At this point, the holding company stepped in and fired the whole of the senior management team and some of the line management!)

It is a function of senior management generally and the steering committee for a systems development project in particular, to ensure that *all* relevant objectives are included in the user request and that these objectives are complementary. Without senior management involvement at this early stage, the project will become bogged down with internal politics and conflict during the later stages.

Rational management

This means, simply, that management are prepared to set objectives, maintain their adherence to them, whilst recognizing that some objectives may change. It also means that management will use their energy and best endeavours in trying to meet the objectives.

Figure 6.4: Sample contents of a user request

---

1. *Objectives*: quantified targets which the system must help achieve
2. *Boundaries*: where the solution is (and is not) required
3. *Constraints*: what the new system must not do
4. *Timescales*: when the new system is ideally required
5. *Mandatory reports*: new operational documents which must be produced or old ones which must not be charged; management reports which must be produced
6. *Identified problems*: problems in the environment which will, now or in the future, prevent or endanger the objectives being met
7. *Potential solutions*: possible solutions to be considered in the feasibility study

---

The user request (Figure 6.4) will go through the application selection procedures, thence to a feasibility study, and this in turn will, possibly, lead to detailed development work. There is always the temptation to keep the objectives secret and not to promulgate them throughout the organization. Within reasonable limits of corporate confidentiality it is important that *all* staff know why new methods are being sought. Only in this way can user staff as a whole play a cooperative and constructive role in the development and *operation* of the new system. A possible problem with this approach is that, because of poor management–staff relations, any specification of objectives will be met with hostility. A senior manager in a large chemical company was considering releasing a slightly abbreviated and rewritten form of a complete user request which would probably result in a major new system. This would be the first time that the company had taken this approach. Management–staff relations were poor. He was sceptical about this idea, and he put it this way:

> 'About one third of the staff wouldn't care less about it. Their attitude would be: "We're here to work and to do what we're told; this is management and nothing to do with us." The remainder would probably be hypercritical about objectives and proposed plans. I suppose my decision is this: do we have *now* one big battle or do we have a series of on-going skirmishes throughout the whole of the project.'

His point was that acceptance of the need for change at the outset would ease tension during the project. It would, hopefully, lead to active user participation. Not to face up to this problem at the start would mean disagreements and lack of cooperation later.

Finally, a word of caution about using the problem-oriented approach to the user request. Listing problems can be taken as a negative approach, implying criticism of existing methods *and staff*. This is especially true of the 'creeping crisis' situation (Figure 6.2(c)), less true in the other two cases. Some organizations have resolved this as follows:

1. Express problems in a positive form—as improvements that should be made.
2. Don't specifically refer to them as problems—refer to them by a euphemism, such as 'opportunity areas'.
3. Where possible, express the problem as a result of the situation *not* the individual.
4. Don't dwell too much on the past, look to the future.

The production and agreement of the user request is thus a first step to ensuring user involvement by establishing common aims towards which all staff on the project can work.

Using liaison officers

Many organizations have (or are considering) the use of liaison officers, appointed representatives of user departments. Some companies have had great success with this method.

The liaison officer (also called a sponsor or contact) can have a number of roles, depending on the organization. Sometimes he is simply a user to whom queries can be addressed. In other cases he acts as the project leader to whom systems staff report.

The typical objectives of a liaison officer are:

- to ensure that the views and interests of the user department are adequately considered during systems development
- to minimize the time spent on consultations and authorizations during systems development
- to act as a trouble-shooter during and after the implementation of the system.

A range of duties and responsibilities for a liaison officer is shown in Figure 6.5. The use of liaison officers can be a very effective aid to systems development, provided that the job is described correctly and that the appropriate man is appointed to the job. Three situations in which liaison officers were a hindrance rather than a help are described below. If such problems can be avoided, then the use of liaison officers will be beneficial to a project.

Example 1

A local authority was undertaking a major project: preparing an eight-year computer development plan, including the feasibility of adopting on-line working. The managers of each department (there were 12) appointed a liaison officer. Liaison officers were vital because systems cut across department boundaries.

Figure 6.5: Duties and responsibilities of a user liaison officer
(list in approximate ascending sequence of magnitude of responsibilities)

1. Arranging the distribution of, and feedback on, all interim and final documentation
2. Briefing user staff on the project and affecting introductions
3. Organizing user staff training courses
4. Providing all information to the analyst during investigations
5. Channelling all maintenance requests to the data processing department
6. Coordinating user resources during conversion and implementation phases.
7. Arranging all consultations during analysis and design phases.
8. Conducting all negotiations with senior management.
9. Advising on the suitability of system methods from the user point of view.
10. Authorizing system implementation after systems testing/user acceptance trials.
11. Authorizing work to proceed to next step/phase after all checkpoints.

There were two major problems: First, the liaison officers were senior men. They were extremely busy and could not devote all the time that they would have wished to the project. Second, being senior, they were out of touch with what was happening at the grassroots level, and were thus only involved at formal checkpoints. In this case, therefore, the liaison officers were really a low-level steering committee for decision making at checkpoints.

Example 2

In a medium-sized engineering company a liaison officer was appointed in each relevant department for the duration of the project. The corporate policy was that all contact with a user department had to be through the liaison officer. Systems analysts were rarely allowed to consult and negotiate with any user other than the liaison officer. There were three problems with this situation:

1. It was no secret that the men designated as liaison officers were 'has-beens'. User managers appointed the oldest and most dispensable members of the department, someone they wanted to get rid of from a line position.
2. Liaison officers were drawn from one area of the department, and were relatively senior. They did not have current working knowledge and experience of their department. Nor were they trained in system techniques. Analysts were not permitted to contact other user staff direct during an

investigation so they had to rely on the inadequate information supplied by the liaison officers.

3. Although the post of liaison officer was a full-time job, they spent little time in consultations with other user staff. The views given during the analysis and design phases were those of the liaison officer and did not represent the views of user staff.

This situation resulted in awkward clashes between user managers, their staff, the liaison officers, and the systems analysts.

Example 3

In a large insurance company, the liaison officers were competent, were given adequate time to do the job, and received training in systems techniques. Analysts were allowed direct contact with users, with the liaison officers simply opening doors and trouble-shooting. A liaison officer was involved in all intermediate checkpoints and was closely involved during design. The major problem was that although the liaison officer was given the responsibility for approving work at the checkpoints and in design, he did not have the *authority* to do so. The liaison officer was often over-ruled by his superiors. Liaison officers and systems analysts became more and more frustrated as the project slipped and work had to be constantly re-done.

Based on these bad experiences, and successes in other organizations, we can lay down some guidelines for the appointment and use of liaison officers. These are described below.

Provide adequate training

If the liaison officer is to play his role in the project to the best advantage, than adequate training *must* be provided. This training should cover two areas: computer-based system techniques and system development methods. The first can be done by a computer appreciation course concentrating on computer jargon.

Training on system development methods is harder to arrange. The course should cover the techniques used in all phrases of the project (i.e. all 11 steps in the standard development cycle, with the exception of programming). This will enable the liaison officer to participate actively in the project, such as conducting some fact-finding interviews during investigation. It will also enable him to give general support to the analyst, especially when problems arise.

One such training technique used by the author is as follows: designated liaison officers first attend an in-house, three-day, non-residential course on computer appreciation. This is hardware- and software-oriented, explaining the jargon. The follow-up course is also in-house, but this time it is an intensive, three-day, residential course. Delegates spend 40 per cent of their time on lectures and 60 per cent on a comprehensive case study. The phases covered are investigation, analysis, design, and a review of testing, conversion, and implementation. The liaison officers are treated as though they are systems analysts. For example, on the case study, they do the job of a systems analyst. The case study contains a range of problems representative of what can happen on a project, and includes the specification of record keeping, control, *and* management information requirements. Given a brief description of the project, the delegates carry out an investigation, with the lecturers playing the roles of the users. The users (managers, supervisors, clerks, and manual workers) react across the spectrum of apathy to antagonism. Based on the results of the investigation, analysis is performed, and then design. At the end of the course the delegates produce an outline system design, which is then criticized by the lecturers.

Seven conditions are built into the case study situation:

- ill-defined and unquantified objectives
- over-restrictive boundaries
- lack of user involvement in investigation
- no interim checkpoints with users
- pressure to computerize everything
- superficial procedural problem analysis
- poor management–staff communication.

The impact of these conditions on the design is then reviewed and solutions discussed.

Providing good training for liaison officers will not only enable them to play an effective role in the project, it will also demonstrate to them that their managers consider their liaison job important.

Make time available

If the job of liaison officer is considered important, then sufficient time must be allowed to do it. A liaison officer may spend all his time on the project at certain stages. A liaison officer performing all the functions in Figure 6.5 may spend on average half his time on the liaison job throughout the life of the project. In some cases it may be deemed satisfactory to expect the liaison officer to work planned overtime. Ideally, he should be relieved of most of his other duties. No matter how carefully defined the job is and the amount of vigorous training provided, the liaison function will fail if insufficient time is provided for it.

Define meaningful job responsibilities

The eternal triangle of 'manager/staff/system analyst' and its problems have been discussed earlier. Changing this to an eternal *quadrangle* of 'manager/staff/liaison officer/system analyst' can create further problems with little or no benefit unless responsibilities are defined carefully. A good way of defining the job of a liaison officer is to list the functions he will be involved in during a project and to annotate them as

- arranges for............
- is consulted on ....
- advises on ....
- decides on ....
- authorizes ....

Great care must be taken to define the authority and responsibility assumed by the liaison officer at each major phase of the project. For example, if he is given the responsibility for *approving* a specification (as opposed to *commenting* on it) then he should have the authority to do so. He should consult with superiors and subordinates but it is pointless to give a decision-making function to a man whose decisions are then consistently over-ruled.

Similarly, care should be taken to ensure that his job definition does not inhibit the work of the systems analysts. An example of this is where, during an investigation, the analyst is blocked from approaching users direct. Unless the liaison officer has had considerable training in and experience of investigation techniques and computer systems, he may inadvertently introduce inaccuracies, delays, and confusion.

The traditional approach of one liaison officer on one project or to a department is being modified in some companies to one liaison officer *per working group*, e.g., for each small section. For example it has been argued that motivation of the individual is preferable to motivating teams of people (L. C. Meginson, *Personnel: A Behavioral Approach to Administration*, Richard D. Irwin, Inc., Illinois, 1967). Further, the more people involved in decision making, the greater the pressure for conformity (as opposed to creativity) and, in any event, the creative thinking of the group will rarely be better than the best person within that group.

Organizing checkpoints

The importance of checkpoints was discussed in chapter 1. There may be considerable user involvement during any one phase but, at the end, there is a formal review of the results before work proceeds to the next. Checkpoints thus require careful planning and organization. Figure 6.6. summarizes the main requirements for organizing checkpoints.

Checkpoints must be planned as early as possible in the project, such as in the project plan which is part of the system proposal, the output from the feasibility study review. Remember that checkpoints are activities, *not* events, because they consume resources. They must therefore be shown on the project schedule and included in the development costs. For example, a schedule which shows 'system designed by Wednesday, programming starts Thursday' is ridiculous. The project is bound to miss its targets because the systems specification review has been omitted.

The project plan should give all user staff adequate prior warning of what will be required of them and when. To reinforce this statement, consider the following two cases where this was *not* done.

Company X was developing a new, computer-based production control system. The implementation date for the introduction of the new system was geared to two other important changes: a reorganization of production facilities and a major revision in computer hardware. Because of contractual obligations and financial liabilities, the implementation date for the new system was critical. No planning of checkpoints was done during the feasibility study. First, as the project progressed, it became apparent that the

Figure 6.6: Guidelines for organizing checkpoints

---

plan and agree in advance:
- the relationship between informal user involvement and the formal checkpoint
- the objectives of each checkpoint
- who will be involved at each checkpoint and their responsibilities
- the content and format of the documentation which will form the basis for the checkpoint
- the time allowed for the checkpoint

ensure at the checkpoint that:
- the documentation is comprehensible to all readers
- sufficient information is presented for decision making
- users realize the importance of the checkpoint

---

systems team had been counting on a one or two-day turnaround at *all* checkpoints. The material was far too complex to be reviewed in this time. Second, the time of production staff was committed to reorganizing production facilities. Checkpoints were largely neglected with user staff becoming more and more resentful that the formal review and consultations were dispensed with. Not only did this situation result in considerable dissatisfaction, but it also caused a very high expenditure on subsequent system maintenance to rectify errors, omissions, and ambiguities.

Company Y was developing an order processing system. A tight development schedule had been proposed, but there was some latitude in moving the final implementation date. Checkpoints had not been planned. Conscious of the tight schedule, systems staff worked extremely hard to produce the systems specification on time. The programming team was set to start programming a day or two after the systems specification was produced. With great difficulty, additional machine time was found for testing; some programmers changed the dates of their holidays, more staff were recruited and trained for the job.

The systems specification was duly completed on time but a five-week delay followed. Two key user managers were on holiday, one was on a course, and other important staff were busy standing-in for their absent managers. Senior managers insisted that work had to stop until the checkpoint was satisfactorily completed. The result was a complete collapse of morale in data processing. The five-week delay at this point lead to a seven-month delay in implementation.

The seven-month delay was caused by more than just the checkpoint delay. Many user staff misunderstood the function of the checkpoint. They assumed that whatever was discussed or agreed during the work that led up to it was all provisional, was background, and was of little account. All problems, uncertainties, and decisions would 'come out in the wash' at the checkpoint. This meant that a considerable amount of additional work had to be done after the checkpoint to modify the design.

On the one hand, a checkpoint must not be seen as a rubber stamp. The whole rationale behind a checkpoint is that it does allow for a careful review, which might generate more work to modify or correct the specification. The chances of a major revision should be minimal. On the other hand, major revisions to the specification are to be expected if there was little or no consultation or joint decision making prior to the checkpoint.

A problem occasionally encountered is a reluctance, sometimes a refusal, by the user to sign-off on a checkpoint. Data processing staff sometimes react to this by applying a stick. This can take several forms:

> 'To enable us (d.p.) to keep to our schedule, if we don't get the spec back in three days, we'll have to proceed anyway. If errors and omissions come to light later, then you'll just have to pay for the maintenance. And that can be expensive.'

> 'If you don't sign-off within five days, we'll have to charge you for idle systems and programming staff time.'

> 'You are holding the job up, so I'll by-pass you and get senior management approval to proceed.'

The reluctance to sign-off may be genuine concern that the specification should be reconsidered. It could be that the user had no prior warning that the specification was coming, he had insufficient time to review it, he didn't know what he was supposed to do with it, or he didn't understand it. All of these are valid or at least realistic reasons for delay. An invalid reason, of course, is that the user is trying to block or sabotage further development work because he is against the project.

The carrot is invariably better than the stick in this situation. The best solution is to avoid the problem in the first place. Following the guidelines in Figure 6.6. will help.

The best way to handle checkpoints is to present users with a series of specific decisions to be taken. A statement such as 'approve results of investigation' is too vague. Expressed as a series of specific decisions, however, it will make the user focus his attention on key aspects of the documentation. An example of this is shown in Figure 6.7. This memo was sent to users with the documentation produced from the data organization step, after a complete investigation had been carried out.

Figure 6.7:   Example of decisions at a checkpoint

'Attached is a report which describes the existing order processing system, its growth, and the future information requirements for the new system. This report will be used as the basis for analysis and then design. According to the agreed schedule, we hope to begin analysis on the 5th June. It is therefore important that this report is carefully reviewed and corrected as necessary.

The agenda of the next project group meeting will contain an item "that the Investigation Report be approved and further work on the next phase be authorized". In making this decision the following should be considered:

1. Does the report contain a description of *all* the procedures?
2. Are all the occasional procedures included (e.g., errors and exceptions)?
3. Are the descriptions of the data and its uses accurate?
4. Are the current volumes accurate?
5. Are the estimates of growth volumes sound (remembering that the capacity and costing of the new systems will be based on these figures) over a five-year period? Do you think better estimates can be made?
6. Do the management reports described in this report meet your requirements in terms of accuracy, timeliness, and content?

I would be grateful if you could let me have a specific *yes* or *no* decision on the above questions, not later than 20th May. If the answer is *no* on any of these points, please let me have a correction, or call me to discuss the problem.

In this way we hope that the appropriate decision to proceed can be taken formally at the next project group meeting on the 3rd June.'

Project Leader

Where a decision is being taken that directly affects the speed or scope of the project work, or the operation of the new system, then special care must be taken in how this is presented to users. The major decision points are based on the feasibility study and the systems specification. The decision can be expressed as:

feasibility study:
What solution should be adopted to meet the requirements?

systems specification:
Should the system as defined be implemented, and can authorization be given for the subsequent development and implementation tasks?

In both cases there must be sufficient information to ensure that a reasoned decision can be made. Initial decision-making steps which might take place without extensive prior consultation present special problems at checkpoints. The first rule is not to pre-empt the user management decisions. The best approach is to present users with a range of options, backed-up by the objective information for selecting one. (This was illustrated in the approach to feasibility study described in Chapter 1, and shown in Figure 1.6. This presented a range of possible solutions and actions; it was the user management who chose.) If a user manager makes a decision, and knows he is making it, then he will support that decision, especially when problems arise in subsequent work. Choice is important. If only one option is given, the manager can either accept it, reject it, or refer it back for an alternative. Presenting a *range* of actions or *alternative* courses of action clearly demonstrates that the decision is his. This will only work if the description and evaluation of each course of action has been clearly and objectively described. A recommendation may be given but this should not obscure the range of possible actions.

User involvement at conversion and implementation

The step from systems testing to live running of the system can be a big one. In most cases there will be an existing system of some kind. Not only must the implementation of the new system be considered, but also the support and phasing out of the old one. This is thus a major area for ensuring that all user staff participate in the transition from old to new system.

Two major tasks in converting from old to new systems are *file conversion* and *user training*, but there are others. The new system may require the installation of special hardware, such as terminals and teleprocessing facilities. New office equipment may have to be acquired, new staff recruited, and new forms printed and issued.

Preparing for the changeover to the new system can begin in parallel with programming. The tasks and responsibilities for conversion must be defined with the same thoroughness as the specification of the new system. Ideally, a comprehensive conversion and implementation plan should be incorporated in the systems specification. At the checkpoint users are thus accepting not only the design of a new system but also a method for implementing it.

Our primary concern here is with user training; however, this cannot be considered in isolation from the overall conversion method.

Conversion methods

There are four main ways of implementing a new system:

- parallel
- pilot

- gradual
- immediate.

The principle of parallel running is shown schematically in Figure 6.8(a). The new system is run side by side with the old system. Output from the old system is still issued for use; output from the new system is vetted to monitor its operation.

This method has many advantages. It provides an excellent buffer between systems testing and live running, with an opportunity for further debugging during simulated live running. New computer-based files can be built-up, checked and brought up to date before live running begins. Parallel running provides an opportunity for on-the-job training in the new system, enabling all staff to familiarize themselves with new forms and procedures.

It is not surprising, therefore, that parallel running is the most favoured and most commonly used method for implementing a new system. But there are several misconceptions about its use, and there can be some serious problems and disadvantages from the people point of view. Let us deal with the misconceptions first.

One misconception is the ease with which outputs can be compared, i.e. comparing, item by item, the output from the new system to the corresponding output from the old system. This is certainly possible where the new system is a computerization (or re-computerization) of the old, where both old and new systems are identical or very similar in that they have the same outputs, functions or processes and operating cycle (daily, weekly, etc). An example is a weekly payroll system. In most instances the basic record-keeping processes and data will be identical, with possible variations in the statistical or summary reports. Outputs from the record-keeping systems could certainly be compared.

In other systems, however, the old system may not produce the equivalent control reports as generated by the new system. Indeed, the justification of the new, computerized system might be that new management reports are produced which are not available from the old. The author once saw a conversion plan produced by a user which advocated parallel running. The main objective stated for this was that it would be a further step to prove the new system: 'Direct comparison of outputs will be used to validate that the new system is operating satisfactorily.' The job was concerned with scheduling and resource allocation. The objective of the new system was to increase throughput, increase plant loading, and to produce control reports to measure its success. The latter could not be 'compared' anyway because (a) outputs from the new system would not be actioned, and (b) there was nothing to compare them with anyway! The old system produced schedules weekly; the new system produced schedules daily. The old system used very rough and ready techniques for work allocation. The new system used far

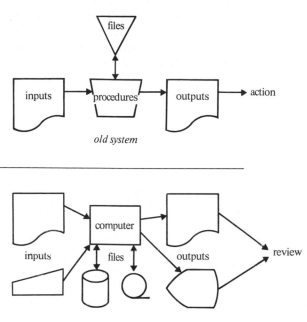

old system

new system

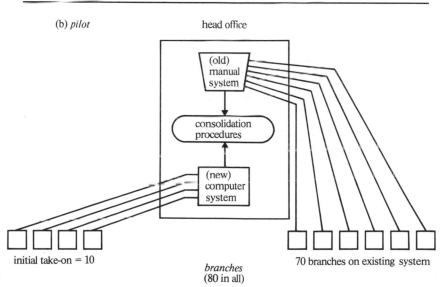

head office

initial take-on = 10

70 branches on existing system

branches
(80 in all)

Figure 6.8:   Parallel and pilot conversion

more sophisticated methods such as smoothing work peaks. The users should have been very concerned if the output from the new expensive system was identical to the output from the old!

The second misconception is concerned with the idea of simulation. If the two systems are not identical in cycle, frequency, currency of data, and functions performed, special procedures will have to be incorporated just to allow them to run side by side. These temporary procedures may distort the system to such a degree that no conclusion can be drawn about the new system running alone because it is running in parallel with the old. Again, if the two systems (old and new) *are* identical or very similar, the simulation might be quite realistic. Only when the outputs of the new system are actioned in practice will it be known with 100 per cent certainty whether the new system will achieve the claims made for it.

If reasonable simulation *is* possible, then it is ideal for final testing and debugging. But parallel running is no substitute for well-planned and controlled system testing; rather, it is an extension of basic systems testing.

Now to the disadvantages of parallel running. The most obvious is the duplication in effort and cost. Because the new system is not actually being used, no benefit will be realized from running it. This leads to a very important rule for parallel running: it must not take place for longer than is absolutely vital. The conversion process must thus be carefully planned and controlled. There have been instances where systems are run in parallel for one or two years at incredible cost and effort. This has been caused by a lack of user confidence, poor systems testing and a lack of planning and statement of objectives for the conversion process. If the two systems have different, incompatible inputs, some form of 'buffering' function will be needed. Consider the case where two systems are to be run in parallel. The old system (O) requires the use of form X, the new system (N), form Y. Forms X and Y are incompatible, in terms of format, content, and frequency of preparation. There are a number of possibilities:

1. Get users to complete two forms, both X and Y; unrealistic and unacceptable in most cases.
2. Set up a special procedure to transcribe and edit from form X to Y; pass Y to new system, X to old.

If the forms are only marginally different, then either X or Y can be used, preferably Y to give the users exposure to the new form.

The responsibility for reviewing the output of the new system is commonly given to the users who are currently running the old one. If this is a manual system, operating under pressure, then the additional task of reviewing output may be the straw that breaks the camel's back, unless considerable overtime is worked or additional temporary staff employed.

Lastly, if the whole of the new system is run in parallel with the old, the 'trouble-shooting' staff (both users and data processing) might be spread very thin indeed, with too many problems and too little effort to sort them out.

Despite the disadvantages listed above, parallel running is a useful means of implementation. But there are situations where parallel running is neither necessary nor practicable. In some cases, a compromise is necessary. For example, the best time to prepare for live running (such as creating the computer-based files) might be at the year end, so that live processing can begin at the start of the new year. This may, however, be the worst time as far as the user staff are concerned. They may be working extremely hard at the special year-end jobs, leaving little time for dealing with the input and output of the new system. It may be possible to use parallel running in conjunction with another method, e.g. pilot running.

PILOT RUNNING

Pilot running is the introduction of all or part of the system into *part* of the organization; see Figure 6.8(b). In this example, there are 80 branches each making returns to the head office. The system does not include any direct communication between individual branches; the information flow is via the head office. Ten branches are brought on to the new system and additional staff will be used to consolidate the results of old and new systems. When the ten are successfully transferred to the new system, another ten are chosen, and so on. The transfer to the new system in the pilot branches may be by parallel or immediate conversion.

The major advantage of pilot running is that it enables 'trouble-shooting' and additional temporary clerical resources to be concentrated on selected areas. It enables last minute problems to be sorted out in a selected part of the organization, rather than in the organization as a whole.

The choice of pilot running must be made very carefully. The first consideration is that the area selected must be independent. In the example shown above, it was stressed that there was no inter-branch communication in the old and new systems. This means that one group of 'barrier clerks' in the head office consolidated the results from the old and new systems. Now consider the case where the new system (different from the old) involves an information flow *between* branches. In this case, an interface must be created in each branch to allow both old and new system data to be processed and consolidated. If pilot running is used on a group of products, or one type of business, then there must be some way of separating inputs, directing some to the old system and some to the new system. Similarly, there must be facilities for merging outputs. Compatibility between old and new systems is very important here. If the timescale or cycle of an operation in the new system is different from the old then anomalies or contradictions may occur in pilot running. This is similar to a plan to change over from driving on the left of the road to the right of the road on a pilot conversion basis—buses on Monday, cars on Tuesday, bicycles on Wednesday!

This can be used in conjunction with parallel, pilot, or immediate conversion. It is the introduction of *part of the system* into whole or part of the organization. A system consists of a number of logically independent parts: procedures and programs. These procedures and programs may be implemented at different times. For example, consider a raw material acquisition and allocation system. The first set of procedures and programs deals with recording material receipts and issues. The next could produce notifications of out-of-stock situations, with replenishment requisitions produced by the existing system. The next phase could be using the new system to produce the requisitions; thence to payments of suppliers and so on. The system may be developed and tested as a whole, but implemented step-by-step.

At times the most expedient way to implement the system is by direct, immediate changeover. Processing by the old system is suspended and the new system introduced at a set time on a set day. Obviously, immediate conversion can be used effectively if there is no corresponding existing system. It is also used when other methods such as pilot or parallel running are not viable, or when a time constraint prevents their use.

The prime requirement for using immediate conversion is good systems testing. A limited form of parallel running may be used during system testing. The major problems of immediate conversion is that it allows little or no chance for on-the-job user training during a transition period. Immediate conversion can be used after parallel running a file, rather than the whole system.

There are difficulties in using immediate conversion when there is work-in-progress to be captured. For example, a system acquires and issues raw materials, schedules jobs and specifies machine loading. The latter task is done weekly and is based on new jobs to be done and progress reports indicating status of jobs in production, i.e. jobs completed, jobs not started, jobs partially complete and at what stage of manufacture. Before the scheduling and machine loading procedures in the new system can be implemented, details of work-in-progress must be captured on a computer-based file. If immediate conversion is used, this may mean a special work-in-progress 'stocktaking' exercise in a short space of time. This can be achieved if the whole plant closes for a set holiday period during the year. Another alternative is to close the plant for a special period and this is not possible in most cases. The last approach could be to parallel run the file, if not the system.

User training for the new system

Any training has one aim: a modification of behaviour. In the introduction of a new computer-based system, training is sometimes seen simply as giving instruction in how to run the system. This could be a series of do's and don'ts, how to fill in forms, how to use a VDU, how to correct errors, and so on.

Training should be the logical extension of the pre-implementation systems development work. If there has been minimal user involvement in development, then training assumes a very different role from that in a situation where the system has been developed as a joint project. Without prior involvement, training becomes a job of persuading and cajoling staff to operate the new system. It will probably be used by the staff as an opportunity to change the system, or to register their disapproval or antagonism to the system.

Problems in organizing training sessions and difficulty in conducting them will probably not be due in whole or even in part to the training methods. More likely, they will be caused by previous shortcomings in consultations, in the ways other changes have been introduced, and in the structure of the system itself. No amount of effective and persuasive training will make a system work if it is too complex or unsuitable for operation in the environment.

A training programme for a new system may span many weeks or even months. (It is stressed that we are concerned here with training for a specific system. Many companies have an on-going computer *education* programme.)

If the reader is confused about the difference between education and training think of the following example. If your 11-year old daughter came home from school and said that she had been having sex *education* you might well be pleased with the progressive teaching method of the school. But if your daughter came home and said she had been having sex *training*, your reactions will almost certainly be different!

Step 1: General instruction in methods to be used in new system. This will be aimed at managers, supervisors, and key operations personnel. This could be, for example, explanations of on-line working and its advantages and disadvantages, demonstrations of equipment and visits to other installations using similar techniques.

Step 2: Formal presentation of why the new system is being introduced (a review), a description of how the new system works, and of their specific role in it.

Step 3: Formal instruction in the operating procedures of the new system, together with practical sessions: filling in forms, coding input, operating terminals, and so on.

Step 4: On-the-job training, running the system under controlled conditions, as in parallel running.

Step 4 leads on to the actual operation of the system as part of the changeover process, as described previously. Note that this training programme is a step-by-step approach working towards the live running of the system. Step 1 could take place as early as systems design (5) in the system development cycle, step 2 in parallel with programming (6), and step 3 in parallel with the end of systems testing (7).

The training methods available are summarized in Figure 6.9(a) and their application in Figure 6.9(b). On-the-job training techniques include *exposure* ('sit by Nellie') for staff joining after the system has gone live and *coaching* for individuals or small groups working with the analyst or previously trained supervisor.

Figure 6.10 lists guidelines for organizing training sessions. This list is not exhaustive but shows areas which are often neglected.

Figure 6.9:   *Summary of training methods*

(a) Methods (not mutually exclusive)

	participation of learner	feedback of performance	stimulii	practise in task
1. Lecture	no	no	yes	no
2. Films/TV	no	no	yes	no
3. Conference/discussion	yes	no	possibly	possibly
4. Case study/role playing	yes	yes	possibly	yes
5. Simulation/demonstration	yes	yes	possibly	yes
6. Programmed instruction	yes	yes	yes	yes

(b) Application   *Method*
- *Step 1*: familiarization, preparation for project   1,2,3,4,+visits
  work (e.g. for user liaison officers, users
  participating in design)
- *Step 2*: initial presentation of system   1,2,3,
- *Step 3*: instruction in system operation in detail   1,2,5,6

TIMING

Scheduling training sessions is always difficult. The analyst is often faced with a dilemma: if training is given too far in advance of the system going live, much will be forgotten before it is used and the impact of the training will be diluted. If training is given just prior to the system going live, insufficient time may be available for practice and this will be at a time when all staff are committed to other important tasks.

The analyst and user management must plan the timing of training sessions carefully. The four-stage approach described earlier is an effective solution to the dilemma.

DON'T BE TOO PAROCHIAL AND DEMONSTRATE

The best training explains, rather than tells. Parochial training describes what happens in one small part of the system, for example, demonstrating how an individual completes a form or inputs a message on a terminal. What happens before and after this stage remains a mystery.

The introduction of a batch computer system using conventional data preparation techniques (e.g., keyboard transcription) often imposes strict rules on data collection form filling. For example:

- write neatly in capitals
- differentiate (using standard conventions) between similar characters
- form line counts and hash totals, use check digits, etc.
- right justify all data, with preceding zeros where appropriate
- use correct codes.

Figure 6.10: Guidelines for user system training

- choose the timing of training sessions carefully
- don't be too parochial in describing systems
- demonstrate where possible
- provide training on output as well as input
- training must include standby and recovery procedures
- remember future training needs

The rules may be specified in great detail. They will probably be applied more diligently if the staff understand why they are required. The training session could thus take the following form:

1. Description of overall system—how all the procedures fit together.
2. More detail on procedures and documents relevant to the group.
3. Basic rules given for the submission of input.
4. Visit to the data processing area, seeing data control, data preparation, and possibly, demonstration of part of the job being run on the computer.
5. Reasons for the rules summarized.
6. At the end of the training session, users are asked to complete sample documents both following the rules and 'beating the system'.

This represents the first day's training. Two or three days later the staff reassemble. Examples of how the good and bad data went through the various stages in the system are reviewed. For example, rightly and wrongly punched cards are shown, error listings displayed, and the impact of error correction time delays and processing faults discussed. The requirements for the operation of the new system are again described. This training approach is, of course, expensive in terms of user time and data processing operations effort and resources. It can, however, be very effective. The staff have not only *seen* what will happen in the new system, but also appreciate what happens after data leaves their offices.

Consider another example. Users will, in the new system, be operating VDUs and teletypes in remote locations. The procedures for operating the new system are described, terminals are provided for practical demonstrations and trial runs. But is this enough? On one project the author gave a preparatory two-hour talk on how the network was put together. It described in very simple, but not condescending or insulting, terms how the whole network operated: the function of the modems and linesharing adaptors, the arrangement of leased lines and their capacity, how messages were handled on the computer and how files were stored on disks. Although the impact of this briefing could not be measured in quantified terms, users appreciated having the system explained to them. It helped in dealing with the network faults that occasionally developed—users could understand the status and progress reports given by the technical staff.

PROVIDE TRAINING ON OUTPUT

Most of the examples given previously have been related to input procedures. Most training sessions bear down heavily on this aspect of the new system, but training in the meaning and interpretation of output is also important. In one large engineering company, for instance, there were exhaustive training sessions on input procedures, but the output side was almost totally neglected. When the system eventually went live, one report caused chaos because of the many different and conflicting decisions being taken. This report showed stock holdings of raw material. The report was headed by a date, and it was this that caused the confusion; some of the interpretations were:

- stock holding on that date
- cut-off date for submission of input
- date report produced
- date report circulated.

The poor design of headings was aggravated by inadequate training on input.

TRAIN IN STANDBY AND RECOVERY

This is especially important in on-line systems. Temporary procedures to be used when the main system is not available must be designed, tested, and documented with the same thoroughness as those that make up the main system. Failure to do this will mean chaos and confusion when the system goes down. This can be accompanied by, at the least, disorganized recovery and, at the worst, panic and loss of data. Training must therefore be given in all standby and recovery procedures, preferably simulating this in training and demonstration sessions.

The training should not, however, overemphasize this aspect too much. Would you fly with an airline that issued you with a parachute as you boarded the aircraft?

The rate of staff turnover may be a major consideration in designing the new system. For example, a high rate of turnover will limit the complexity of techniques and the simplest procedures (and possibly the most expensive) will have to be used. Where staff turnover is more stable, there can be more scope for drawing on their experience and using cheaper methods.

The initial programme will be concerned with the training of staff *en masse*. When occasional new staff join after implementation, greater use can be made of the exposure and coaching on-the-job training techniques. The future training methods must, however, be considered. This means that training literature and demonstration material must be preserved and kept up to date.

Special problems during system changeover

The actual changeover to the new system is a trying time. Invariably there are technical teething troubles, such as residual bugs in programs and problems with new hardware as it settles down. In addition to this there will be problems of people adapting to new methods, documentation, and equipment.

The magnitude of the problems encountered at this time will depend mainly on how the system was developed and the pre-implementation training. If there was little user involvement, poor investigation and analysis, and machine-biased design, then the changeover will be rife with problems. The shortcuts taken in development such as the suppression of user involvement, failure to agree objectives, and hurried checkpoints, will simply move the problems from development to implementation, a time when they are least welcome. If the rules and guidelines given earlier in this book are followed, the problems at implementation will be minimal. Figure 6.11 lists guidelines for avoiding the problems which can occur during the changeover period. These are discussed below.

Warn staff of unusual, temporary conditions

Exceptional conditions can arise in the first operating cycles of a new system. This can span days, weeks, or months depending on the system. The exceptional conditions are caused by abnormal processing loads or methods which are *not* expected to continue once the system settles down. Examples of these exceptional conditions are:

1. A higher than normal incidence of errors in output, caused by erroneous data on file, left there after file conversion. This may have been pre-planned by the use of adjustment procedures on quantitative data (e.g., reconciliation of physical stock to file balance) or as a result of too hurriedly collected indicative data.

2. A sudden rise in stock holdings when an inventory control system is implemented, because the new system now looks at every record in the stock file every day as opposed to only a limited selection of records being examined each day in the manual system.

3. A much slower response with an on-line system because of a higher than usual number of messages.

It is important to identify the exceptional conditions that can arise *and to warn users in advance that these can happen.* If these conditions are encountered by users without prior warning, the new system can get off to a very poor start indeed. Systems staff can lose credibility (because they apparently didn't know this was going to happen), users become despondent and dissatisfied (thinking this level of service will persist in the new system),

Figure 6.11:   Guidelines for implementation

- warn staff of unusual, temporary conditions
- monitor reactions of staff carefully
- be there, but don't look over their shoulders all the time
- establish one trouble-shooting point of contact
- show and explain; but avoid doing

---

and user management may panic for more resources to improve the level of service. The following extract is from a presentation given by the author to user staff who would be operating a new, VDU-based on-line system.

'So that summarizes the operation of the new system. You will have ample opportunity to practise on the VDUs before we commit to the new system. Now, the first few weeks in the life of a new system can be pretty traumatic. We're bound to hit snags. But there is one thing we must all be clear about. It is this. As you know, the new system is geared to give a fast response. The time between hitting the "send" button and getting back the display shouldn't exceed three seconds. Most of the time it shouldn't be more than a second or so. Now, designing the computer system was like designing a completely new switchboard. We have to work on an assumed workload – number of messages hitting the computer from your terminals. In a system like this, we must expect that the workload will be much higher than usual in the first few weeks or so. For a start, there'll probably be special training sessions going on for those people who missed the formal training programme. Some people are bound to be "browsing" using the enquiry transaction; just making certain that all is going well, and getting confidence in the new system. There will be a higher error rate; fumbling at the keyboard and retransmission of correct data. Experience has shown that all this will eventually settle down to a normal workload. It means, however, that during the first few weeks the response time could be much longer than that planned for normal operation—anything up to 10 to 15 seconds. This is unavoidable, unless we'd got sufficient line and computer facilities to handle the increased workload. But if we'd done that, then much of the kit would not be used in normal operation. Perhaps the long response times won't happen, but they probably will. So don't panic if you have to sit and wait.'

Without prior warnings the effects of possible problems will be much worse. But such warnings must *always* be accompanied by explanations. The potential problems and reasons can thus be explained in a positive way. To express them in a very negative way will be to invite doom and despondency. Remember the example in training on standby—'Who would fly with an airline that hands out a parachute to each passenger?'

Monitor reactions of staff carefully

This must be taken in conjunction with the third guideline of not being too obvious a critic. Some analysts try to withdraw from the project shortly after testing. Some analysts' interest is consumed in the analysis, design, and testing phases. Other analysts prefer to retire to an office and to spend their time on technical trouble-shooting and not facing up to the user tasks and problems.

Consider the following examples of user staff reacting to the new system:

1. No adverse comments—complaints or grievances—referred to analyst.
2. No questions asked of the analyst seeking clarification of procedures or further information.
3. Analyst is in constant demand to discuss, explain or clarify.
4. Arguments and moans among staff, possibly referred to the analyst.

These are empirical statements describing reactions to the new system. Many inferences can be drawn from them. In the first case perhaps the most natural or obvious inference would be that all is well, that the system has been accepted by the staff and is running smoothly. Alternatively, it could be the quiet before a storm of protest, or it could mean that a 'make do and mend' attitude is being taken. In the second case it could mean that the system is running without problems and has settled down. Or it could mean that people are reluctant or afraid to show their ignorance or uncertainty. In an extreme case, it could be a rejection of the analyst and the system.

An analyst in constant demand may feel flattered, especially when he sees this as being respect for his knowledge and expertise. But examination may show that staff are hesitant about using the system, that the system is too complex, or that they see it as the data processing department's system. It could be that the staff are referring questions to the analyst which should be referred to their supervisors and managers. This is typical of where the analyst has, albeit unintentionally, usurped the manager's authority. Arguments are not necessarily indicative of low morale, friction, and rejection of the system. This could be ebullience and the apparent arguments could be high-spirited feedback of new ideas and comments.

The analyst should not, therefore, take user reactions at their face value nor draw only the most obvious inferences from this behaviour.

Be there, but don't look over their shoulders all the time

This is a simple warning not to consider the system in and running until sufficient operating cycles have elapsed. During this time the analyst should personally check on how the new system is going. But this should not be an obvious intrusion, with staff under constant, critical surveillance.

Establish one trouble-shooting point of contact

Both minor and major problems can cause delays and even panic. This guideline is especially important in a large or complex system, such as terminals at decentralized points on an extensive network. The user staff are given a few, but preferably only one, point of contact when problems arise. This might be a full-time network controller, a senior person in data control, or the systems analyst. The point of contact will refer to or draw upon the expertise of other staff as appropriate to correct the problem.

Show and explain; but avoid doing

The new system is being used, but delays are occurring; one or two critical procedures in the new system are not working as they should. Under pressure to keep the system running, there is always the temptation to do the procedures oneself, or create a special experienced group to do them. This can cause two problems in the future. By doing the job, rather than explaining what should be done, the user staff may never really understand the procedures. Even more serious is that someone else doing the job may be taken as a precedent—and the user never does get to do the job in the future. Or, there are later personnel problems when the time is considered right to move the job into the user area where it was always planned to be done.

For example, in a batch system, the error listing produced by the data vet or validate program is returned to a user department for examination. It is their function to resubmit corrected data. The new system goes live and users claim they are busy on other activities; they are also having trouble understanding the report and the correction procedures. In the interests of keeping the new system running to schedule, the task of correcting invalid data is assumed by data control. Two or three months later, data control (busy now with other work) ask the user department to take over the job of error correction. The user department is reluctant to accept this job, or even refuse to do so, on the basis that

> since the system went live they have taken on more work in place of the correction job
>
> they don't understand how the correction job should be done and they have no experience
>
> data control has done a marvellous job, the system is working well so why change anyway.

Another example is where users operating VDU terminals have never been thoroughly trained in recovery procedures, or where some training has been given but the recovery procedures are very complex and (hopefully) have been rarely used. The system (cpu, disk files, lines) goes down for two to three hours. The user staff have become reliant on the on-line system, a backlog of work is building up, and problems have arisen in the standby manual system, again because users have had little or no experience in using the standby procedures. They begin to become flustered and to panic. The on-line system becomes available again and they ask for assistance in going through the recovery procedures. The pressure of time and lack of data processing staff to cover all terminal points means that the analyst and other staff cannot guide the users through the recovery procedures. Rather than explaining and showing what should be done, the data processing staff move in and do the recovery. This could well mean that user staff never become conversant or confident in running the recovery procedures themselves.

It is, of course, a difficult compromise to balance the expediency of keeping a system operating and the need to explain to staff what should be done and why. Good pre-implementation training will certainly help. But remember, overcoming a short-term problem of maintaining a system in operation may create the long-term problem of ensuring that users play their part to the full.

This, then, is the role of the analyst in the changeover to the new system. Throughout this phase he is acting as an adviser and as a trouble-shooter. But, as in his role in the previous development work, he must not pre-empt the authority or responsibilities of the user management.

Summary

1. This chapter has considered five key aspects of user involvement:

> the importance of setting and agreeing the aims of the project
> the use of liaison officers
> the organization of formal checkpoints
> ● user training in the operation of the new system
> personnel problems during the changeover to the new system.

2. User liaison officers are personnel assigned to providing a link between the data processing department and the user area. They can provide a valuable service in ensuring that a project proceeds smoothly with adequate involvement. This can only be achieved *if*:

- their terms of reference are clearly stated and they encourage rather than inhibit consultations
- their responsibility and authority to do the job correspond
- adequate time is allowed for them to carry out their liaison function
- appropriate training is given in system development methods and computer-based system techniques.

3. The definition and agreement of the aims of the system are crucial to encouraging constructive and meaningful user involvement. Quantified objectives must be set and agreed as the first stage of the project, i.e., in the user request. A problem-oriented approach has been described, in which current/future objectives are compared with the current/future environment. Where the two do not agree, the fault or shortcoming in the environment must been isolated. A problem has thus been identified and it is this that the subsequent system development work attempts to solve.

4. Formal checkpoints, at which the quality and quantity of work done are reviewed, are an important part of the system development cycle. They are not meant to replace user involvement during a phase. Checkpoints will only give valid results *if*:

- adequate prior notice is given of what they are, when they take place, who is involved and how they are to be organized
- time is allocated to them in the project schedule
- specific decisions are taken at each checkpoint
- the documentation is both comprehensive and comprehensible
- time is allowed for change and correction.

5. At critical checkpoints, such as the review of feasibility study, user decisions must not be pre-empted in the report. Decisions must be taken, *and be seen to be taken*, by user management, although recommendations should be made by the data processing staff.

6. Conversion and implementation procedures and the assignment of responsibilities should be planned with the same thoroughness as the design of the new system. Conversion methods include parallel, pilot, gradual, and immediate running.

7. Training will be a major task in the conversion and implementation phase. The magnitude of the problems encountered during the training of staff in the operation of a new system is a direct function of how the previous system development tasks have been organized. The selection of the training method, and its timing, are important to the success of the new system. A range of methods has been discussed.

8. The analyst has a responsibility to ensure that the new system actually operates effectively and efficiently. Systems development *does not* finish with pre-implementation training. Guidelines for system changeover are given in Figure 6.11.

7
Systems designed for people

Systems design encompasses many disciplines and involves many considerations. It is thus impossible to produce a list of rules, which, if studiously followed, will produce the optimum design for a given situation. The quality of the system will be dictated by many factors, such as:

- the thoroughness with which investigation and analysis have been done
- the constraints placed upon the analyst, what he is not allowed to change or do
- the experience and imagination that the analyst can bring to bear.

In this chapter we will look at aspects of system design that have a common theme, the impact of a system on people. We are not concerned with the technicalities of hardware and software other than as they affect the people side of the systems. The chapter starts with a general discussion on the nature of job enrichment in systems design, concentrating on a comparison of traditional batch techniques and on-line working. We then consider input and output, data collection, and the specification of management reports. Finally, methods of studying and analysing errors are discussed.

The need for considering impact of the system design on people was described in Part I. It is sufficient to summarize these arguments with the following quotation:

'The "utility" of humanizing procedures is not apparent from cost/benefit calculations but arises from the point of view of the quality of life—not only of our own but also of future generations who will be saddled with the systems which are designed and implemented today. The wish to keep these systems humane and dignifying must take its place with the desire to keep the air breathable and the water drinkable as a necessary countermotive to the drive of government and industry to be as efficient and cost-conscious as possible' (Theodor D. Sterling, *Guidelines for Humanizing Computerized Information Systems: A Report from Stanley House*, Communications of the Association for Computing Machinery, pp. 609–13, November, 1974).

The nature of job enrichment in systems design

Job enrichment means creating more satisfying and meaningful jobs. In Herzberg's terms, this is bringing the motivator factors into play, as described in chapter 3; i.e. those concerned with the content of the work itself. They are:

1. Achievement
2. Recognition
3. Meaningfulness (of work)
4. Responsibility
5. Advancement and growth.

For the designer of a computer-based system, job enrichment is significant in two ways:

1. To preserve the meaningful content of a job, and never unwittingly to destroy or dilute it.
2. To enhance the meaningfulness of a job, thereby improving productivity via better employee motivation.

If there is a job enrichment programme currently in operation in the organization, then the design work should fit in with the aims *and methods* of this programme. Alternatively, the redesign of jobs may be linked only with the system design phase in a computer systems development project.

Since the middle of the 1960s, job enrichment has been applied in many organizations and there is a welter of documented case studies. Two are listed below to illustrate the nature and impact of job enrichment.

Case 1: American Telephone and Telegraph Company

(Based on Robert N. Ford's articles in the *Bell Telephone Magazine*, 'Motivating people', July–August 1968, pp. 2–9, and 'The art of reshaping jobs', September–October 1968, pp. 28–32.) AT & T had a large department which dealt with letters and telephone calls from the company's three million shareholders. Although shareholder records were computerized, many staff dealt with the clerical and administrative tasks of creating new records, altering existing records, dealing with enquiries, and so on.

The staff worked under close supervision, especially when correspondence with shareholders was involved and their work was double-checked. The staff were female, highly intelligent and most had a college education. Prior to the job enrichment exercise, they were dissatisfied with their jobs and with the company. In consequence many errors were made, staff turnover was high, and productivity was low.

In 1965, the job enrichment experiment began, removing the restrictive controls and close supervision. For example:

Before experiment	After experiment
Close scrutiny of work done (checks, etc.)	Close checks removed
Letters signed by supervisors	Sign own letters
Calls dealt with by carefully structured dialogue	Answer calls on own initiative, in own manner
Close limits on specialization	Encouragement to increase expertise in own choice of work

The result was that satisfaction with the job and the company increased, represented as a drop in absenteeism and staff turnover, a rise in productivity, and a sharp decrease in error rates (to about one-third of their previous levels).

Further job enrichment experiments were carried out involving some 300 people in the Bell System. All showed considerable gains, in one case doubling throughput with fewer resources.

Case 2: Federal Home Loan Bank Board

(Based on W. J. Stuart Jr's *An Experiment in Data Processing Management*, Datamation, June 1968, pp. 64 and 65.) The Board's data processing installation was organized in the classical structure by function: analysts, programmers, operations. The installation ran a number of major applications, but with major problems, such as excessive overtime and re-runs, backlogs of work, staff shortages, and depressed morale. An attempt was made in 1967 to change the organized structure and job content.

It was an interesting, if radical, change. A totally project-centred approach was adopted in which a team took full responsibility for a project. This included not only initial development, but also programming, testing, conversion, implementation, *and operations*. The creation of more meaningful jobs had very positive results, such as halving errors and doubling productivity. Also noted were the obvious disadvantages including the inefficient use (and occasional abuse) of equipment.

The characteristics of job enrichment

The work of Herzberg and the cases cited above have a number of common characteristics. The first is that motivators come into play when an individual is given a complete function or meaningful unit of work. Secondly, the onus for performing an error-free job rests firmly on the individual. It is impossible to eliminate mistakes or errors completely so feedback on errors is provided direct to the individual who corrects them. Working against this idea of job enrichment are the short- to medium-term considerations: increasing throughput by taking a highly specialized assembly line approach, and reducing training time and costs.

Herzberg is practical in his approach to applying job enrichment (see 'One more time: how do you motivate employees?', *Harvard Business Review*, January–February, 1968, pp. 53–62). He states that it should be used when improved motivation will be of benefit, when job design will not be too costly, and when attitudes are poor, and the maintenance or hygiene factors are costly.

He draws an interesting distinction between 'horizontal' and 'vertical' job loading. Horizontal job loading is adding unrelated tasks to the employees' jobs, and should not be used as the basis for changing job content. Vertical job loading, on the other hand, is the addition of logically related tasks, making the job more complete and meaningful.

Figure 7.1: Principles of vertical job loading (Herzberg)

---

1. Remove some of the controls from the employee's work while retaining accountability for accuracy.
2. Increase the accountability that an employee carries for his own work.
3. Give the employee a complete 'natural' unit of work, such as building a complete assembly rather than just adding a few components to an assembly.
4. Give the employee more job freedom, for setting goals, solving problems, etc.
5. Make periodic reports—on schedule, cost, and quality—directly to the employee himself instead of just to his supervisor.
6. Give the employee new and more difficult tasks, to encourage growth and learning.
7. Assign the employee specific or specialized tasks in which he might desire to become an expert.

He suggests several principles for vertical job loading, as shown in Figure 7.1.

Consideration of the job content of user staff should be an integral part of systems design. It can proceed in parallel with technical design (preparation of program specifications, etc.) after initial design has been completed. Most user job restructuring will be concerned with data capture, manual data validation and correction, and actioning output reports.

Production line batch systems versus direct entry on-line

Perhaps nowhere else in data processing does job enrichment come more to the fore than in comparing batch and on-line techniques. A well-designed batch system can be a relatively inexpensive but effective way of running record-keeping systems and producing valuable management reports. Poorly designed batch systems, on the other hand, encourage user discontent and perpetuate suspect business practices.

Figure 7.2 summarizes the steps common to a batch system using the traditional method of data preparation, such as key punching cards or paper tape, or key-to-tape transcription. The potential danger of a batch system, from the people point of view, is that it can become a de-personalized assembly line. An example is shown in Figure 7.3.

Figure 7.3 shows an expenditure reporting and control system in which departments are allocated a budget at the beginning of a financial year.

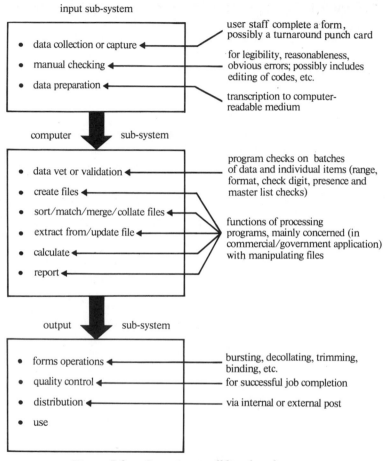

Figure 7.2:   Steps in an off-line batch system

During the year user departments commit expenditure by placing orders on outside suppliers, petty disbursements, charges from other departments, paying staff, and so on. Expenditure was extremely tightly controlled against functions and departments, projects, and types of expenditure by resource. An elaborate coding system was used against each item of expenditure. With the exception of those charges registered in other systems (such as payroll), an expenditure docket followed the path shown in Figure 7.3. Eventually, the

192

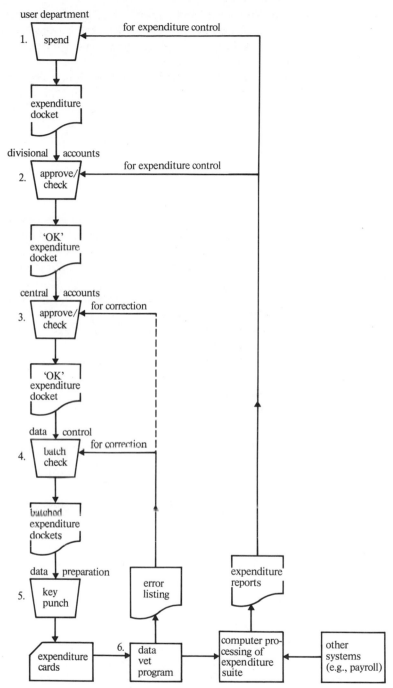

Figure 7.3: Example batch system—expenditure control

user department received an expenditure report which listed expenditure, cumulative year to date and current period, analysed by the various levels of code. Note that steps 2, 3, 4 and 5 are all concerned with checking and correction.

Before the batch computer system was implemented, each user department had its own manual expenditure system with limited checks being made by the accounts department. The reason for going to the batch system was to cut out clerical costs by centralized record keeping, to rationalize interfaces with other computer systems, and to enable more comprehensive management reports to be produced.

The problems in the batch system were legion; they included the following:

1. The quality of the data on the expenditure dockets was appalling. Users had little or no interest in, or concern for, the quality of the data. After all, they were not to be trusted; why else have the subsequent four checking steps? If they made a mistake it would be picked up at these steps, so why worry or spend time on the accuracy and completeness of the dockets anyway?
2. Accounts and data control staff scorned the user staff as 'incompetent idiots' for the errors made. Tension developed.
3. User staff had only (2) above as feedback on their performance. Note that errors were referred to steps 3 or 4 for corrections, never back to step 1.
4. The time delay between step 1 and the return of the expenditure report could be up to eight working days. The user departments thus preserved their manual procedures to record expenditure incurred between the cut-off point for input data and the return of the computer-produced report. In fact, most of the pre-computer system was retained in the user department, and the reports produced by the computer were little used.

Discussions took place to see if the situation could be improved. On-line working was considered in which terminals would be put in the user departments with direct entry to the computer. This could be expanded to on-line updating if required. The initial discussions were between selected user management (involved at step 1), accounts management (involved at steps 2 and 3), and data processing management. Accounts insisted that giving users direct access to the computer would be a folly. The current level of inaccuracy of the expenditure dockets was offered as evidence. Accounts also insisted that correct expenditure recording was one of their responsibilities—it always had been and always should.

Users put forward their problems together with the fact they were caught in a three-way trap by being asked (as they put it) to run one system for the computer, one for accounts and one for their own purposes. To the users, the computer system removed the job interest and provided a worse service than in the manual system. On-line working was suggested as a means of using the power of the computer, but with a return to the level of service and job content prior to the introduction of the off-line batch system.

In the expenditure system, modifying the batch procedures was considered essential because the problems were so serious and fundamental to its operation. The advantages of using a direct on-line link from user areas were seen as being an increase in morale in user areas and more accurate, up-to-date expenditure information. This would be generated by the following:

1. *Greater responsibility on user staff:* all manual checks would be removed; rigorous checks would be made by program on each input message. Most files would be updated batch overnight and further machine checks and reconciliations would be done at this stage.

2. *Reduction in duplicate (manual) systems and more interest in producing expenditure data:* the level of service demanded by users could be satisfied and thus the collection and processing of expenditure data on the computer would become more relevant to the user staff. This would also mean that the manual systems currently duplicating the work of the computer could be abandoned.

3. *More feedback on user performance:* for the batch system, there was no feedback to users from either the pre-computer accounting checks or computer data vet program. Direct entry would allow immediate feedback of errors to the terminal operator who could then correct them. Similarly, detailed analysis on individual performance could be produced from an analysis of the message log and control reports from the overnight batch update runs.

4. *Greater integration of computer procedures with the job:* expenditure reporting and control was mostly considered a sop to finance. The local procedures were seen as being an additional chore. A new system would only be of use if a user management education programme accompanied the introduction of on-line working. At a lower level, expenditure reporting would cease to be an activity separate from the day-to-day work.

5. *Applying user-oriented input methods:* the use of framing, scrolling, paging and conversational processing techniques would simplify data entry. By using computer driven dialogue and minimizing the use of complex codes, the possibility for error is reduced.

Against these possible advantages would be the increased cost for terminals, lines, and communications equipment, the additional core for communications software and application programs, increased capacity of more sophisticated disks, costly security and back-up procedures, and longer program development times. The general disadvantages would be as follows:

- the difficulty of cost/benefit analysis
- the 'gamble' element

- the problem of integrating senior-level policy making and systems design
- the difficulty of dealing with group versus individual reactions.

The major quantifiable benefits from on-line working come mainly from improved utilization and control of some form of stock: currency for foreign exchange dealings, products in a warehouse, material in a store, seats on an aircraft.

Assessing the benefits in the type of system described above, however, becomes far more difficult. A financial analysis of the problem will pose the following questions:

1. What is the benefit of the current expenditure reporting system?
2. What will be the additional benefit if the currency of expenditure data were improved?

The potential interest and satisfaction of the staff in the new system would contribute greatly to realizing these benefits; indeed, they will be a prerequisite for (2) above. Beyond that it is impossible to quantify the major advantages.

The conventional approach to job redesign is to set up pilot runs (controlled experiments) in which morale and productivity are carefully monitored. If the job redesign is associated with a computer system, this is prohibitively expensive, introducing a 'gamble' element—the uncertainty of whether or not the new procedures will be acceptable to the staff, or will have the desired effect. The new system can be subjected to rigorous testing to prove that it is *technically* viable, that hardware and software function as planned, but this is not the same as testing operational suitability as far as user staff are concerned.

Returning to the example expenditure system, suppose that a decision is taken to implement the on-line VDU system. Will it *really* improve job satisfaction and attitude of user staff? In practical terms, will it really lead to better data accuracy, or give a level of confidence and service that will lead to the manual system being discarded? As the accounts management put it 'What guarantee is there that the ludicrously high error rate of 40 per cent will decrease to less than even 2 per cent?'

A pilot scheme was proposed in which, say, one or two user departments would go on-line was disqualified on both cost and technical grounds. The cost disqualification was on the grounds that the system and program development, terminal/line equipment, communications software, additional disc storage, etc., would not fall far short of that required for the complete system. The technical problems were those of integrating the records of the on-line and batch systems. A commitment to the pilot project would be a commitment to the implementation of the system itself.

The work of Lawrie *et al.* provides an interesting insight into how terminals affected staff in one company (J. W. Lawrie, J. M. Ryan and A. Carlyle, *Terminals and their Impact on Employee Motivation*, Datamation, August, 1974, pp. 59, 60 and 62). The study was concerned with the reactions of tellers to terminals in a large mid-Western bank. Two groups of seven branches each were used as samples—a terminal-using group and a non-terminal-using group. By means of questionnaires, feelings about jobs were analysed (see Figure 7.4(a)). There was little increase or decrease in

Figure 7.4: *Terminals and their impact on employee motivation* (Lawrie, Ryan, and Carlyle). Reprinted with permission of DATAMA-TION ® © Copyright 1974 by Technical Publishing Company, Greenwich, Connecticut, 06830.

(a)

feelings about:

the work itself	XXXXX OOOOO	(terminal) (non terminal)	XXXXX OOOOO	
sense of accomplishment	XXXXX OOOOO	XXXXX OOOOO	XXXXX OOOOO	XXXX OOOO
personal development	XXXXX OOOOO	XXX OOO		
feedback on personal performance	XXXXX OOOOO	XXXXX OOOOO		
co-workers	XXXXX OOOOO	XXXX OO		
responsibility for quality	XXXXX OOOOO	XXXXX OOOO	XX	
	10	20	30	40

(b)

attitude cluster	change over time
the work itself	no change
sense of accomplishment	slight decrease
personal development	no change
feedback on personal performance	increased
feelings toward co-workers	increased
responsibility for quality	no change

morale between terminal and non-terminal groups. But the terminal group showed more *positive* attitudes about co-workers and personal responsibility for quality. A further analysis was carried out, this time taking into account the length of time tellers had worked with terminals (Figure 7.4(b)). Withdrawal characteristics, tardiness, absenteeism and turnover were taken as indicators of morale and measured in both groups. As the authors report:

> 'No significant differences were found. Evidently the terminal did not cause the tellers to withdraw from their job; neither did it "enrich" the job such that withdrawal was reduced.'

The risk element is not unusual in on-line systems, where terminals are to be located in user areas and operated by user staff. A careful study can narrow the odds. Carefully planned on-line systems can improve staff job satisfaction—the answers to the questions posed earlier for the expenditure system are often 'yes'.

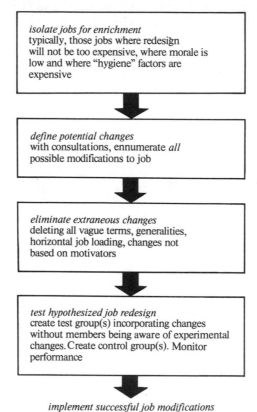

implement successful job modifications

Figure 7.5:   Steps in a job enrichment programme

Applying job enrichment in systems design

The classical role of job enrichment is job design or job redesign in which the 'motivators' are brought into play to increase productivity and morale. The general sequence of steps in applying job enrichment has been described by Herzberg and many others. Based on practical experience, a five-point plan appears to be necessary as summarized in Figure 7.5.

Job design for the computer-based system is mainly concerned with defining the user's relationship with the automated procedures, and with specifying the job content on the input data collection and output report usage procedures.

It is difficult to separate job content from systems design as a whole. Figure 7.5 shows, however, that management and staff involvement is considerable. In this context a formal job enrichment programme may overlap with system design.

Figure 7.6 present a ten-point checklist of factors to be considered in the design of procedures. These apply to both user personnel and data processing operations staff. Note that many of these factors (especially 1, 2, and 3) are based on Herzberg's motivators.

Figure 7.6:   Considerations in job design

Job is a series of tasks. In designing tasks, for each task:
1.   What must it achieve?
2.   Is it necessary?
3.   Is it complete, meaningful, and satisfying?
4.   Will new conditions be required?
5.   Is it practically viable?
6.   Is it required purely for the sake of the computer?
7.   Will it require new skills and are they available?
8.   Is the training required feasible?
9.   What is the expected/required quantity of work?
10.   What is the expected/required quality of work?

Data collection procedures

Data collection or data capture will be the first step in any computer-based system. The exact nature of the step will depend on the system. It could be, for example:

Form filling: completing a pre-printed form for later key transcription to a computer input medium by data preparation
Document marking: completing a pre-printed form for later automatic direct reading (mark sense cards, OCR/mark reading, etc.)
Automatic data capture: as a by-product of some other activity, such as a paper tape punch attached to a cash register, or as a very simple activity such as a badge reader or wand reader
Keyboard direct entry: typing messages which go to an off-line storage device (such as key-to-cassette) or direct to the computer (such as a visual display unit or teletype)

The percentage of user time spent on data collection activities and its relationship to their other work is extremely important. The data collection task could be associated with some form of enquiry processing. Some jobs will have data collection as the primary activity; to many, however, it will be a secondary (or lower level) task. This is illustrated in the following examples.

Primary function:

   —order entry clerks capturing orders via telephone calls on order forms on VDU's

   —clerks checking lost/stolen credit cards via VDU's from telephone calls

   —stock clerks completing special forms recording stock movement (issues and receipts)

Secondary function:

   —salesman (primary function = selling) recording orders, calls, etc.

   —project staff (primary function = developing systems) completing progress sheets, expense forms, etc.

   —machine operators (primary function = setting-up and running machines) recording work done, scrap, time, etc.

   —health inspectors (primary function = visiting and actioning health problem cases) recording visits made and actions to be taken

   —drivers (primary function = loading and delivering) filling in log sheets and recording status of deliveries

The relationship between data collection as a secondary versus primary task is of vital importance.

If the data collection and ancillary enquiry procedures are primary activities, the procedures will form the greater part of the job, the design of the new system will have a major impact on the job. The system designer will probably expect a high level of quality and quantity of data. He must take care that the job deals with a meaningful unit of work, and that adequate feedback is provided on quality and productivity. On the other hand, the quality of the staff could be low and the boring nature of the job makes for a high error rate and low productivity.

Where the data collection is a secondary activity, the designer must understand the *entire* content of the job, not only that part which is concerned with data collection. The best approach will be to integrate the data collection activity with the primary activity such that the latter is improved. Another approach is to minimize the extent of the data collection function where it occupies a high percentage of user time but is still a secondary function of the job. But user dissatisfaction can result, for example, with complaints that there are not enough hours in the day to do the job, high error rates, and missed schedules.

There are no short-cuts to the design of data collection procedures, no techniques which if applied in all circumstances will give good results. Only careful analysis of a specific job and the imaginative selection of techniques from those available can give a satisfactory design. OCR with mark-reading might work well in one case and be a disaster in another; user completion of a punch document may be a success in one instance, and unsatisfactory in another.

The design of a computer-based system is an iterative process of initial design, test hypothesis, redesign, retest hypothesis, etc., with the design formulated in greater detail at each step. The sequence of design steps and their iterative nature is important. A computer system falls into the following pattern as was shown in Figure 7.2:

- input sub-system
- computer sub-system
- output sub-system.

Some analysts take the following approach:

1. Design *output* first—based on what the system must produce.
2. Design files and computer processing requirements—based on that necessary to create output in (1).
3. Design *input* last—based on that necessary to maintain files and process as in (2).

This will rationalize the input to the computer, producing (probably) a machine-biased system. The iterative process of design would be to analyse (3) critically from the users' point of view and to redesign accordingly. The starting point of design (input versus computer versus output) is less important than applying the iterative process to design. The problem with the approach shown above is that the designer forms an emotional and intellectual commitment to the design at steps (1) and (2), and is loath to reconsider input at step (3). A better approach would be:

1. What outputs must be produced from the system?
2. What data can be said to be reasonably available for input?
3. What files and computer processing are necessary to go from (2) to (1)?

It is difficult to sub-divide the input data collection design process into a number of neat self-contained compartments. For the sake of explanation, however, we can sub-divide the design of the input sub-system into two stages.

1. *What* data is to be input and *when*.
2. *Who* inputs the data and *how*.

Although these two points are inseparable during design as part of the iterative process, *what* and *when* are taken to be part of the overall function of the system. An initial checklist of data elements to be input could be developed independently of the *who* and *how* questions. It is these latter questions which concern us here.

Figure 7.7 shows a checklist of questions to be answered at the *who* and *how* stage, given that a first approximation has been made as to *what* and *when*.

RELEVANCE

Subject to other criteria listed in Figure 7.7, relevance will be an important factor in determining data accuracy. The worst case of data collection (in terms of quality and quantity) is where a user is expected to record data which does not aid his own immediate task, does not provide him later with management information, and where he does not see how the data will be of use later in the system. In this case there is no incentive for the data to be collected accurately, if at all. For example, a salesman is requested to complete a lengthy product classification code which does not aid delivery of an order; it is used for management reporting elsewhere in the system.

Figure 7.7: Data collection guidelines

---

1. *Relevance*
What does the data collection function do for the collector?

2. *Suitability*
Can the method be used in the working environment?

3. *Completeness*
Is all the information to hand?

4. *Clarity*
Are all the options clear and the action for each option obvious?

5. *Checking*
What additional checking is necessary?

6. *Feedback*
How will feedback on quality and quantity of data be arranged?

7. *Rationale*
Is this method (or aspect of the design) being used simply for ease of data preparation or ease of computing?

Another case is the capture of data which is not immediately used in the system. It is to be used in the future, possibly in the production of management reports, as yet to be defined.

In the first example, it *may* be possible to persuade the salesmen that the information is valuable for the continuing success of the company—and his rise in commission! In the second example it is dubious whether anything but threats would have an effect, if then.

Ensuring that users collect only that data which is relevant to their job may complicate the system, with more complex file designs and programs in the computer system.

SUITABILITY

The data collection method must be geared to the user's working conditions. At its simplest, this could be ensuring that an adequate writing surface is to hand for filling in forms; for example, not expecting construction workers to complete mark sense cards whilst swinging from scaffolding! Similarly, it could be unrealistic to expect men on a factory floor, working in messy conditions, to complete a punching document neatly. The designer must have a good working knowledge of the users' environment—there is little excuse for designing a system which is unsuitable for the user's working conditions.

COMPLETENESS

This requires a careful study of the sources of data to be collected. If a code is to be entered, what is the source of the code? Is the source to hand and easily accessible to the user? Users working under pressure will not complete information if they must rely on remembering or must resort to a complex look-up procedure.

As a last resort, the designer may have to consider introducing a separate editing procedure, in which another function adds information to the original document. Although this will add to the cost and timescale of the operation, it may be the only effective way in which data is collected accurately.

CLARITY

Many data collection procedures present the user with a number of options. Different data is recorded depending on the events. This is often expressed as a series of 'if . . . then' conditional statements such as:

> 'If home order, then enter A,B,C, and E and sub-total A and C. Prefix A by code 12. If export order, then enter A,C,D, and F; sub-total E and C. Prefix A by code 27.'

And so on.

The options must be clearly stated, with access to appropriate instructions. The designer must decide how to deal with these complex situations. One approach is to have one document (or display) for each transaction-type. The user thus makes *one* decision: to use form A (home order) or form B (export order). Once this basic decision has been made, the user follows the field descriptions and instructions as shown on the form. There is, of course, a limit to this approach; an unwieldy procedure with too many different forms because of many conditions should be avoided.

CHECKING

The degree of checking and *double-checking* required will depend on the type of system. Wherever possible, the responsibility for ensuring data accuracy should be the user's. The detrimental effect of having too many checks was illustrated earlier.

FEEDBACK

If the data collection task is relevant to the user's primary function, then feedback on data collection will provide him with information about this primary activity. In a clerical or administrative system, error correction should be a user function (rather than data control) if time permits. Note that feedback is necessary for both bad *and good* results.

This is a close examination of the reason why the user is being asked to do a job this particular way. Is the data to be collected and method to be used the easiest and simplest from the user's point of view? Or is the method selected because the computer-based system demands that it be done this way for efficiency? The answers to these questions will determine the type of system produced as measured on the Systems Matrix in Chapter 2, with the associated gains and losses.

Report design

The same attention must be devoted to the design of output reports and displays as that devoted to input design. This requires careful study of the job as a whole, and of the aptitude and attitude of the people doing it. The questions posed in Figure 7.7 are also relevant to the design of output.

The contents and format of record-keeping documentation are dictated by the functions which the system must perform. Management reports, on the other hand, present special problems for the systems analyst. The information reported will depend on the reporting structure of the organization, the management climate, the quality of management, and their decision-making style.

Relevance of information is extremely important. Is the information provided:

    —of the right content and scope?
    —in the right timescale?
    —to the appropriate degree of accuracy?
    —in an acceptable format?

To ask a user the question, 'What information would you like out of the system?', and then to build these reports into the system without any critical analysis, is hazardous. It presupposes that a user has analysed his control and decision-making functions and related this to information availability. The good analyst will be a catalyst to stimulate the user to think about information requirements.

One method of formalizing a critical approach to studying information needs is the '*so what?*' test. As the need for a management report emerges, analyst and user together produce a dummy. (This can be done as early as in the feasibility study.) The dummy report should be completed with a full range of sample entries. As each entry is noted, the analysis tests as follows (here expressed as a dialogue between analyst and user):

    Analyst: 'If you saw this on a report, what would it mean, what would you do?'

User: 'That's ridiculous, that could never occur.'
Analyst: 'Not ever?'
User: 'Never.'

The analyst could then ask supplementary questions to find the basis of the user's definite 'no' reaction. For the next entry:

Analyst: 'If you saw this entry on the report, so what? What would you decide to do?'

The user agreeing that the entry was practically possible, could react as follows:

User: 'I wouldn't be interested in that', followed by a reason.
or
User: 'Well, I would do the following . . .', followed by a description of the action. The analyst checks that sufficient information is available for the decision or action to be taken.
or
User: 'If I saw that, I'd ask . . .', followed by a description of the additional information required.

By using these practical examples, some items of data may be eliminated and others may be enlarged or added.

The following example illustrates the importance and use of the *so what?* test; it is quoted from a senior analyst who worked for a medium-sized furniture manufacturing company.

'The project concerned the development and implementation of a simple production control system. The system was being developed following an edict from the production director. It was a very tense and difficult situation; I was dealing with the production manager, who wasn't consulted by the director. The PM was against his boss, the project and, by association, me. In that situation there was little or no investigation and no analysis.

The project finally went live and I retired to my office, to hide and finish my nervous breakdown. About two weeks later I was summoned to the production manager's office. I went there, really shaking at the knees, fearing that the balloon had finally gone up. When I entered his office, the production manager warmly welcomed me. He went on at great length about how wrong he had been: that computers were an invaluable aid to management and that he couldn't think how he'd managed without them. He even apologized for his resistance to the project. He then produced a copy of the "scrap" report. "Take this report", he said, "Marvellous. Very useful. Look at this." He jabbed his finger at an entry that read something like this:

quantity material used	quantity used last week	scrap last week	per cent scrap
1234	10 000	1000	10

"I never knew", he went on, "That as much as 10 per cent of material 1234 was scrap. Wonderful things, computers. Now, one small point. Having been given this piece of information, I feel duty bound to do something about it. So, what I'd like you to do is to take the report away and just make one simple change. I'd like to know *why* it's scrap; percentage operator error, design error, machine error, material fault and so on."

Just a small change! It was a completely new sub-system, a very difficult one to design. If I'd dummied-up a report and applied the "so what?" test, I'm certain this wouldn't have happened.'

We now come to a problem which has no simple solution. Is it possible to design the format and content of a report *independently* of the person who will be using it? Why is it that manager A demands one report in a particular format and manager B (who replaces A for some reason) demands a report with a slightly different content and a radically different format? It could be caused by two different interpretations of the decision-making function in the job. Or, two different styles of decision making, one based on very formalized reporting and the other informal, by general feedback and hunch. It could be totally different personalities—one a numerate manager with a wide span of comprehension and a good feel for trends, the other with a far narrower span of attention, a desire for more detail with general, graphical summaries.

Using a report generator program, a format change will incur some expenditure, but it will simply require a modification to the reporting program. Changes in content, however, can be far more expensive and have far more wide-ranging implications. Is the data for the new report on file, has raw data been kept for the new report, is the data coded or cross-referenced in a manner suitable for the new report? The data for producing the new report may not have been included in the file, or has been coded in such a way that different items of data cannot be correlated. It may not be possible to produce the report without going back to the original hard copy documents. For example, the raw data in a system is customer orders. These orders are held on disk for two or three days before being summarized into monthly sales statistics and held on magnetic tape for comparison purposes. The user later requests a detailed weekly report. The intermediate disk files are not available and the monthly summarized statistics are not suitable.

A system which is totally flexible, capable of meeting the demand for any user report, is a technical impossibility unless every single item of raw data is recorded and preserved, and every possible relationship between the data items has been defined.

206

There is no simple solution. Careful analysis of management reporting needs is essential. The cost of altering reports because of personal preference should always be stressed.

Privacy

Privacy in this context means the exercise of control on personal data about employees. We are not concerned with the wider issues of holding personal data about people outside the organization, such customers or the general public.

Many organizations who have computerized their payroll are now considering putting personnel records on the computer. A payroll file will hold the minimum of personal data: personnel number, rate of pay, tax, other contributions, name, etc.; personnel records contain more sensitive data. For example:

- —age
- —family history
- —marital history
- —employment history
- —educational qualifications
- —official grading
- —employer's rating
- —medical summary
- —credit rating.

Some organizations have succeeded in computerizing such information with little or no opposition from individual employees or their staff association or union. In others, the employees have been obstructive and openly hostile. Indeed, some trade unions have threatened industrial action.

Open hostility comes where there is mistrust of management and a lack of consultation. The opposition to a computerized personnel records project is sometimes an emotional reaction to the idea that 'Big Brother' will be watching. If the records are to be on-line, the control of access is a major problem.

Arguments from the employee's point of view, as put forward by a staff association, for example, can be as follows:

1. Management must expect some benefits from putting these records on the computer. This can only be by limiting the number of people, paying them less, or getting more work out of them. Therefore, we stand the chance of being exploited, especially because we won't have the same sophisticated methods and information available to us in negotiations.
2. We don't like the idea of being manipulated by a machine.
3. Some of this information is highly personal and not all of it appears to be relevant.

4. A computer system can bring this information (which is currently decentralized) to one point.

5. We are not satisfied that access is going to be controlled effectively, especially in view of point 4 above.

Some of these points go to the very heart of management–staff relations. They are matters of culture, custom, and convention as discussed in Chapter 4. Points 1, 2, and 3 must be discussed at the user request stage. Staff reactions will probably be more hostile if they are not consulted early. Some organizations have encouraged the staff association or trade union to become users of the records in the same manner as management; so that they can have access to the same summary reports as management.

In one company, the staff association insisted that each employee should have access to his own record including his manager's comments. Management refused on the basis that this wasn't practised in the manual system and that the computer-based system was no different in principle.

Human errors in input and processing

The importance of accuracy

The accuracy of data is vital to the operation of any computer-based system. The GIGO principle of Garbage In, Garbage Out is probably the first principle we all learn about computers. In this part of the book we are going to examine human errors, their cause, analysis, and prevention. An error is defined here as a failure in accuracy. Accuracy is a wide subject in itself and we shall limit the discussion to three of the most important aspects of accuracy in a computer-based system:

- accuracy of data entry (as in form-filling or the operation of a VDU, etc.)
- accuracy of data transcription (as in data preparation keyboard operations)
- accuracy in following procedures correctly.

The first two cases are concerned with the recording of data, the last with processing the data.

Data accuracy can be defined as that which conforms to the standards set for the system and that which is realistic. A data error is thus any item of data which does not so conform with the system processing standard or with reality, such as the following actions of a VDU operator:

1. Operator types in date as 01/0570 which accurately records the date (1st May 1970) but which does not conform to input rules (should be 01/05/70).

2. Operator types in product code 12-37/A which conforms to rules—two numerics, hyphen, two numerics, slash, alpha, but does not conform with reality. There is no product 12-37/A on file.

3. Customer requests 73 cases of product 1234. Operator types in 73×1324; 1324 is a valid product code (conforming to rules) but does not conform to reality.

4. Operator receives notification of stock receipt, 15 cases of product 1234. Operator calls up ISSUE transaction and types on 15×1324, not conforming with either rules or reality.

Before examining the causes of human error we must first discuss four important concepts:

- currency versus accuracy
- tolerance
- subjective assessment
- conscious versus unconscious errors.

CURRENCY

Currency of information is a measure of how much it is up to date, to what degree the data on files reflect the reality of the events or resources they describe. In computer system terms this is the *accuracy of the file*, as opposed to the *accuracy of the input data*. The former is determined not only by the performance on an individual during data capture, but also by the hardware and software techniques used.

TOLERANCE

Tolerance is the measure of the margin of permissible error in conforming to standards or reality. The tolerance must be determined by looking at the use to which information is to be put. One item of data may have different tolerances, depending on different usages. For example, value of sale will have to be 100 per cent for billing, and perhaps ± 0.1 per cent for payment of commission (on pounds sterling only, ignoring pence) and ± 5 per cent for cumulative, monthly sales statistics. A single data capture point will have to work to the finest tolerance.

SUBJECTIVITY

Subjectivity is where there can be more than one definition of what reality is. For example, basic rules could be defined for the allocation of expenditure codes. There could be an implied error tolerance ± 10 per cent. The exact allocation of an expense to a code is left to the discretion of a manager. In some cases, no two managers may allocate the same charge to the same code.

CONSCIOUS VERSUS UNCONSCIOUS ERRORS

Conscious errors are detected immediately they are made, before any check brings them to light. Unconscious errors are those which the operator does not realize he has made until they are revealed by an independent check.

Conscious error: VDU operator realizes that a key just pressed was wrong.

Unconscious error: VDU operator presses wrong key and receives error display for correction.

The difference between these two types of error can be very important. If the majority of errors in the on-line system above are conscious, then most will be corrected by off-line character or line insertion and deletion. If the majority are unconscious, however, there can be considerable traffic for re-transmissions for error correction. Similarly, in an off-line data collection procedure, the greater the number of unconscious errors, the greater the time and effort for reconciliation and correction in verification or from the data vet error listing.

Causes of errors and their avoidance

Throughout this book, the importance of creating meaningful jobs and of designing systems geared to the capabilities of people has been stressed. This is the first line of attack in ensuring data accuracy. Below are reviewed a number of specific causes of errors. These are:

- transfer of learning
- fatigue and boredom
- anxiety
- complex logical relationships
- resistance
- incompatibility.

TRANSFER OF LEARNING

In 1961 a report was published on pilot errors. It was noted that there were a large number of errors leading to accidents and near-accidents when pilots changed from one type of aircraft to another. Many of the errors were simply that the pilot operated the wrong control; he operated controls in the new aircraft as he had been accustomed to doing in the previous type. This is an example of *habit interference in the transfer of learning.*

When faced with a situation in which we must use new methods or skills, the effects of our past learning and experience come into play. In the example quoted above, there was a *negative transfer of learning*—habit interfered with the selection of the right controls at the right time. A positive transfer of learning is where past and present learning can be correctly applied to the new situation.

Error rates will tend to be higher in a negative transfer situation than in a positive one. In a positive transfer situation, new methods will be learned more quickly. To minimize errors, therefore, the designer should seek a positive transfer of learning whenever possible. This can be done by adopting the axiom 'When it is not necessary to change, it is necessary not to change.' New methods should be compatible with old.

210

On a repetitive job, an employee will get tired and bored. His performance will deteriorate accordingly, with an increase in errors and a decrease in throughput.

It has long been realized that this consequent deterioration in performance is due to reduced motivation rather than ability. As discussed in Chapter 4, motivation in the business sense is the willingness to do a job and to give of one's best (see Figure 7.8). The performance of operators was measured under test conditions and under operating conditions. Note that the capacity

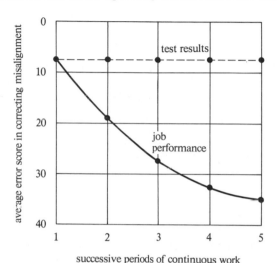

successive periods of continuous work

Figure 7.8:   Capacity versus performance

of the operators in terms of their ability was a constant score of 7 to 8 over five successive work periods of continuous work in test conditions. Their performance on the job, however, was well below the established capacity. The difference is attributable to the fact that operators were highly motivated in tests and less well motivated in the operating environment. The increased motivation in test conditions would probably be caused by the same factors as those discussed in the Hawthorne Experiments in Chapter 3.

Fatigue and boredom without a very high degree of motivation will lead to carelessness and lack of concentration and attention. The latter will probably lead to a corresponding rise in unconscious errors.

From the designer's point of view there are two important considerations:

- the working periods
- the repetitive nature of the tasks.

There is a limit to which attention can be maintained in the everyday situation, though the period after which concentration tends to lapse, and the errors made depends on the task and working conditions. It is difficult therefore to give general rules. A useful guide is as follows:

> '... For tasks involving careful attention without much physical exertion, cycles of 40 or 50 mins of work alternated with 8 to 10 mins of rest are best. In general, total work periods should not be longer than 4 hrs with 1 hr of rest' (Clifford T. Morgan, *Human Engineering Guide to Equipment Design*, p. 31, McGraw-Hill Book Company, Inc., New York, 1963).

Although this guide was based on a military environment, it is a good *initial* rule of thumb for estimating productivity in a commercial data processing system. Longer continuous work periods may well introduce a higher error rate.

The impact of repetitive tasks on fatigue and boredom is a matter of some controversy, For example:

> 'Simple tasks that must be done over and over again are boring. Where possible, provision should be made for some variation in tasks to be performed' (op. cit.).

This is descriptive of any continuous on-line data capture or off-line data preparation activity. There is another school of thought which says that this work should be made as simple and as repetitive as possible. This is often expressed in the adage: 'never expect a punch operator to think'.

Many studies of data preparation activities have shown that there is a positive correlation between *high* key rate and *low* error rate. Further research indicated that a feature of high quality input was data that were absolutely clear and legible, with no decisions left to the operator. The good, experienced operator on the one hand, was one who could scan a document, press keys whilst at the same time hold a conversation with a neighbour or think about something totally different. This happens when the keying activity is reduced to a reflex operation, not requiring the conscious concentration of the operator.

There is thus no clear cut answer to the conflict of simplification versus variation. The design decision must be based on the particular group involved and their working conditions.

The following example provides a summary to this discussion.

A company with a very high card punching workload operated a nine-to-five data preparation shift. Because of the volume of work, a special three- to four-hour evening shift was arranged. This was staffed exclusively by married woman, most of whom had young children. On the evening shift, the working conditions were far more informal than the prime shift. The evening shift punched from the same documents as the day shift.

The operations manager was struck by three interesting differences between day and evening shifts:

1. The number of key strokes per operator hour was on average almost twice as high on the evening shift.
2. The error rate (per cent key strokes) on the evening shift was a fraction of that on the day shift.
3. The noise of conversation in the punch room was far louder in the evening than in the day.

The operations manager had originally instituted this special shift as a last resort to clear the backlog. He had expected productivity to be far lower, and high error rates to be a problem. After all, these women would:

—have already spent an exhausting day with children, and housework, and would be fatigued
—not have the constant practice of the day shift
—not be subject to the same feeling of involvement and loyalty to the company
—not be 'inspired' by the data preparation supervisor.

The superior performance of the evening shift could have been caused by any or all of the following:

1. *Better quality operators* who could reduce punching to a reflex level, thereby not suffering from fatigue and boredom. This could be because conversation was not discouraged in the informal atmosphere of the evening shift.
2. *A shorter working period* in which quality was not affected by fatigue and boredom.
3. *The informal, social nature of the group.*

To determine the exact causes would have taken many months of controlled experiments to isolate the variables.

ANXIETY

This can depress productivity and increase errors. It has two main causes in computer-based systems:

● loss of control or security
● lack of information

Loss of control can occur in several ways. The user may feel that the computer is taking over, he does not have confidence in its processing logic. For example, the computer is used to allocate staff to jobs, plant and stock to customers, and raw materials to production. The user *'feels'* he is losing control: he doesn't understand the allocation algorithm, he has lost his local visual records, he is remote from the processing. If there is *no* manual override, then the user probably *has* lost control. To a user operating a VDU with a more direct link to the control process, this feeling of a lack of control may be even more acute. The same anxiety about loss of control can occur in the typical full-time VDU operator, when he is faced with a long response time and mass of work, where he feels 'locked-in' to a transaction. The only way to prevent these feelings of anxiety and frustration at a loss of control is to provide, where possible, a temporary manual over-ride or by-pass.

Similarly, some users and operators feel that their job security depends on whether they get on well with the machine. This can be aggravated if people feel that they are being evaluated by machine. If these feelings are strong, then the threat of the machine will almost certainly result in a high error rate.

A lack of information is a contributor to a loss of control. This is a common problem when a fault develops in the system. When will the system become available again? What do I do with my backlog? How do I start? Will I get away on time tonight? And so on.

Anxiety can be caused in many simple ways: abrupt, rude or critical error messages and failure to give positive, comprehensive acknowledgements of data acceptance or update.

Removal or reduction of anxiety will play a major role in minimizing errors.

COMPLEX LOGICAL RELATIONSHIPS, RESISTANCE TO THE SYSTEM, AND INCOMPATIBILITY OF PEOPLE AND SYSTEM

All these factors have been discussed previously. Taken together, they mean that the system is not geared to the employees and has been developed in conflict to their attitudes.

Understanding the potential causes of errors is the first step to minimizing them. Designing totally error-free systems is almost an impossibility. Designing systems with minimum errors requires a careful analysis of potential causes, isolating those which might apply and then seeking solutions. This may require the use of experiments or pilot studies to test hypotheses.

Error analysis

In designing a system, the analyst is faced with a series of iterative steps:

- basic design
- estimating performance: throughput and errors
- testing hypothesis: measuring throughput and errors
- modifying design/proceeding to next level of detail.

One approach is to start by estimating the lowest error rate at which the system would become untenable. That is, the quality of data reaches such a low level that:

- if the erroneous data was applied to the files or output, the results would be meaningless
- excessive delays would be caused for correction
- an excessive amount of effort would be needed for correction.

This could be established, for example, as a 5 per cent error rate; over this the system would be unworkable. This assessment of whether or not the design is satisfactory must be made very carefully. There is always the danger that the designer may become emotionally and intellectually committed to the design, lose objectivity and make false assumptions that prove the system is acceptable.

Ideally, experiments or pilot tests are carried out to determine whether or not the assumptions are correct. In some cases this is not possible. Creating, for example, a controlled pilot test of an on-line system can be prohibitively expensive. In many cases, however, setting up a controlled test will be an invaluable exercise (at reasonable cost) in arriving at an optimum design. The obvious problems are the logistics of arranging such tests, such as cost and user staff availability. The tests must be made at the system design stage, i.e. before the system specification is prepared. Some organizations have carried out these tests of *method* as part of the conversion or even the implementation phases. If unsatisfactory results are obtained at this stage, there is little or nothing that can be done because too great a commitment has been made to the system. It may be possible to make minor changes, but this is tinkering with the system rather than having the flexibility to redesign if necessary.

There are three major problems with setting up a controlled test:

- simulating live running conditions
- allowing for extraneous factors which distort the results
- extrapolating from a limited number of measurements to the system as a whole.

The latter is perhaps the easiest to solve. Established statistical techniques can be used to interpret the results. Most measurements of human characteristics and performance vary according to a normal (Gaussian) distribution. They can be plotted on a bell-shaped curve. For example, in the measurement of errors made by people, we must make another distinction: between *constant* and *variable* errors (see Figure 7.9). *The Human Engineering Guide* (p. 20) mentioned on p. 212 gives a good example of these. No two tests of visual acuity, for example, give exactly the same results on one person. When error is measured by a normal distribution, the mean of the distribution is a constant error, and the standard deviation is a variable error. Various analyses may be made on the incidence of errors, the major types and possible causes. (A wide range of texts are available which describe the statistical methods and their application. One excellent

aim: test of visual acuity

situation: riflemen shooting at target

results:
rifleman A comes close to hitting bull first time,
hits second time, complete miss third, etc.

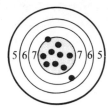

this is *variable error*

rifleman B: all shots off bull, clustered right

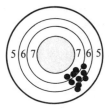

this is a *constant error*

Figure 7.9: Constant versus variable error

Figure 7.10: Pilot versus actual system differences

---

1. Is the reason for doing the task (as explained to staff) the same as in the new system?
2. Is the task being done exactly as it will be done in the new system?
3. Is the pressure under which the task is done the same as in the new system?
4. Are the results of doing the task the same as in the new system?
5. Is the level and type of supervision for doing the task the same as in the new system?
6. Is there more involvement of the analyst than in the new system?
7. Does the task add to the staff's workload in the test situation?
8. Is the volume the same as in the new system?
9. Are the people doing the task representative of the people who will do it in the new system?
10. Is the feedback on errors the same as in the new system?
11. Do the staff know the expected results of the test?
12. Do the staff (in principle) support the idea of the new system?
13. Have any special rewards or incentives been promised for the test?

---

text is E. F. Lindquist's *Design and Analysis of Experiments in Psychology and Education*, Houghton Mifflin Company, Boston, 1953.) From a limited range of readings, assumptions can be made about the system as a whole, and the design can be modified as necessary.

Creating a near real-life simulation and allowing for special conditions will take careful thought and planning. The fact that the exercise *is* an experiment can distort results as, for example, in the Hawthorne Experiments and in the simple tests shown in Figure 7.8. One way of assessing the differences between pilot versus real-life environments is to make a detailed checklist as in Figure 7.10. Rarely is there time to make detailed studies of the impact of these differences and to screen out interference from the factors specific to the test situation.

Summary

1. This chapter has examined the people-related factors in designing computer-based systems.

2. The nature of job enrichment has been explored in many research studies and it has been applied in many companies. The *principles* of applying 'motivators' are relevant to many jobs associated with computer-based systems. The function of systems design may be allied to an overall corporate job enrichment programme. Examples of job enrichment have been given.

3. An effective systems design is generally one which creates meaningful jobs, and avoids creating a number of tenuously linked assembly-line procedures, as is the tendency in off-line batch systems.

4. The potential of on-line systems permitting a direct link between user and machine has been discussed under five main headings:
- greater responsibility on user staff
- reduction in duplicate (manual) systems
- more feedback on user performance
- greater integration of computer with user job
- more user-oriented input techniques are available.

5. Data collection is a user, labour-intensive task. It can be either a primary or secondary function. If it is a secondary task it must not be allowed to interfere with the primary function; rather it should aid or support it. Figure 7.7 gives guidelines for designing data collection procedures.

6. The design of outputs requires the same attention as that devoted to data collection. The *so what?* test is a useful practical means of analysing management report requirements.

7. Privacy, in terms of information about the organization's own employees, can present problems. The aims of the personnel system and the safeguards to

be included should be discussed with employee representatives as early as possible in the project.

8. The importance and definition of accuracy was discussed and the types of errors reviewed. Special causes of errors are:

- transfer of learning
- fatigue and boredom
- anxiety
- complex logical relationships
- resistance
- incompatibility of user/system.

9. The system must include methods and techniques for minimizing errors. The agreement of tolerable error rates and the testing of the design against these error rates is an integral part of the design process. Where low error rates are crucial and new techniques are being used, a formal pilot scheme is desirable.

8
Handling a project team

The systems analyst as project leader

In addition to his analysis and design responsibilities, the systems analyst commonly assumes a project management role. A senior systems analyst is frequently a project leader, with several systems analysts and, possibly, programmers reporting to him. In this chapter, the role of the analyst as project leader is discussed. In keeping with the rest of the book, we are concerned here with the people side of project leadership, not with the general management and technical aspects which are often associated with the job. These include, for example, estimating and scheduling, costing, technical trouble-shooting, and advising on hardware/software selection.

The scope of the project manager's responsibilities, his freedom in decision making and his management style depend on many factors. Not the least is the organization of the data processing department as a whole, the system development methods, project control standards, and the general 'management climate', as defined in chapter 1.

The role of the project manager can be viewed in the same way as that of any manager: objectives, environment, and constraints, as shown in Figure 6.1. In this case the environment is the project team. The short term objectives are the project plan, the medium-term objectives are raising (or maintaining) levels of productivity generally, as well as reducing (or holding) development costs. Longer-term objectives will affect more senior project management staff, such as maintaining staffing levels, reducing staff turnover, improving staff skills, and so on. The project leader's task in the context of this chapter is ensuring that the *people* environment is geared to meet the objectives. We will assume the general project management objectives are as follows:

> 'To develop systems (or programs) of acceptable quality at an economic rate in the timescale required.'

The only real asset that a project manager has is his people. The four main aspects of his job can therefore be described as:

1. *Acquiring and retaining the asset:* through effective recruitment and employment policies.
2. *Developing the asset:* through effective on- and off-the-job training and career development.
3. *Creating an environment in which the asset can be put to work:* through good methods standards and effective management.
4. *Putting the asset to work:* through effective management to get the best out of the asset.

The systems manager or equivalent will certainly have responsibilities for all these. The more junior the project manager, the fewer responsibilities he will have in this area. For example, a project leader in a junior position can have responsibilities only for (4), with no hire or fire responsibilities (1), only marginal influence on career development (2), and only a limited involvement in standards development (3). This chapter will concentrate on the leadership aspects of (3) and (4). For this reason the term project *leader* will be used in the remainder of this chapter.

In considering the project leader in terms of the management diagram in Figure 6.1, we must not forget the constraints which are fundamental to how the project leader does his job and the problems he faces. An example list of constraints is shown in Figure 8.1. Constraints are those factors over which the project leader has no control. They are imposed by the policy of the company, by the immediate superior management, and by external factors such as the state of the labour market. Constraints are not, of themselves, necessarily bad. Employment policies and methods (implied in 3 and 7 in Figure 8.1) are essential to the operation of most organizations but they can create a difficult situation for the project leader. The more unrealistic the constraints, the more impossible the project leader's job becomes. For example, there may be established personnel practices for professional staff working overtime which, although suitable for most of the staff, are not suitable for systems and programming staff who work (occasionally) excessive overtime and late hours as during testing and conversion.

A far greater constraint, in terms of the morale of the project leader, is whether or not he has direct or at least reasonable control over his own staff. A project is proceeding more-or-less on schedule, the staff are working enthusiastically and well. Then, on the instructions of superior management, a key member is pulled off the project to work on a maintenance job. This is frustrating and damaging to the morale of the team.

No job is perfect; every supervisor and manager has constraints placed upon him. They are part of the job, indeed they may form part of the challenge of the job.

Before studying styles of leadership and decision making methods and their impact on the team, it is useful to examine project leadership from the team member's point of view.

On a wide range of project leadership courses involving hundreds of analysts and programmers, the author asked the following: 'You've all worked for at least one project leader. Most of you have worked for several project leaders. Think of the best and worst leader you have worked for. Fix a specific person in your mind. From your point of view, what one or two

Figure 8.1: Example constraints placed on the project leader

---

1. No control over the deployment or allocation of own staff.
2. No control over the composition of own team.
3. No variation permitted of conditions of employment or working conditions of own staff.
4. Project deadline (usually unrealistic) imposed from outside with little or no consultation.
5. No flexibility over the availability of other resources.
6. No flexibility in dealing with commitments previously made to staff.
7. No control over working methods.
8. Limited staff available (based on state of job market, corporate head-count freeze, etc.).

Figure 8.2: The leader from the subordinate's point of view—good and bad

---

+ *Technically competent*—can understand my job and my problems

+ *Unflappable*—remains pleasant and calm no matter what the crisis

+ *Let's me get on with the job*—doesn't spend all his time looking over my shoulder but exercises reasonable control

+ *Listens to what I've got to say*—doesn't necessarily do what I want, but at least gives my views a fair hearing

+ *Takes decisions and lets me know*—doesn't sit on the fence or pass the buck and I know what's happening

+ *Fair and honest*—doesn't hold personal grudges or let prejudices interfere with decisions, and plays it straight with staff

− *Inconsistent*—is continually changing his ideas, pace, and direction

− *Doesn't support his staff*—will always take our opponent's stand against us

− *Makes commitments without consultations*—leaving us to pick up the pieces; generally, never says 'no' to users

− *Takes all the credit and none of the blame*—when things go wrong, they are told it's our fault

− *Doesn't believe in the 'rule of law'*—I never know what I'm supposed to be doing and get penalized for being wrong when the rules were never laid down

− *Doesn't lead*—he sits behind his desk doing not managing; we're on our own doing his job, but without the authority

---

points stand out in your mind that made him the best or worst?' A list of responses, usually 15 to 20, was then put up on a blackboard, identified as '+' for good and '−' for bad. Although this represented a range of highly personal reactions and incidents, a hard core of common responses usually emerged. The most frequent + and − reactions are shown in Figure 8.2.

Remember that what one team member expects of a leader is not necessarily the same as another. A man with all the pluses and none of the minuses for each member of the team would be a paragon indeed.

Leadership

The nature of leadership and the question 'What makes a good leader?' have been the subject of much research and debate. An answer to this question would enable a leader to be identified and trained. The first studies of leadership concentrated on the *personality approach*. This involved categorizing those qualities which appeared to differentiate the leader from the follower. 'Shopping lists' of personal traits of leaders were thus developed. For example, much of the early research was financed and undertaken by the military and a constant characteristic identified was *courage*.

The personality approach to defining leadership had a number of shortcomings. The first was that there was little agreement between the entries on various independently compiled lists, with noticeable exceptions like 'courage'. The second problem was that observed results (where a leader was appointed with the characteristics as listed) did not correspond with the expected results. The lists did not take account of the law of the situation. For example, what was the relevance of 'courage' identified for a platoon leader, to a management job in industry? A man would be an excellent leader in one situation and a disaster in another. Finally, it implied that a leader was born and could not be made. How, for example, can 'courage' be taught? McGregor has given an excellent analogy: that leadership is no more a property of a *person* than gravitation is a property of *individual* objects.

Later studies have taken a *behavioural approach*. Rather than asking 'What are the *personal characteristics* of a good leader?', this approach asks 'What does an effective leader *do*?' In talking about a style of leadership, therefore, we must *not* consider the leader in isolation from the group or the situation; leadership cannot be considered in a vacuum.

Early ideas of leadership tended to see the leader as someone who set the goal, headed in that direction and, based on his personality, the followers followed. The behavioural approach, because it now considered the dynamics of the group, lead to a greater emphasis on *group* decision making and action. This in turn caused a reaction against the 'autocratic' to the 'democratic', involving such terms as 'job satisfaction', 'involvement', and 'participation'.

This has led to an interesting paradox as seen by some managers. On the one hand, the vogue of democratic management requires greater participation in decision making. This *may* be taken as a sign of weakness. It will certainly require time and effort on the part of both leader and group. On the other hand, the leader and his followers are expected to be efficient and this dictates that to save time and effort, the leader should decide alone.

The amount of authority that lies with the leader and with the group defines to a large extent the decision-making style of the leader (see Figure 8.3). There is no one style which is inherently 'good' and another which is inherently 'bad'. The law of situation must apply. This means that the area of authority retained by the leader and group will vary not only between different leaders and different groups, but it will vary from situation to situation in the same group. Pressure and time are often quoted as the major factors in determining decision-making style; heaven help the platoon

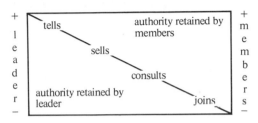

examples

    tells: leader identifies problem, selects solution, and announces decision.

    sells: leader identifies problem, selects solution, explains decision, and is persuasive in getting it accepted.

    consults: leader identifies problem and lets members influence selection of solution. He reserves the right to select solution himself.

    joins: leader becomes one of the group, who select problems and solutions on a "majority" basis, within freedom allowed by supervisor.

Figure 8.3:   Leader–group authority

sergeant under fire who consults! In the day-to-day decision making in the computer room, the shift leader must invariably work at the 'tells' level. Where there is more time and pressure is eased, the 'sells' or 'consults' situation could well be used: considering new rest-room facilities, future training programmes.

There are other factors besides just pressure and time, as shown in Figure 8.4. This list is by no means exhaustive and the entries are complementary rather than mutually exclusive, but it provides a useful checklist for studying project leadership styles in data processing.

The project leader's decision-making style

The major factors that affect the decision-making style of the project leader are discussed below. There are:

1. Incompatible objectives
2. Freedom of action

3. Interest and expectations
4. Knowledge and experience.

Figure 8.4: Factors in selection of leadership style

The leader

- his personal beliefs, values, and previous experiences
- his confidence in the group members
- his confidence in himself
- his knowledge and experience of the subject matter

The group

- their knowledge and experience of the subject matter
- their expectations
- their personal beliefs, values, and previous expectations
- their interest
- their relationships with each other

The situation

- pressure and time
- traditions and expectations of the organization
- freedom of action of leader permitted by superiors
- frequency of decision making (by type)
- compatibility of leader's objectives and group member(s)'s objectives

---

INCOMPATIBILITY OF OBJECTIVES

This means that leader and group are working towards totally separate goals. In such a situation, the leader is forced to dictate to the group because consultations would produce results totally at odds with the leader's goals and methods. This is illustrated in the following quotation:

> 'I was a project leader at a consulting company. My team normally consisted of five or six people, of which two were programmers. I inherited these programmers from another part of the company. Dealing with these programmers was difficult and time-consuming. My objective for the team was to turn in a job of reasonable quality, on time and on budget—and thus at a profit. The two programmers, on the other hand, were the programming "backroom boys"! Their satisfaction came from putting the machine and the software through their paces. They were classic examples of the type of programmer who would spend three days finding a way to save three milliseconds. There was enough day-to-day conflict without compounding this with conflict in decision making.'

In this example, the project leader was, as a major part of this job, trying to change the goals of the technical perfectionists. Until this could be achieved, consultations were more frustrating than fruitful. Neither side would compromise their views.

The personal goals and preferred methods of each group member might vary, but the members and the leader must have an agreed sense of direction. The inculcation of common objectives is a primary function of a project leader. Only when this is achieved can the decision-making style become truly democratic—if that is the preferred method.

FREEDOM OF ACTION

This means simply that the greater the limitation on the range of actions available to the leader, the less important his decision-making function becomes. The more restricted the freedom of action, the greater the use of the 'tells' style. For example, the leader's superiors and the users decide that:

1. The new system must be implemented by the year end.
2. No more staff are available for the project.
3. Machine time is restricted but external facilities cannot be used.
4. Standard hardware, software, and development methods must be used.
5. No paid overtime will be authorized.

In this case, the leader was not consulted, and he must 'tell' or 'sell' the above points to his team. But the leader may then consult on the basis of: 'That's what we have to do and the tools we have for doing it. Any ideas how we apply the tools?' Again, if further limitations are imposed there will be little else to do but 'tell'.

INTEREST AND EXPECTATION, KNOWLEDGE AND EXPERIENCE

These vary from member to member and from group to group. Some members take the view that a project leader is there to lead and the group is there to follow, that decision making is a management function, and that managers are paid to manage whereas workers are paid to work. Although this is perhaps true of some groups, most systems development staff are *interested in* the project and *expect* to participate in decision making.

Knowledge and experience of members and leader will influence the decision-making style and the distribution of authority. For example, the author once assumed control of a group engaged on an information survey as part of a data base development project. The group had been in limbo for some weeks—they didn't know where they were going, nobody had tackled a project like this before, and morale was at rock bottom. This was a case for limited consultation; what the group really wanted was to be 'told' and 'sold'.

Another example was where a user, with little technical experience, was appointed as project leader of a team which consisted of three analysts and six programmers. (The rationale for this approach was that because the work of the team was providing a service to the user, the user should be in control.) The technical and management knowledge and experience of the leader was such that he 'joined' the group.

In some situations, the project leader consistently uses the 'tells' or 'joins' style so that he can pursue his own interests. This can happen if the project leader is appointed not because of this management potential but because he was the *best technician*. This can mean that he concentrates his time and attention on the technical aspects of the job, not on the people side of running a team. Because he enjoys the technical content of the work and feels at home with it, he spends his time on technical decision making. He 'tells' the group of technical decisions because he thinks he knows best. When non-technical decisions are made he 'joins' the group because he has little interest in or knowledge of the subject matter.

DELEGATION

There is another dimension to decision making which is not shown in Figure 8.3. This is *delegation*. Delegation is giving a member a job to do and decisions to make. Delegation of responsibility implies delegation of authority. It does *not* mean that the leader gives an opinion and then seeks the opinion of the group members. Nor is it asking for a recommendation of action to be taken. True delegation can be expressed as: 'You decide and inform me afterwards'.

If delegation is used then, in all but very unusual circumstances, the leader does not change the decision once it has been made. Again, a practical instance to illustrate this:

> 'I worked on a team in which the leader prided himself in his use of delegation. Regularly he'd say, "Right, John, you decide this". I would make the decision and start to implement it. When he heard about what I was doing he'd say "No, don't do that, do this instead." It was worse than that. We all felt that he had secretly decided what was going to happen before he "delegated". No matter what I'd decide, the boss would do what he originally wanted. In the end, this turned the whole thing into a giant guessing game of trying to predict what he'd decided already.'

A decision to delegate is an important one and must be taken carefully. True delegation is not 'buck passing'. The superior remains responsible for the actions of his subordinates. This means that the leader must have confidence not only in the member to whom he delegates but also in himself.

Practical research findings indicate the following characteristics about decision making by senior management.

- The prior consultation method is used more than any other. Delegation is least frequently used.
- Subordinates tend to overestimate the degree of influence they have.
- The more experienced a manager is, the more he tends to let subordinates have influence.
- A manager with a large span of control tends to use time-saving methods (e.g., 'tells' or delegates).

For the project leader, we can draw the following general conclusions:

1. *The good leader is flexible.* He will examine a range of decision-making methods choosing that method which best meets the needs of himself, the group, and the situation. The leader must be consistent. If two comparable decisions are to be made, and one is taken arbitrarily ('told') and the other with participation ('consults'), the members will mistrust his motives. It means that he will 'tell' when he must, 'consult' when he can and 'join' when it's necessary.

2. *The good leader will let members know how much influence they will have on any decision.* With a consistent choice of method, the members will soon realize how much influence they have. At the beginning, however, the leader should state positively how much influence the group will have in any particular decision.

3. *The project leader must always stay in control.* If responsibility for quality and quantity of development work is delegated to the project leader, he must remain in control.

4. *The good leader examines his style and seeks to improve it.* Under pressure of work and with no major problems in sight, the leader can become complacent. The good leader will *think* about leadership. He will critically examine the forces in himself, in the group and in the situation.

Hints for better project leadership

There can be no such thing as a cookbook approach to good project leadership. There is no one set of rules which if carefully followed will give an effective leader. There are, however, a number of principles for guidance. The first requirement is a recognition that leadership is a function which must be studied and analysed. The bad leader is one who occupies a leadership position but never devotes sufficient time and effort to the function nor appraises and improves his performance.

Figure 8.5 lists ten *hints* for better project leadership. They are not formal rules but guidelines for consideration by the leader. They are discussed below.

Be consistent

Inconsistency in the project leader is unsettling for the team. Consider the following quotations from students on courses.

'My boss gets fads and it makes our life difficult. For example, a few months ago he went on a decision table course. When he came back, it was decision tables for this, decision table standards for that, and so on. A month or so later, it was back to normal and nobody used decision tables any more. Then he went on a project management course, and for weeks it was special reports for this and performance feedback for

227

that. Then, again, it was business as normal and we all went back to the old methods.'

'The inconsistency of my boss was that he continually changed job allocations and priorities. Part of it was because of the chaotic maintenance situation but mostly it was because of bad planning and the tendency of the leader to panic. For example, he'd give me a job and say that it was top priority, that it had to be done by a certain date. I'd be sweating my guts out, working overtime, taking the deadline seriously, when in he'd come: "Drop that", he'd say, "This job is more important. It must be done by . . . ." Then, a few days later, it was all changed again. In the end, I just gave up.'

Figure 8.5: Ten hints for better project leadership

---

1. Be consistent
2. Provide support
3. Don't make promises you can't keep
4. Praise in public, criticize in private
5. Beware of morale danger points
6. Set realistic deadlines
7. Set perceivable targets
8. Explain and show, rather than do
9. Don't rely just on formal control reports
10. Encourage a good team spirit

Inconsistency of decision-making style can also create problems as discussed earlier. Consistency implies forward planning. It means that any change must be carefully evaluated; if a course of action is worth taking, it must be applied and followed up. If a course of action is to be discontinued then a formal announcement is usually preferable to just letting the new method die and fade away. Inconsistency can destroy the respect and credibility of the leader in the eyes of his team.

Provide support

'When you get right down to it, one of the most important tasks of a manager is to eliminate his people's excuses for failure' (Robert Townsend, *Up the Organization*, Coronet Books, Hodder-Fawcett Limited, London, 1971, p. 55).

This is one of the best definitions of the role of the leader. Excuses for failure in a system development project could be no machine-time available for testing, the failure of users to sign-off on a specification or the late arrival of test data from users. Support for team members means that the leader, because of his more senior position, uses his energies and best endeavours to ensure that the members have the tools and means to apply them to do the job. Another relevant quotation from Townsend is:

> 'True leadership must be for the benefit of the followers, not the enrichment of the leader. In combat, officers eat last. Most people in big companies are administered, not led. They are treated as personnel, not people' (op. cit., p. 90).

In some organizations, the job of a project leader is seen as a sinecure: the reward for hard work is leadership which is an escape from it. When an analyst becomes a project leader, he will probably still be expected to play a productive role on the project. His additional authority will give him a privileged position, which if he abuses for his own self aggrandizement, will cause resentment of his staff.

Don't make promises you can't keep

A broken commitment or agreement, no matter what the reason, will damage the team's trust in the leader and his credibility. Again, an illustration of this point:

> 'By the time system testing started, the project was six weeks behind. We got additional time on a remote machine. Our team leader promised that we could all have time off commensurate with the overtime we worked. The project went in—more or less on time. None of us got our time off. We never could have had it: it turned out that it was against company policy and another project was due to start immediately anyway. Our accrued time off was equal to about a month's holiday.'

A promise must be kept; if it can't be guaranteed, don't make it. (The same applies to promises made to users!)

Praise in public, criticize in private

The attitude 'Unless I tell you otherwise, you're doing OK' is a very negative one. People need to know where they stand and they like to be told. Praise is a type of reward, provided it is used meaningfully and sparingly. Differentiate, therefore, between *praise* for a job especially well done and *reassurance*, that the project is proceeding along the right lines and is on target. Both are necessary.

If the leader works alongside the team, the members will get reassurance informally. Where the leader is remote, more formal reassurance will be necessary, as in a weekly meeting.

Any good words said by outsiders about an individual or the group should be passed on. If the user, for example, compliments the leader on a report which is the product of one member of the group, a special point must be made of telling him about it.

The most important part of praising is to do it in public. Complimentary remarks should be passed on at a team meeting or in the presence of the superior manager. If the occasion warrants, the praise should be put in writing. For example, when a user is especially complimentary about an individual's work, he should be asked to write a memo about it. If such letters and memos become part of the individual's personal file, so much the better.

If the most important part of praising is to do it in public, the most important part of giving criticism is to do it in private. Many people hate to criticize and will postpone doing so as long as possible. It is never a pleasant task and may open the door for bad feelings and hostility. But it is inevitable that there will be a situation where a word of criticism and correction is most definitely called for. The first thing to remember is that when this occurs, the person involved is quite likely to know that he should be criticized. If the leader puts it off and remains silent, he may lose some respect.

Excuses and rationalizations should not be demolished at a stroke. As long as the person knows what he did wrong and is willing to try to correct it, that is sufficient. Simply, don't rub his nose in it.

If there are other people involved as, for example, a complaint to the leader's manager or a complaint from members of the user department about an individual he should be defended as much as possible and he should know that this has been done. After the team member has been seen by the leader, even if the individual has been severely criticized in private, the leader should pass over the incident lightly with the third party denying its importance by his attitude. Criticism should never be completely negative; it should be constructive, presenting alternative courses of action for the future.

Beware of morale danger points

The very nature of systems development work means that there are peaks and troughs of pressure, as in waiting for users to sign-off on checkpoints or the quiet after the storm of testing. Without adequate planning these sudden quiet periods can present problems where 'the devil finds work for idle hands'. Making work specially to fill the time is never really satisfactory. The time can be spent on planning and preparing for the next phase or project. Some project leaders encourage group members to take leave.

Other morale danger points can be a sudden reversal in policy, a project being scrapped or one or two key people leaving. The project leader must never become complacent about the satisfactory morale of his team. It can be very high one week and come crashing down the next. Anticipating such crises in morale is infinitely preferable to suddenly being faced with the loss of key staff, a fall in productivity, a rise in absenteeism, as well as destructive arguments.

Set realistic deadlines

The ideal way of setting a deadline is to evaluate the quantity and complexity of the workload and the resources available, and to set the target date accordingly. This is not always possible, because deadlines can be enforced by external factors such as the needs of the business and previous promises made by managers to users. But if the team is given impossible targets, they are bound to fail.

The importance of setting realistic and *honest* deadlines is illustrated in the following story. A project leader had three totally different schedules. The first contained targets promised to users; they were realistic and easily attainable with a wide margin of safety. The next schedule contained the estimates which were made by the project leader, based on his assessments. This was what he *expected* to happen. The last was a schedule from which he allocated deadlines to his staff. This last bore no resemblance to the commitments of the first. The reasoning behind this schedule was that taking 25 per cent off what was expected (second schedule) stretched people—giving them challenging targets which, though never attainable, were desirable in getting the maximum of production in the minimum of time. Staff soon became disillusioned with never meeting their targets. They were enraged when the deception of the three schedules was eventually discovered.

Certainly, there is nothing inherently wrong with setting targets which are not too easy. But setting totally artificial and unrealistic objectives is counterproductive. Staff should always be consulted about targets; a target which staff feel they have had a part in setting will have their support. This does not mean that the project leader is dictated to by the group; this would be the equivalent to 'joining' as in Figure 8.3.

Set perceivable targets

Targets must not only be realistic, they must be practical, short-term goals. Progress to a distant goal is best made by setting and achieving short-run targets along the way to it. People normally respond well to short-term goals, because they may be accomplished comparatively quickly, within their span of attention and will-power.

A project team undertaking an information survey as a prerequisite to data base design could spend a year on investigation. A year of intensive interviewing is a hard, sometimes frustrating, job. Setting a deadline one year ahead of 'Complete Information Survey' is by any definition a distant goal. At the start of the project, most of the staff couldn't conceive of this phase of the project being completed. Five intermediate goals were therefore set. The final goal was always present but most of the team worked from one short-term, intermediate target to the next.

Each target must be a meaningful unit of accomplished work. The elapsed time between targets depends on the project or the group. Most people appear to respond well to goals not more than two to three months away. The target should have some practical significance, such as giving a report or presentation to a user or getting a decision. Targets and progress towards them should be expressed in visible, preferably graphic form. A master progress chart available for all the team to inspect will encourage their interest in the project. Moving a line on a chart may be the only way in which progress on the project is perceivable to the team members.

If a target is met, time should be allowed for a reward and a feeling of achievement engendered. If a target has been missed the leader must be realistic about it. The team member should be encouraged to analyse what went wrong, to take corrective action, and then to set to a new goal. It is essential that re-scheduled targets are reasonable. As discussed above, continual failure is bad for morale, and if there is never any success, people will stop trying.

Explain and show, rather than do

On-the-job training and personnel development is an important part of any project leaders' job. At the project checkpoints, the quality and quantity of work done by each team member is reviewed.

What should happen if, at a checkpoint, the quality of work is not up to standard? The first point to consider is whether or not the team member *knew* the standard required. What is poor or suspect quality to the leader may be seen as satisfactory work by the team member. Each member of the team must thus know what the expected standard is. Systems development methods and documentation standards will help in this respect. But no formal set of standards will explicitly cover every aspect of systems and programming work. Improving quality, therefore, is an iterative process, of work done, review and critique, re-do work, and so on.

If work is below standard and project deadlines are tight, there is always the temptation for the leader to re-do the job himself or to pass that aspect of the job on to someone who has proved success in doing it. If this is done consistently the under-performing team member will never have the opportunity to learn and practise. Getting the job done will meet the short-term objective of getting the project in on time, but it will also create long-term problems of staff capability.

Don't rely just on formal control reports

Every installation needs project control standards, which will include formal progress reporting documentation. This will include reporting on time, percentage of project complete, and special problems encountered. These reports are especially important if the team members are in different locations. They should not in any way, however, be seen as replacing the face-to-face review of project successes and failures at a target checkpoint. Some project leaders prefer, in addition to this, a weekly or fortnightly review meeting with the whole team. This is certainly important if the team is scattered about. The objectives and tone of this weekly or fortnightly meeting are important. It can be used for the leader to announce or explain points of administration and review project progress overall. It can also be used for any team member to raise problems with his work, the project as a whole, or with the company generally. But remember the following:

1. The meeting is for the benefit of the members as well as the leader.
2. If the team work in proximity, they could well have had discussions on problems and progress among themselves. Result at meeting: they're bored.
3. It is dangerous to fix a constant duration for a meeting. On some occasions the material will be covered in less than half-an-hour, in others three hours are required.
4. It must be decided and announced in advance, the type of problems which can be discussed at the meeting. If the leader says 'anything goes' then he must be prepared for personal gripes from the individual about his salary, working conditions, and so on. Many of these are best discussed in private. So the ground rules for the meeting will probably be 'any problem which affects the project specifically or the whole of the group generally'.
5. At a review meeting, mechanisms must exist for decision-making, follow-up, and work allocation (as discussed in Chapter 10).

Encourage a good team spirit

A good team spirit can be equated with high morale. An apparently well-functioning group need not necessarily indicate high morale. There may be a highish level of productivity, conformance to standards, neatness and orderliness, and a lack of conflict in the group. These can be engendered by management by coercion, but with the team still unhappy, frustrated, and totally devoid of a good team spirit.

If the characteristics of a well-functioning group as described can be obtained by rigid discipline and coercion from above, what is the advantage of a good team spirit and high morale? There are many. With coercion, turnover of the group will probably be high, enforcement by management will require constant effort and will be inefficient, and team members will give the minimum but tolerable level of performance. When additional effort above and beyond the call of duty is required as in testing, conversion, and implementation, this will not be readily forthcoming. The frustration and unhappiness of the team members will also lead to buck-passing.

A good team spirit or high morale is not directly perceivable from the basic productivity of the group. It is seen from the level of staff turnover, absenteeism, and the reaction of the group under pressure or in a crisis. Additionally, there are indications of high morale from how team members interact with each other. For example:

> 'Some signs that the individuals are working well as a team, with high morale and a good group spirit, are:
>
> ● Members ask each other's advice and consult often to make decisions and solve problems.
> ● They defend each other against outsiders: "We can solve our own problems": "I don't care if Bill (a team-mate) was right or not, John (not a team member) shouldn't criticize him."
> ● There is a general feeling of optimism: "We can do it."
> ● Standing private jokes develop that are not comprehensible to outsiders.
> ● Members call each other by nick-names that outsiders are not allowed to use.'

(Susan Wooldridge, *Project Management in Data Processing,* Petrocelli Books, New York, 1975.)

The prerequisites for high morale and a good group spirit are the basic compatibility of members, the sharing of common goals, clearly stated and realistic targets, and fair and just management. Another interesting factor is that of *elitism*, that the team and its members are a cut above the average.

This feeling of being special or at least different in a superior sort of way is a good morale booster. It may emerge from the well-functioning group naturally, or from some prompting by the leader from time to time. Examples are given by Susan Wooldridge (op. cit.):

> 'There is a wide range of possible characteristics that members of a team may take as evidence that they are an elite. They may be the most experienced group in the department, or have a history of past success—notches in their belts. Their project may be the toughest one yet undertaken in the department, or the one with the most potential benefit to the company. They may be the biggest project team, or the smallest and most cohesive, or the most difficult to join. A reverse scale of values is possible, too: they may have the nastiest users, the most incompetent manager, or the lowest priority on computer time for testing, i.e. they face greater obstacles than other teams.'

As Susan Wooldridge goes on to say, it does not matter if the belief of an elite conforms to reality or not, as long as all members of the team subscribe to it. It becomes yet another strong, positive belief shared by the members of the group, providing a common bond.

High morale will be encouraged by the leader applying an appropriate decision-making style, and considering the hints shown in Figure 8.5.

Summary

1. Many systems analysts are required to assume some project leadership functions. The job of the project leader and the techniques used require the same analysis and study as the technical job content of investigation, analysis, and design.

2. The job of a project leader can be seen as the same as that for any manager, as shown in Figure 6.1. The major asset that the project leader has is his people. He must therefore consider their acquisition, their development, the provision of a good working environment, and an effective way of putting them to work and monitoring their performance.

3. The responsibility and authority of the project leader varies from organization to organization. The greater the constraints placed on the project leader (as in Figure 8.1), the more his freedom of action is reduced. Too many constraints may eliminate the leadership function altogether.

4. The personality approach to leadership has to a great extent been replaced by the behavioural approach. This recognizes that effective leadership depends not only on the forces in the leader, but also those in the group members and of the situation.

5. Good and bad characteristics of the leader from the typical analyst's point of view are shown in Figure 8.2. The good leader is flexible in choosing a decision-making style to suit himself, the group and the situation.

6. The decision-making style depends on the amount of authority retained by the leader versus that assumed by the group (Figure 8.3). There is no one inherently 'right' decision-making style. The consultation method appears to be most suitable for data processing personnel.

7. Ten hints for better project leadership, as in Figure 8.5, were described. The most important factor is that the leader thinks about his role as a leader and does not become simply a super-technician.

Part III

Communication techniques

Note to Part III

Communication is an important part of any analyst's job. It includes communication with his team, his management, his colleagues and with all levels of user staff.

This part consists of four short chapters which present techniques for the following:

- presentations
- reports
- group meetings
- special illustrative techniques.

The techniques are presented as a series of checklists, supplemented by a discussion in the text.

9
Presentations

There are many occasions when the analyst is called upon to make a presentation. A presentation could be required to supplement a report at any checkpoint shown in Figure 1.5 as, for example, to present the findings of the feasibility study to users. The analyst will probably have to organize and present pre-implementation training sessions to all levels of user staff. He may also have to present training sessions to his own management and colleagues. Designing and delivering a presentation are thus important aspects of the analyst's job. A good presentation makes a satisfactory conclusion to a project phase. A poor presentation can damage or destroy weeks of carefully planned and conscientiously executed project work.

The key to a successful presentation is thorough preparation. This can be difficult because if project work is behind, the only time which can be made up is in the preparation of the report or presentation which comes at the end of the phase. One solution to this problem is to begin preparation as early as possible in the phase and not to leave it as an afterthought. For example, the basic strategy and the sequence and form of the material can be designed early in the phase and the material organized accordingly as work proceeds. This means that the preparation of the presentation at the end of the phase is a tidying up operation, slotting the facts and figures into place.

Organizing the material

There are many factors in the design of a presentation as shown in Figure 9.1. The material from the project work is to be presented; the amount of consultation during the phase will determine the presentation content and style.

The objectives for the presentation must be set out very carefully. These are what the presentation must achieve, not what the presentation is going to do. For example, 'To explain the findings of the feasibility study' is not an objective but a statement of what will happen during the presentation. An objective could be: 'To present the findings of the feasibility study so that user management can make a rational decision as to the action to be taken.' We must distinguish between formal objectives and the analyst's personal thesis. For example, there could be a supplementary objective to the above which couldn't be announced at the beginning of the presentation: 'To show that we've done a good job so far, we know what we're doing, and we can be trusted with future work.'

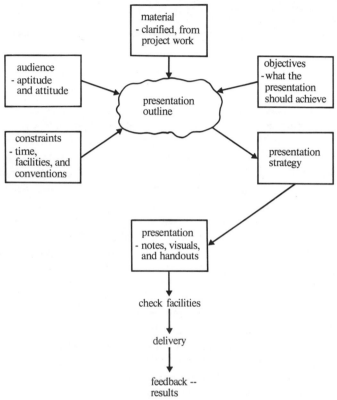

Figure 9.1:   Organizing the material

The duration of the presentation will normally be limited, and matching the material against objectives is the acid test as to whether it is included. The objectives will also be used to determine the strategy. Far too many presentations have no real form, but are a serial succession of facts and figures. Examples of strategies are shown in Figure 9.2.

The audience should be consulted in advance whenever possible. The development of presentation should not be like the preparation of a Budget Speech, cloaked in secrecy, a guessing game between analyst and users. Again, whenever possible, the presenter should say something of interest or promise to each individual in the audience; but he must never make promises that cannot be kept. Generally, management and workers should not be mixed at one presentation.

Preparation

With good understanding of the material to be presented, clear objectives, a defined strategy, and an understanding of the audience, detailed preparation can begin.

Figure 9.2:   Presentation strategies

Poorer:

1. *The strategy of direct assault*: prove how terrible the old method was and how much better the new (computer) solution will be.
2. *Put the burden of proof on the audience*: 'We challenge you to show our ideas are no good.'
3. *Shift attention to minor points*: especially effective in diverting attention away from what will not bear examination; for example, demonstrate how the terminal works to prevent questions about how much it will cost.

Better :

4. *Use the opposition's arguments*: acknowledge limitations, problems, and faults *before* they are brought to your attention. Very disarming.
5. *Intentional concealment of objectives*: present the evidence to support the conclusion before stating the conclusion. Leave the main point to the end. Use this one carefully.
6. *The strategy of withholding proofs*: use your weakest justification first. When that is questioned, bring out the next strongest one, etc., saving the most effective argument for the end.
7. *The horns-of-dilemma strategy*: start by presenting a seemingly insoluble problem: 'The present system will break down in six months, but a computer system will take at least a year to develop.' What to do? Then present your heroic rescue.

The presentation must follow a logical sequence, with each argument built up with all the premises being revealed which support the conclusions. One of the best ways to build a case is expressed in the old adage:

- tell 'em what you're going to tell 'em
- tell it to 'em
- tell 'em what you've told 'em.

This is a good guide, but it must not be overplayed otherwise a very stereotyped and stylized presentation will result. If the presentation is too contrived and slick, the audience will think they are being oversold, and will react accordingly.

Special attention should be paid to the introduction. This should include the objectives of the meeting, a summary of method, and the time allowed, how questions will be dealt with, and the role of handouts.

Not only must the material to be presented be prepared, but also back-up material which will not form part of the formal presentation, but will be held in reserve for questions should be assembled.

The form of presentation notes is important. They must be usable. One method is to use key words which describe the major topics. The notes should be a *guide*—it is important that the analyst does not become note-bound, e.g., that he is thrown by a question which interrupts the flow and sequence.

The presentation should be rehearsed but not memorized. Most presentations are not speeches that must be written out word-for-word and

Figure 9.3:   Summary of visual aids and their usage

Blackboards	Used effectively as a 'scratch pad'
	Don't leave awkward silences while you write
	Don't write complete sentences—use key words
Flipcharts	Used effectively for checklists and some diagrams
	Can be prepared by analyst
	Better than a blackboard because they can be prepared in advance
	Be careful how you limit the amount of material on one page:
	too much—will be confusing and will lose attention
	too little—presentation will be 'bitty'—it will look like an amateurish 'hard sell'
	Ensure visuals can be seen at the back of the room, that the stand is stable, that you can turn pages easily without going on tip-toe and doing yourself an injury
Overhead slide projectors	Used effectively for complex diagrams (flow diagrams, costings, etc.)
	Can normally be prepared by analyst
	An overhead projector allows the speaker control and can be used in an un-darkened room
	Practise in advance and check visibility
	Treat a slide projector as you would a loaded gun—switch it on only when it is being used and use it only when there is a point to be made
	Have plans for what you do when the projector doesn't work
35 mm slide projectors	Used effectively for illustrations of equipment, complex completed documents or displays, etc.
	Must be used in a darkened room
	Sequence of slides can be controlled automatically
	Must be prepared professionally

then read. A dry run is useful to test the timing, although the value of other conclusions that can be drawn from it is debatable. Some dry runs are very successful followed by disaster on the day; others are disasters in rehearsal and very satisfactory on the day.

Visual aids

Visual aids are an essential part of any presentation. The basic facilities include blackboards, flipcharts, overhead projectors, and 35 mm slide projectors. More sophisticated equipment can include film projectors, models, and magnetic boards. We will concentrate here on the basic facilities.

Variety is important, with a selection of methods being used, but the

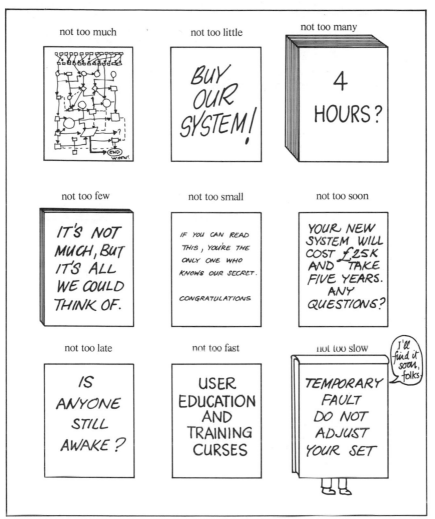

Figure 9.4: Guidelines for preparing flipcharts (From: Successful Presentations, *Keith London, London, 1973.)*

analyst must not become a gadgeteer, using visual aids just for the sake of it. A summary of facilities is shown in Figure 9.3.

For any pre-prepared visual aid, consider the following:

- Choose the amount of material per visual and the number of visuals carefully, as in the guidelines for flipcharts in Figure 9.4.
- Check the sequence carefully.
- Practise in advance.
- Talk to the audience, not the display.

The facilities

If at all possible, the facilities should be checked by *the presenter* before the presentation. There is nothing more frustrating, or apparently unprofessional, than to be caught out by minor irritations of faulty equipment and poor accommodation. A checklist of points to watch is shown in Figure 9.5.

Delivery

Most people have the ability to stand on their feet and to talk to an audience, making at least a reasonable attempt to get their point across. To improve on

Figure 9.5: Checking facilities

---

1. Check the room out for basic facilities:
    —seating
    —size
    —noise
    —access
    —acoustics

2. If there is to be a small group (less than 12) in a management presentation, consider the use of a horseshoe arrangement—it will encourage discussion.

3. Check the sight lines to the blackboards, flipcharts, screen, etc.

4. Practise with the equipment that will be used on the day. (Can you change the slides without spreading them on the floor and shuffling them on your hands and knees? Can you move from one blackboard to another, wearing a throat microphone, without garrotting yourself? Can you move freely to all your visual aids/notes without giving the impression that you are tackling an obstacle course?)

5. If you are taking your own equipment, check that it can be used in the room.

6. If you are using other people's equipment, check (just before the presentation) that it is all in working order. This will get round the blackboard collapsing in the middle of your crucial summary, as well as avoiding a hernia when you lower the screen, etc.

---

this basic ability requires practice, as in using exercises in voice modulation. Rules for delivery should polish one's natural style, not inhibit it. Guidelines for delivery are given in Figure 9.6.

Problem situations

The three situations frequently identified by analysts as problem areas are nerves, dealing with questions and the use of handouts.

Nerves

Most experienced and accomplished speakers get nervous before an important speech or presentation. Nerves are simply anxiety and apprehension about the outcome of the presentation. They can give the analyst an edge, that extra sparkle in the performance. They become a problem when they interfere with his delivery. One way of dealing with nerves is to try to understand the reason for them:

'I don't want to make a fool of myself.'

'I've worked on this project for three months and I don't want to muff this final part.'

'The audience will contain some very difficult people who will be gunning for me.'

Figure 9.6: Guidelines for delivery

---

1. Work out *in detail* what you are going to say as opening remarks. Also, work out your closing remarks—don't just trail off.

2. Every word, action (such as a pause), and diagram will count. Be mindful of the overtones of your message.

3. Learn your peculiar mannerisms—and distracting idiosyncrasies. Cultivate those that are useful—try to stop those that are bad. This goes for repeated words as well—'you know', 'OK?', 'basically'.

4. Enthusiasm, interest, and pace go a long way in keeping the audience's attention and getting your points across.

5. Vary the pace (but don't have too much contrast). Above all try to vary the tone of your speaking. There is nothing worse than listening to a monotone—except having every word/ statement starting and finishing with a flourish of 'ummms', 'ahs', etc.

6. Speak with authority and keep control—don't treat your audience like under-fives.

7. Speak clearly—your words must be understood by everybody present. But don't be too artificial with your enunciation. (Try to avoid those words which you have difficulty pro nouncing.)

8. Look at the audience—try to get feedback—but don't stop and query every smirk, scowl, puzzled frown, etc., or fix a particular member of the audience with a beady stare.

9. Make certain that your actions support your words, that you cover what you say you are going to cover.

It won't cure nerves, but it will probably enable the analyst to live with them. The best way to get nerves under control is to be well prepared and to work out in detail what to say in the first few minutes. This will enable the speaker to get over the first few moments of shock and get into his stride.

Questions

Answering questions is one of the most effective ways of presenting information and persuading people. How questions are to be dealt with during the presentation should be announced in the introduction. Questions which seek to clarify material should never be inhibited, e.g. never say 'No questions until we've finished'. On the other hand, 'time for a general discussion has been allowed at the end after you have seen the system as a whole so please leave general comments until then,' is a reasonable request.

The reasons which lie behind a question vary. For example, at a management presentation, a question can mean:

'Look, I'm awake.'
'Look, I know more than he does.'
'Look, I actually understand what he's saying.'
'I'm setting him up by asking him a loaded question—when he answers, I'll get him.'
'I want to know something.'
'I'm selling something.'

The apparent motive behind the question must be considered when the answer is given. The timing of the answer is important. To some questions an immediate answer should be given; to others a pause for thought will be more effective. Some questions are better answered with a question to clarify the terms or assumptions of the questioner.

If the analyst doesn't know the answer, he should be cautious of giving an instant opinion. If it really is a tough question, the questioner should be thanked for raising the point and told that it will be looked into—after the presentation.

The *heckler* or persistent questioner can be a menace. If the presentation is going well (and he is not the managing director) the audience will take care of him. Another problem is the *idiot questioner* who asks a very basic point that was covered in depth earlier in the presentation. (Also included is the question that has no possible relevance to the point being covered.) There are no shortcuts in this situation—except not to lose one's temper or humiliate the questioner. One technique is to purposely misinterpret the question or to ask the questioner for further information about what he's getting at.

Handouts

Most presentations are accompanied by a full report. There is often the need for a handout prepared specifically for the presentation. For example, the sequence of material covered in the report may be different from that in the presentation. The handout should include copies of all visuals; the text is best organized into checklists with the full narrative given in the main report.

Should all the handouts be distributed at the start of the meeting? Some experts say no—it will distract the audience from the presentation. If the presentation is so poor that it doesn't hold the audience's attention, they will find something else to distract them anyway. If the material to be covered is new to the audience, they will be curious about the handout; a quick review of the material during the introduction will probably remove most of the temptation to shuffle the papers during the actual presentation.

10
Reports

Types of reports and the role of standards

Data processing reports can be divided into three basic classes as shown in Figure 10.1. In this chapter we are concerned with the construction and narrative for class 1 and 2 reports. The contents of class 3 reports are usually controlled by rigid standards, such as by the use of pre-printed forms which must be completed in a highly stylized format.

There is one major difference between a presentation and a report. A presentation is (or should be) a two-way process, with the analyst seeking and reacting to feedback from the audience. A report, however, tends to be a rather more passive one-way means of communication. In a presentation the analyst has the users in one place and can hold their attention not only by the content of the material itself, but by means of attractively presented material and by his own personality. The preparation of a report thus requires the same type of careful planning (if not more) as that required for a presentation. The diagram in Figure 9.1 is also applicable to report writing. The following require special attention:

- *Know your audience*: be sure you know who will be reading the report. Find out as much as you can about what their attitudes might be, as well as what knowledge and experience they have.
- *Know your own attitudes*: what is your attitude toward your readers? For example, if they are known to be hostile to the idea of a computer system, however irrationally, this can cause you to be hostile, negative, or condescending. Be careful not to let such attitudes show through in your writing.
- *Decide on your purpose and tone*: as a general rule, the writer of a business report should be 'invisible'; his personality and prejudices should not be obvious or obstruct the objective message of the report. There is some latitude within this restriction, however.

Defining the objectives of the report and its strategy is as important as for a presentation.

To prepare a report, the analyst must have to hand not only the material but also the house-rules and standards. These should cover the house-rules and the standards for the specific report. Examples of these are shown in Figure 10.2.

House-rules and report standards should help rather than inhibit, the analyst's writing. For example, a standard table of contents for each report will act as a guide not only during the writing of the report, it will also provide an outline which the analyst can work towards during the project. This means that the material can be accumulated during the project work in

Figure 10.1: Types of data processing reports

Class 1: States case for a management decision; mainly narrative. Examples:

- user request
- feasibility study
- post-implementation survey report
- hardware/software procurement and development plans

Class 2: Describes a situation for general approval or reference; narrative with diagrams.

- results of fact-finding interview for user agreement
- training manuals
- standards

Class 3: Specifies a system for action; very rigid, stylized format.

- input, output, file specifications
- operating instructions
- system/program logic

---

the sequence and format of the report. Report writing thus becomes a task of tidying up the material, putting the final touches to its organization and presentation. (This is important; as discussed in Chapter 9, it is the presentation or report which will usually suffer if project work slips.)

Within the house-rules and standards, the analyst will have considerable freedom in the organization of material and style, especially in class 1 and 2 reports in Figure 10.1.

Steps in report writing

Figure 10.3 summarizes the steps in preparing a report. Note that each of these steps is an activity and will therefore require facilities and time. Without adequate planning and scheduling, delays and frustration will result; for example, the draft is prepared and no typing facilities are available, the final copy is ready for proof reading and the analyst is on a course, or the final copy is produced and reproduction facilities are not available.

The outline

Preparing an outline for a report is similar to preparing a program flowchart before coding. The flowchart is a check that all conditions/actions have been included, the logic is valid and the sequence is correct. It is easier to use an outline flowchart to correct an error and test the logic than it is the coding. When a flowchart has been proved, the programmer can focus his attention

Figure 10.2:   Report house-rules and standards

For all reports
- Identification
- Amendment procedure
- Page/paragraph numbering
- Cross-referencing
- Illustration numbering
- Page layouts and spacing
- Typestyles
- Weights of heading
- Diagram standards for
  —cost tables
  —timing tables
  —decision tables
  —system flow diagrams
- Standard abbreviations
  (e.g. VDU as V.D.U.)
- Standards for
  —spelling (disc versus disk)
  —hyphenation (real-time versus real time)
  —numbers (3 or three)
  —capitals (RJE versus rje)
- Reproduction and binding

For each report
- Objectives
- Distribution list
- Table of contents
- Contents and format by chapter
- Title and identification
- Length
- Special forms and techniques
- Examples

on the coding knowing that he is working from a sound base. By analogy, a report outline is used to ensure that all relevant material is included and extraneous material excluded, that the sequence is correct and that there is a logical development.

There are any number of systems for preparing an outline. A popular one is to identify the headings as:

```
I ....
   A ....
      1 ....
         (a) ....
            (1) ....
               (i) ....
```

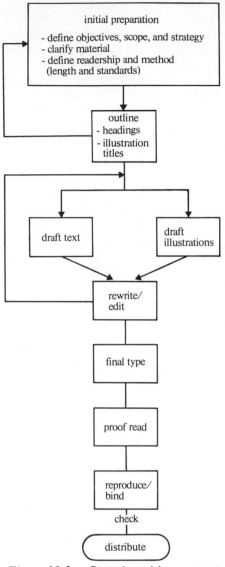

Figure 10.3:   Steps in writing a report

Entries of the same weight should be of the same level of importance and expressed in the same grammatical form. For example, if A is a noun, B, C, etc., should be nouns.

There should be no single entries; for example, if there is (1) under (a), there should be at least (2) as well.

The outline is edited against the criteria of objectives, strategy, and readership. For each entry on the outline, two questions are asked: 'Is this item absolutely necessary?'; 'Is this item in the right sequence?'

Determining the length of a report is never easy. An example from a senior systems analyst:

> 'We did ten man-years of work in a local government authority. The senior management insisted on a six-page summary report. How could we do justice to all this work in six pages. How could we show that we'd done a good, thorough job?'

It is *content* that matters, *not bulk*. The answer here was to produce a summary report as requested and to send this with a comprehensive (and impressive) supplementary report. The latter had to be produced for junior management anyway. Nobody really expected senior management to read the supplementary; it showed by detail that a thorough job had been done.

Another example, from a consultant:

> 'Some clients measure the tangible product of an assignment—the length of the report—as well as the findings and recommendations. The client pays £20 000 for advice. Give him a 20-page report which says only and exactly what we want to say and he looks at it, does his sums and says 'Good heavens, that's £1000 per page!'

Again it is the quality of the content not the quantity of content that counts. If there is the attitude that value = length then the author's advice is:

● Drop the fee marginally and explain at the beginning of the job that a short report will be submitted, and
● explain that for an extra fee, tidied-up working papers can be provided as a supplementary report.
● Hire a large van (anyway) and deliver four full filing cabinets of all working papers.

The first draft

How many computer programs compile first time without any diagnostics? How many complete programs work 100 per cent correctly on all test shots first time? In a typical commercial installation, the answer is very few, if any. By analogy, very few first draft reports are completely satisfactory. In contrast with programming, report writing is for human not machine consumption and the English language is being used rather than a highly artificial programming language. The conclusion is that the secret of the first draft is to get the material down on paper. The first draft concentrates on the *ideas*. Later editing and rewriting can correct the grammar and spelling, and improve the style. Working from the outline, the writer develops the material by using sentences and paragraphs.

The paragraph is the basic unit of composition. It can be thought of as a whole work in miniature. A paragraph should be unified; it contains the development of *one main idea*. Paragraphs can correspond to sub-headings on the outline, although several sub-headings may be covered in one paragraph or several paragraphs may be used for one sub-heading.

As a general rule, a single sentence should not form a paragraph. Exceptions are where a paragraph acts as a transition from one subject to another or for a summary with strong emphasis.

The first sentence of a paragraph should either state or suggest the topic or provide transition from the previous paragraph. For example:

'Punched cards provide greater flexibility.'
'Although punched cards provide greater flexibility, paper tape has its advantages too.'

The sentences which follow should give details and examples.

How the paragraphing will look in print is also important. Long blocks without a break are daunting for the reader; it may be necessary to break one paragraph into two or more, at some logical place. Too many short paragraphs can look disorganized and be distracting.

There are many excellent texts on writing style. The best, invaluable for any writer, is *Elements of Style* by William Strunk, Jr, and E. B. White (Macmillan Company, New York, 2nd edn, 1972). From the author's point of view, any advice on writing style would simply repeat the contents of that book! The discussions here, therefore, will concentrate on some general guidelines on style.

The writer of a business or technical report is striving for three things:

1. Clarity
2. Precision
3. Conciseness.

In doing so, the following are out of place in most reports written by the analyst:

    jokes
    puns
    colloquialisms
    slang
    dialect
    poetic or flowery language
    pretension
    condescension to the reader
    double-entendre—intentional or unintentional
    use of the first person
    foreign expressions, except when no English equivalent exists.

The reader is referred to Strunk and White for specific guidelines on style.

Rewriting

If at all possible, the first draft should be put aside for at least 24 hours before attempting to check and revise it. The draft should be read, several times if necessary, looking for the following points:

- adequate development of central ideas
- sequence of ideas
- sentence structure
- paragraphing
- transitions
- grammar
- spelling
- capitalization
- punctuation
- conformance to company standards.

One read through of the report should be devoted to simply reducing the length by *omitting needless words.*

Using scissors, paste, staples, etc., parts of the report should be rearranged as required. Fresh copy should be written out if revisions become so extensive that the writer or typist cannot follow them easily.

Whenever possible, another person should read through the draft and make suggestions for improvements.

Production and reproduction

A badly produced report can destroy its credibility. A neat, clean appearance is important. Remember that typing errors can be magnified out of all proportion in the eyes of the reader. No matter how much pressure there is to issue the report, it must be proof read carefully.

11

Group meetings

Meetings are expensive. A three-hour meeting of a dozen senior data processing staff could cost £200 to £300 (including overheads). It is vital, therefore, that a meeting gives value for money. Meetings which are frequently unproductive or frustrating will bring them into disrepute, making them even more worthless. It will also call the credibility of the manager or group leader into question. This chapter reviews methods for increasing the effectiveness of group meetings.

Types of meetings

Any business meeting will have one or more of the following functions:

1. Define a problem
2. Solve a problem
3. Plan for implementing a solution
4. Set goals
5. Analyse obstacles
6. Make decisions
7. Agree a course of action
8. Gather information.

Individuals attending a meeting, on the other hand, may have other reasons, conscious or unconscious. For example:

1. Air a grievance
2. Exert authority
3. Change attitudes of others
4. Enhance own status
5. Gain admiration
6. Gain sympathy
7. Learn new things.

A clash between the purpose of the meeting and objectives of the individual will be frustrating and counter-productive.

The first requirement is to define clearly the specific objectives of the meeting. The second is to have a chairman or group leader who recognizes and responds to the personal objectives of the members and, where these are in conflict, will attempt some reconciliation.

Setting up the meeting

Figure 11.1 is a checklist for setting up the meeting. The way in which a meeting is organized will influence how people react during it. If the meeting is formal, then there will probably be rigid rules of conduct (such as Roberts' rules of order).

Figure 11.1: The mechanics of setting up a meeting

---

1. Be sure all members know about the meeting, its purpose(s), and the time it is expected to take.

2. If necessary, a specific list of decisions should be circulated in advance (as in the sample memo in Figure 6.7).

3. Make every effort to plan the meeting so all can attend.

4. The meeting room should be:
   big enough, but not too big
   well-ventilated
   comfortable
   private

5. Start on time and keep as far as possible to the time-table.

6. If there are papers, reports, etc., to hand out, have enough copies for everyone.

7. Try to head off interruptions; disconnect the telephone, etc.
   Try to break at a logical point.

8. If the meeting is long, have a 10 to 15 minute break every 1 to $1\frac{1}{2}$ hours. Have coffee, etc., served outside the room during a break.

9. The leader is the 'host' and should have extra pencils, paper, etc., available in case needed.

For a standing committee such as a steering committee, a user liaison officer committee or a standards committee, a major decision will be the role of substitutes. Many hours can be lost in fruitless discussions if this problem is not tackled at the outset. For example, a committee of user liaison officers if formed. One liaison officer cannot attend a particular meeting. Will a substitute be allowed to attend? If the answer is yes, then the following may happen.

● the substitute isn't properly prepared for the meeting
● old arguments are re-opened because the substitute wasn't in on them originally
● the standing member of the committee contradicts the advice or decisions of the substitute at a later meeting

255

This can be prevented by banning substitutes altogether on important committees, or by formally nominating substitutes and allowing time for them to study and prepare for all sessions.

Discussing the optimum size of a meeting is similar to generalizing the number of subordinates that a manager can control: there can be no hard and fast rule. For most meetings, a limit of no more than 10 or 12 members is apparently a frequently quoted number. Perhaps the last word on this subject can be left to C. Northcote Parkinson (the coefficient of inefficiency): that if the number of people exceeds 21, a member must stand to be heard. Once on his feet, the member cannot help but make a speech. At this point efficiency becomes impossible!

The leader and the group

A meeting, formal or informal, is a dynamic situation, where group members interact with each other and with the leader. To understand how and what happens at a meeting, it is therefore important to study the characteristics and attitudes of both leader and members.

Most meetings will have a leader, whether formally or informally acknowledged. There is no one set of characteristics which determines the best leader in all situations. For most meetings in which the analyst will be involved, however, the characteristics of a good group leader appear to be as follows:

1. A well-adjusted personality
2. A basic respect and concern for human beings
3. Sensitivity to the basic trends and needs of the group
4. Reasonable knowledge of the problems being discussed
5. Facility to articulate the ideas of the group
6. Reasonable restraint
7. Vitality
8. Mellowness.

The role of the leader will be to achieve the cooperation of members and thereby further the aims of the meeting. He will probably do this by recognizing people's limitations and rights, *and being seen to do so.*

Voluntary contributions will be encouraged through providing emotional support. Although the leader can join in all discussions on the subject matter of the meeting, he must exercise more self-control when speaking than the members of the group. Any member of the group can act this way and perform these functions. If he is the only one doing so, he will probably become the recognized leader of the meeting.

If the role of the leader can be formally defined as above, a member of the group will probably assume the role informally. For example, the productive roles are:

1. The information giver

2. The information seeker
3. The critic
4. The expediter
5. The clarifier
6. The conciliator
7. The organizer.

The non-productive roles are the member acting as a recognition seeker, as a dominator, or as a pessimist.

An individual may change roles a number of times in any one meeting. The function of the leader is to draw on the productive roles and to suppress the destructive ones.

Figure 11.2: Productive services vital for a successful meeting

1. Initiating discussion
2. Summarizing and transition making
3. Recording the discussion
4. Clock watching
5. Side-tracking irrelevancies
6. Elaborating ideas
7. Seeking further opinions
8. Testing validity of ideas
9. Seeking further information
10. Reality testing
11. Setting standards
12. Pointing out similarities
13. Pointing out differences
14. Resolving conflicts
15. Concluding the discussion

The group at work

Each individual at the meeting will, from time to time, perform some of the functions as shown in Figure 11.2. All these functions are vital to the conduct of the meeting. Where they are not forthcoming from the group, they must be performed by the leader.

It has been found that informal conversations and socializing outside of the meeting are beneficial. Private talks and lobbying outside of meetings are also beneficial, as long as the goals of the group are being furthered. At the meeting, the group should proceed step by step through the circulated agenda. Even the most informal, free-ranging, problem-solving meeting needs an agenda, although in this case it will probably have only one entry: the objective of the meeting, a summary of the problem to be discussed, and the output required from the meeting.

Satisfactory progress will only be made if all participants of the group recognize the following:

1. That an analysis of premises and variables must precede reaching conclusions and most making decisions
2. That an orderly approach is essential to problem solving
3. That facts and opinions must be separated and recognized accordingly
4. That all members understand and subscribe to the group strategy and its goals.

The leader should from time to time ensure that all group members recognize and agree these points. Where the same group meets regularly, the points should be openly discussed, as a way of improving group productivity.

A meeting, like a formal presentation, should never be allowed to tail off. It must end in a positive way. The conclusions of the meeting can include an assertion of intention to act or even challenge or appeal to succeed. The main points agreed should be summarized together with a statement of points of disagreement or things left to be done. A review should also be made of tasks and specific assignments. A record of the meeting (the minutes) should be produced for each session. Only important, decision-making meetings need to be minuted in detail, i.e. an almost verbatim report of the proceedings. Minutes are best prepared by the leader. Each decision taken should be clearly stated. Where tasks have been issued to members, these should be clearly identified, for example, by putting 'for action by . . .' separately in the margin. Minutes should be circulated as soon as possible, e.g. the same day or next day.

Problem situations

Common problem situations are:

- one person dominates the discussion
- one person never contributes
- conflict
- a general lack of interest
- discussion drifts into irrelevancies.

Each of these problem situations has a short-term and long-term solution: short term to prevent disaster at a particular meeting, long term to avoid it again in the future.

The dominator

One person can dominate a discussion because he has a special knowledge of, or interest in, a particular topic. Alternatively, one person can dominate because of a vested interest, a grievance, or a desire to exercise or demonstrate personal power or influence. In either case it is important that domination does not exclude or diminish other people's points of view.

Where one member has a special knowledge or interest, then this should be presented in an organized way. For example:

> 'Fred, before we all discuss this point, I think 10 or 15 minutes from you would be useful because of your special knowledge of. . . .'

This can be done at the beginning or (less desirable) at the end of the discussion of the topic. If the member is notoriously verbose, he can be invited to submit a written paper to the other group members *before* the meeting. The introduction is then:

> 'Fred, you've prepared a paper on . . . which we've all read, so let's get straight on and discuss it.'

The negative dominator, the second case above, is more difficult to deal with. Many dominators speak with airy generalizations; asking for specifics can have a salutory effect in shutting them up. Alternatively, questions can be directed to others. Where this is a recurrent problem, it might be possible to set time limits on speeches, but this is almost an admission of failure. Most domination comes from interjection and general remarks rather than formal statements.

The long-term solution is to correct the dominator tactfully after the meeting. If the seniority and authority of the leader permits, as a last resort, the destructive dominator can be assigned to another job—such as taking notes!

The non-contributor

One person never contributes. It could be that he has nothing to say, that he is hesitant and nervous about expressing his views, or he is dominated by other members of the group. The first rule is never to embarrass him. In the short term, it may be possible to draw him out by asking him a few easy questions, then asking directly for his opinion. Long term, counselling outside the meeting may help. Provided there is no atmosphere of conspiracy, the help of other members of the group can be enlisted to draw him out. If the problem is one of nerves or one of articulation, then a public speaking course may be of benefit. The non-contributor could be suppressed by a dominator, in which case the comments above may be of help.

Conflict

Conflict at a meeting is not necessarily bad. It can encourage new and valid ideas. It can lead to a lively discussion which (at least) keeps people interested in the proceedings. It can, however, be frustrating and personally acrimonious.

The conflict could be a clash of opinion or interpretation, or it could be a dispute about facts. The latter is perhaps best dealt with by asking the antagonists to be specific, not general.

Personality clashes and disputes of opinion are harder to deal with. Some ideas are:

- Backtrack and restate the variables, the facts, and the criteria for the solution—ground rules in their interpretation in making a decision.
- Remind the group of areas where they do agree.
- Use humour to relieve tension.
- Have the whole group list items of disagreement; rank them in order of hostility; then tackle them one at a time, starting with the least difficult.
- Recess and seek to resolve hostility informally.
- Divide the group into smaller groups to separate the antagonists, then have each group try to resolve them.

Each of these methods has its advantages and disadvantages. The last two, for example, can simply suppress conflict, leading to the same or bigger battle later on. It is up to the sensitivity of the leader to select the best solution to be tried at a particular time.

Nowhere is conflict so strong as in small, informal design sessions, where each member gradually becomes more and more emotionally (as well as intellectually) committed to his own particular ideas. This is an inherent problem of the totally free-form, problem-solving sessions which encourage open criticism. Conflict may be ameliorated by the following techniques:

- As a general (but not the absolute) rule, no idea can be criticized or demolished unless the critic can suggest an alternative method or solution.
- In areas where conflict exists between two people with apparently irreconcilable ideas, one member is asked to explain his idea clearly and succinctly, with all the supporting assumptions. The other protagonist is then asked to explain the idea to the satisfaction of the first member. The process is then reversed. This takes place before any further discussion takes place.

The last method can be very useful in heated design sessions. It achieves two things that can go by the board in the heat of the argument: that terms are purposely misinterpreted and that the antagonists refuse to *listen* to each other's arguments.

General lack of interest

There are many causes of a general malaise, leading to a shuffling of papers, yawns, and longer and longer awkward silences. There are a number of solutions to this situation, depending on the leader's assumption of the cause.

- introduce humour
- break a larger group into smaller sub-groups
- have a recess
- drop the immediate topic and move to another
- move towards specifics, away from generalities
- introduce conflicts by, say, asking a controversial question.

Irrelevancies

This situation may be similar to a general lack of interest. It could be that one man's interest (the member's) is another man's (the leader's) irrelevance! Some solutions are:

- use questions to bring them back to the point under discussion
- remind them of the agreed topic
- cite specific cases or examples
- summarize and introduce the next topic
- assign one person to keep the group going.

The leader should be anticipating the problems that can arise and looking for solutions as described in this chapter. He may try an approach which doesn't resolve the situation. In this case he can do one of three things:

- Stop *immediately* and try a different way.
- Summarize and go on to another topic with a comment that he'll think about this and return to it.
- Explain the problem and ask *the group* to decide on a better way of dealing with it.

12
Special illustrative techniques

The role of illustrations

Good illustrations are invaluable in any report or presentation. Illustrations will make a report or presentation visually appealing—people will want to read or look. Many users are bored with reports, with page after page of typed, numbered paragraphs. In some cases, diagrams are essential because narrative is unsuitable. Why do programmers use flowcharts instead of narrative? It is because narrative is unsuitable for describing 'if . . . then' conditions represented by a diamond in a flowchart. There are also occasions when illustrations are not essential but useful. For example, some ideas are best represented in diagrammatic form because less space is required, more information can be assimilated by the reader (i.e., there is a wider span of comprehension), and trends are easily discernible.

Many analysts do not use illustrations simply because they have never been trained in graphic techniques and have never considered their relevance to data processing reports and presentations. This chapter will describe techniques for the following:

- graphs
- histograms and bar charts
- pie-charts
- pictograms (symbol charts)
- decision tables
- summary diagrams.

The relevance of each technique to data processing reports is discussed, together with example uses and rules for its application.

Graphs

A graph is used to show the relationship between two quantities—variables— with a continuous curve. There is a continuous relationship between two quantities when a set of values can be obtained. The graph has discrete values marked on the vertical axis and the horizontal axis. By convention, the independent variable is placed on the horizontal axis and the dependent variable on the vertical axis.

The independent variable is the value which is not affected by the other value, the dependent variable, being measured. An example is shown in Figure 12.1. The independent variable here is time, the dependent variable (value measured) is key punching throughout. The graph shows a continuous relationship between these two variables.

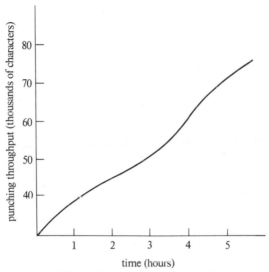

Figure 12.1:   Sample graph

A graph can be used to indicate a general trend or so that a specific value can be calculated. The former is used to show a number of discrete plots and it would not be strictly correct to interpolate between these points. An example is shown in Figure 12.2(a). The purpose of this graph is to show a trend: that over the seven-year life of a system, the cost of the system rises one way, and the value of frauds prevented decreases in another way. It would be accurate to assume that at 3 years 3 months the frauds would be £4,500.

The second case is shown in Figure 12.2(b). This graph shows not only a trend, but can also be used to calculate the estimated run time, given a specific volume of input.

In designing the graph the following must be considered:

● number, identification, and direction of curves
● choice of grid
● scale values and identification.

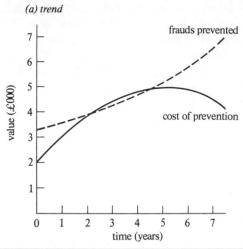

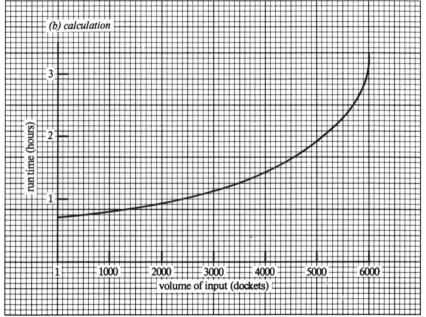

Figure 12.2:   Graphs to show trends versus detail

CURVES

The number of curves should be limited to no more than three or four on one graph. A general trend which could be represented by a family of curves is best shown by a typical curve or upper and lower limits. If the curves overlap and could be misread, solid and broken lines should be used as in Figure 12.2(a).

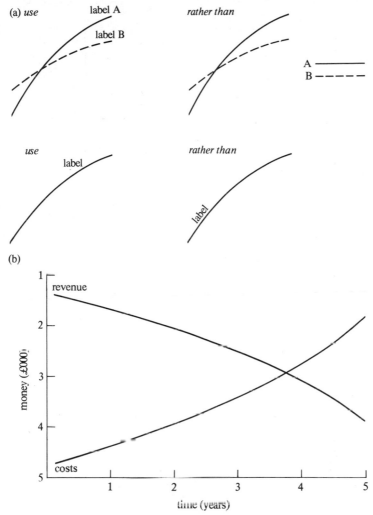

Figure 12.3: Graph curves

Labels are understood more easily and rapidly than legends. Labels should be kept horizontal; if they arc printed on a curve they are difficult to prepare and read. See the example in Figure 12.3(a). The direction of the curve is important. In one report studied by the author, the message was that the system would decrease costs and increase revenue. The analyst had plotted money on a downward, increasing scale on the vertical axis as shown in Figure 12.3(b).

GRID

Very fine gradations should be avoided if the graph is to be published or

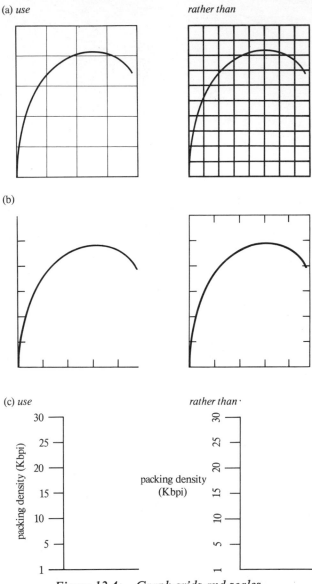

Figure 12.4:   Graph grids and scales

projected at a presentation. Heavy-lined grids will distract from the curves. A skeleton grid showing only essential lines is preferable when a trend is being shown; see Figure 12.4(a). Also useful for trends is the stub grid which can be framed or unframed as shown in Figure 12.4(b). Where there is a wide range of values, such as 0.01 to 1000, logarithmic paper will have to be used.

The scale should be uniform and consistent, otherwise the shape of the curve will be distorted. Scale captions should be kept simple, using key words rather than complete sentences. The unit of measurement must always be shown. The lettering on the caption on the vertical axis should be parallel to the axis, the scale values horizontal to it (Figure 12.4(c)).

Histograms and bar charts

Histograms and bar charts can be used in much the same way, but there is a difference:

- *a histogram* is used for a continuous function of a variable—there is no space between bars
- *a bar chart* is used for plots of data (for comparison) that are not a continuous function of some variable—space between bars

An example is shown in Figure 12.5. The histogram is used when a continuous function of a variable is to be shown but there is insufficient data to plot a continuous curve. In Figure 12.5(a), the histogram shows the error rate against time on job. Time is a continuous variable, but there is no data, for example, for a plot of the error rate for $1\frac{1}{2}$ hours.

The bar chart (Figure 12.5(b)), on the other hand, shows, for comparison, the error rate for four (independent) input methods. Care must be taken when more than two factors are to be shown, as in Figure 12.5(c). In this example there are three factors: error rate, sample, and system. Bar chart (i) has the visual impact of comparing samples, while (ii) that of systems.

Most of the principles that apply to graphs also apply to histograms and bar charts.

Pie-charts

A pie-chart is used to compare data which is not a continuous function of some variable. It is normally used to show the distribution of costs or time among a number of activities or functions. A circle is segmented in proportion to the distribution of resource-to-usage. An example is shown in Figure 12.6(a). The parts of the chart must add up to unity (e.g. to 100 per cent), and the value of the component must be shown, i.e., do not rely on the spatial proportions to indicate exact quantities. Comparisons can also be made between the value depicted by the whole circle, as shown in Figure 12.6(b).

The calculation and artistry required in preparing pie-charts can be considerable, but they are a very effective graphical technique.

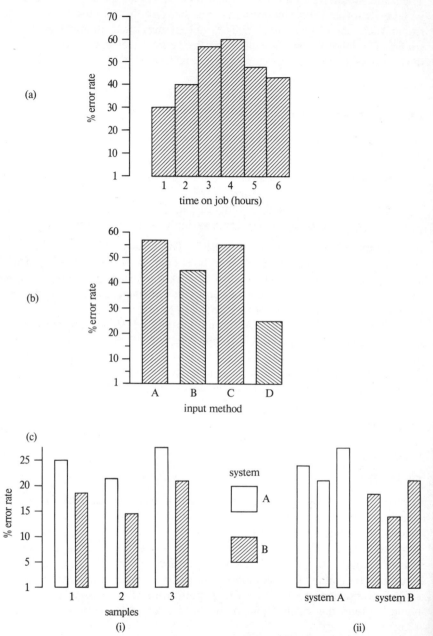

Figure 12.5: Histograms versus bar charts

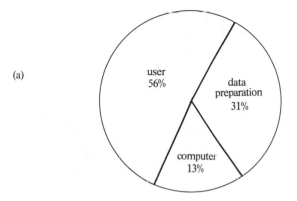

(a)

distribution of invoicing system running costs (1969 to 1971)

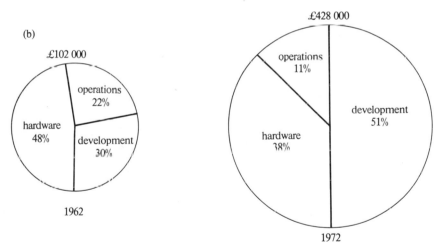

(b)

data processing budget -- 1962 and 1972

Figure 12.6: Example pie-charts

Pictograms

A pictogram or symbol chart, like a pie-chart, is used to compare data. An example is shown in Figure 12.7. Considerable artistry is required in preparing the chart, and the size and shape of the symbols can be misleading.

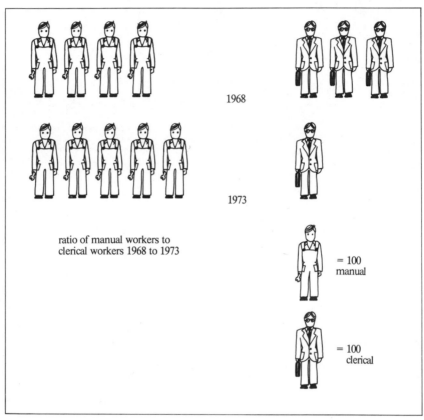

Figure 12.7:   Example pictogram

Decision tables

The analyst is often required to represent complex, conditional logic. This is a description of the conditions to be considered and the actions to be taken for different combinations of conditions. Complex conditional logic can be represented by narrative, flowcharts, or decision tables; see Figure 12.8.

Decision tables have, for people-to-people communication in reports and presentations, considerable advantages over flowcharts; this is shown in Figure 12.9.

narrative

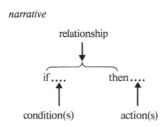

flowchart

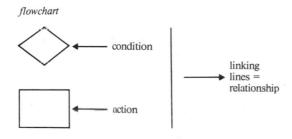

decision table

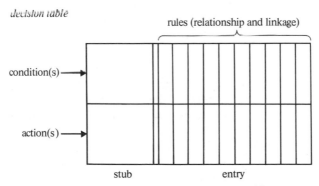

Figure 12.8: Representing conditional logic

We are not concerned here with the value of decision tables in investigation, analysis, technical design specification or programming (as with a decision table preprocessor, etc.). Many installations have developed standards for the technical application of decision tables in the data processing department. Rules and conventions have been established for such features as initialization, recursion, extended versus limited entry tables, the 'else' rule, checking methods and table-linkage. (A complete description of the mechanics of decision tables and their application is given in *Decision Tables*, Keith London, Auerbach Publications Inc., Philadelphia, 1973.) Many, if not most, of these techniques and conventions are irrelevant to the presentation of decision-making procedures to users.

Figure 12.9: Flowcharts versus decision tables

	Flowcharts	Decision tables
Compactness	Tends to spread with a low ratio of 'sense to size'	Compactness, with ease of assimilation
Completeness	Can be omissions because of 'free form nature'	Tends to be more complete because of discipline in construction
Logic sequence	Relies on sequence of decision points/action procedures	Logic can be stated independent of procedural sequence
Artistry	Typing difficult; leads to abbreviation because lack of space in symbols	Simple penmanship; can be typed easily. (Normally, preprinted forms are used.)
Reproduction	Easy on Xerox. Good quality artwork (black ink) if type-set printing is used	Easy on Xerox and other printing methods, provided carbon-ribbon is used in typewriter (and preprinted forms are used)
Maintenance	Redrawing a flowchart can be a tedious and even difficult process	Easy to update (retyping a rule/condition/action); no linking lines necessary
Modularity	Fair. Linkage is on both logic and size	Fair. Form faces modular approach
Standardization	Fair—because of free form	Good—because of structured form

Note that decision tables provide a checklist for the procedure writer where clerical instructions are involved. Tables can be used to set the steps out clearly in the sequence required.

As far as a user is concerned, he needs to be able to see the conditions, the actions, and the relationship between them. Extended entry tables (i.e. those with quantitative values in the rules) are far more effective than limited entry tables (i.e. those with only 'Y'es or 'N'o values in rules). In programming, however, limited entry tables are commonly used. Similarly, many tables which specify a system are consolidated as much as possible by using indifference symbols, but this could be confusing to users. An example is shown in Figure 12.10.

(a)

works?	1	2	3	4
works?	Y	Y	N	N
staff?	N	N	Y	Y
hours >40?	N	Y	–	–
hours <40?	–	–	N	Y
pay base rate	X			
pay overtime		X		
pay regular sal.			X	X
absence report rq.				X

(b)

employee:	works	works	staff	staff
hours worked:	40 hours or less	more than 40 hours	40 hours or more	less than 40 hours
pay:	base x hours	overtime x hours	regular salary	regular salary + absence report

Figure 12.10:   Technically oriented versus user-oriented tables

Summary diagrams

A summary diagram showing the major information flow and activities is important. It can be supplemented with detailed diagrams later in the report or presentation.

Highly stylized flowcharts are admirable in technical documentation and in specifications for users trained in systems documentation techniques. In more general reports and presentations, a pictorial representation of the flow of information and activities in a system is preferable. This avoids the use of standard flowchart symbols, and uses common-or-garden pictures of documents, filing cabinets, vehicles, men, buildings, and so on.

Bibliography

This bibliography lists books only, which are available from a reasonable library. They are listed under major areas of interest for further reading, as opposed to chapter headings. A book cited under one heading can also contain useful information on other topics.

Data processing

Brandon, Dick H., *Management Standards for Data Processing*, Van Nostrand, Princeton, N.J., 1963.

Brandon, Dick H., *Data Processing Organization and Manpower Planning*, Petrocelli Books, New York, 1974.

London, Keith R., *Documentation Standards: Revised Edition*, Petrocelli Books, New York, 1973.

Mumford, Enid, and Olive Banks, *The Computer and The Clerk*, Routledge and Kegan Paul, London, 1967.

Whisler, Thomas, *The Impact of Computers on Organizations*, Praeger Publishers, London, 1970.

Wooldridge, Susan, and Keith London, *The Computer Survival Handbook*, David and Charles, Newton Abbot, 1973.

Systems analysts, systems analysis, and systems design

Chandor, A. J. Graham, and R. Williamson, *Practical Systems Analysis*, Hart-Davis, London, 1970.

Clifton, M. D., *Data Processing Systems Design*, Business Books, London, 1971.

Crawley, Margaret, and Jennifer Morris, *Systems Analyst Selection—A Preliminary Study*, National Computing Centre, Manchester, 1970.

Daniels, Alan, and Donald Yeats (eds), *Basic Training in Systems Analysis: Edited on Behalf of the National Computing Centre*, 2nd edn, Pitman, London, 1969.

Lindquist, E. F., *Design and Analysis of Experiments in Psychology and Education*, Houghton Mifflin, Boston, Mass., 1956.
Milward, G. E. (ed.), *Organization and Methods*, Macmillan, London, 1962.
Morgan, Clifford T. (ed.), *Human Engineering Guide to Equipment Design*, McGraw-Hill, London, 1963.
Rodens, Dereck, *Creative Systems Design*, Arbar Publications, London, 1970.
Wooldridge, Susan, *Computer Input Design*, Petrocelli Books, New York, 1974.

Management and administration

Bower, Marvin, *The Will to Manage*, McGraw-Hill, New York, 1966.
Drucker, Peter F., *The Practise of Management*, Harper and Row, New York, 1954.
Townsend, Robert, *Up the Organization*, Hodder-Fawcett, London, 1971.
Uris, Auren, *The Executive Deskbook*, Van Nostrand–Reinhold, New York, 1970.
Whalley, B. H., *Manual of Office Administration*, Business Publications, London, 1968.

People at work and change

Argyris, C., *Personality and Organization: the Conflict between System and the Individual*, Harper, New York, 1953.
Blake, Robert R., and Jane S. Mouton, *The Managerial Grid*, Gulf Publishing Comapny, New York, 1964.
Blaue, Peter M., and W. Richard Scott, *Formal Organizations*, Routledge and Kegan Paul, London, 1963.
Herzberg, Frederick, Bernard Mausner and Barbara Block Sayderman, *The Motivation to Work*, 2nd edn, John Wiley and Sons, London 1959.
Judson, Arnold S., *A Manager's Guide to Making Changes*, John Wiley, London, 1966.
Kelley, Joe, *Organizational Behavior*, Richard D. Irwin, Homewood, Ill., 1969.
Leavitt, Harold J. and Louis R. Pondy, *Readings in Managerial Psychology*, University of Chicago Press, Chicago, 1964.
Likert, R., *New Patterns of Management*, McGraw-Hill, New York, 1961.
McGregor, D., *The Human Side of Enterprise*, McGraw-Hill, London, 1960.
Sidney, Elizabeth, Margaret Brown and Michael Argyle, *Skills with People*, Hutchinson, London, 1973.
Tannenbaum, Arnold S., *Social Psychology of the Work Organization*, Tavistock Publications, London, 1966.

Interviewing

Bingham, Walter Van Dyke, and B. V. Moore, *How To Interview*, Harper Bros, New York, 1941.

Finley, Robert E. (ed.), *The Personnel Man and His Job*, American Management Association, New York, 1962.

Oldfield, R. C., *The Psychology of the Interview*, Methuen, London, 1941.

Project leadership and supervision

Barnes, R. J., *Principles and Practice of Supervision*, Heinemann, London, 1968.

Brandon, Dick H., and Max Gray, *Project Control Standards*, Auerbach Publishers, Philadelphia, 1970.

Supervisory Management, staff of (eds), *Leadership on the Job*, American Management Association, New York, 1957.

Van Densol, William R., *The Successful Supervisor in Government and Business*, Pitman, London, 1970.

Wodsworth, M. D., *The Human Side of Data Processing Management*, Prentice-Hall, Englewood Cliffs, N.J., 1973.

Wooldridge, Susan, *Project Management in Data Processing*, Petrocelli Books, New York, 1975.

Communication

Carney, James D., and Richard K. Scheer, *Fundamentals of Logic*, Macmillan, New York, 1964.

Chisholm, Cecil (ed.), *Communication in Industry*, Business Publications, London, 1955.

Duerr, Carl, *Management Kinetics*, McGraw-Hill, London, 1971.

Irvine, Alec S., *Improving Industrial Communication*, Industrial Society/Gower Press, London, 1970.

Miller, George A., *The Psychology of Communication*, Penguin Books, Middlesex, 1970.

Oldfield, R. C., and J. C. Marshall (eds), *Language*, Penguin Modern Psychology Readings, Penguin Books, Middlesex, 1968.

Pierce, John R., *Symbols, Signals and Noise: The Nature and Process of Communication*, Harper Bros, New York, 1961.

Reports

Clarke, Emerson, *A Guide to Technical Literature Production; A Concise Handbook of Production Methods*, T.W. Publications, River Forest, Illinois, 1961.

Darbyshire, A. E., *Report Writing: The Form and Style of Efficient Communication*, Edward Arnold, London, 1970.

Hicks, Tyler G., *Successful Technical Writing*, McGraw-Hill, New York, 1969.

Kapp, Reginald O., *The Presentation of Technical Information*, Constable, London, 1973.

Sidney, E., *Business Report Writing*, Business Publications, London, 1965.

Smith, William D., *Business Letters and Reports*, Collins, London, 1968.

Strunk, William, Jr, and E. B. White, *The Elements of Style*, Macmillan, New York, 1972.

University of Chicago Press, *A Manual of Style*, 12th edn, University of Chicago Press, 1969.

Group meetings and presentations

Anstey, Edgar, *Committees—How They Work and How to Work Them*, George Allen and Unwin, 1962.

Cartwright, Rupert L., and George L. Hinds, *Creative Discussion*, Macmillan, New York, 1959.

Jay, Antony, *Effective Presentation: The Communication of Ideas by Words and Visual Aids,* Management Publications, London, 1970.

Olmsted, Michael S., *The Small Group*, Random House, New York, 1959.

Smith, Peter B. (ed.), *Group Processes*, Penguin Modern Psychology Readings, Penguin Books, Middlesex, 1970.

Special illustrative techniques

Chapin, N. (ed.), *Flowcharts,* Auerbach Publications, Philadelphia, 1971.

Enrick, Norbert Lloyd, *Effective Graphic Communication*, Auerbach Publishers, Philadelphia, 1972.

London, Keith R., *Decision Tables*, Auerbach Publications, Philadelphia, 1972.

Index